Competition and Control at Work

By the same author

THE DOCKERS

THE DOMINANT IDEOLOGY THESIS (*with* N. ABERCROMBIE *and* B. S. TURNER)

Competition and Control at Work

The New Industrial Sociology

Stephen Hill

London School of Economics and Political Science

HEINEMANN EDUCATIONAL BOOKS · LONDON

Heinemann Educational Books Ltd
22 Bedford Square, London WC1B 3HH
LONDON EDINBURGH MELBOURNE AUCKLAND
HONG KONG SINGAPORE KUALA LUMPUR NEW DELHI
IBADAN NAIROBI JOHANNESBURG
EXETER (NH) KINGSTON PORT OF SPAIN

First published 1981
Reprinted 1982

British Library C.I.P. data

Hill, S. R.
Competition and control at work.
1. Industrial sociology
I. Title
306′.3 HD6971

ISBN 0-435-82414-7
ISBN 0-435-82415-5 Pbk

Printed by Richard Clay (The Chaucer Press) Ltd, Bungay,
Suffolk, England

Contents

For Jane, Martin and Anna

Preface

Considerable changes in both the real world of industrial relations and the academic analysis of these have occurred during the 1970s. The decay of the postwar industrial peace in this period has once again brought the issue of conflict in industrial organisation to the fore. The successful institutionalisation of class conflict in advanced Western societies during the late 1940s and early 1950s reduced industrial strife to easily-managed proportions for a quarter of a century. The resurgence of more intense conflicts in the 1970s showed that the relative harmony of the earlier era had rested on precarious foundations. Moreover, modern industrial conflict embraces more than the traditional issues of wages and conditions, when people question the very basis of economic and industrial organisation.

Within the world of academic analysis there have also been changes. In the first place, there has been a great increase in the amount of factual knowledge available as the result of the empirical research conducted over the last ten years. In particular, we now know considerably more about Britain, continental Europe and Japan to set alongside the detailed accounts of North American industrial life which were once the empirical basis of industrial sociology. Secondly, the growth of new intellectual approaches has provided new answers to old questions and raised seemingly novel issues as legitimate areas of investigation. The influence of new perspectives is strong even among people who do not support them, because they have successfully structured the agenda of what is held to be worth discussing.

The traditional sociology of industrial organisation written in the 1950s and 1960s began to collapse at the same time as these changes were taking place. Old concepts were unable to cope with the industrial changes, while the new ideas that excited people in the late 1970s were incompatible with existing approaches.

In this book I attempt to reconstruct industrial sociology. I focus on the social relations involved in production and employment and their ramifications both inside and outside organisations. A major theme is the precarious nature of industrial peace given the ineradicable opposition of certain interests; this feature is characteristic of the dominant forms of modern economic organisation. In support of this position I employ a wider range of material than has been hitherto customary in industrial sociology. This includes the historical and comparative study of labour and managerial organisation, the modern theoretical and empirical accounts of class structure and the role of the government in the economy, and the economics literature dealing with trade unions, labour markets and certain aspects of economic theory. Inevitably, the issues that I think are worth discussing and the framework within which this discussion takes place reflect the ideas that are current in sociology. The text draws in places on Weber's economic sociology because I am convinced that this has an enduring importance for industrial sociology which is not sufficiently appreciated. This perspective certainly produces a more relevant framework than the Durkheimian tradition in what used to be the dominant American approach to industrial organisation. It can accommodate a number of the insights of the revived Marxist perspective with which it is often thought to be in competition, as the following chapters demonstrate.

The book has its origins in lectures given to graduate and undergraduate students of sociology, industrial relations and personnel management at the L.S.E., and in a paper I published on the 'new industrial relations' (S. Hill, 1976a) reviewing Harry Braverman's seminal work, *Labor and Monopoly Capital*. Many of my ideas have changed during the course of writing and the text now departs substantially from its origins. I have refrained where possible from treating the subject as a history or thematic review of the various theories and schools that have existed in industrial sociology. This approach has so often led to a narcissistic and abstract sociology of sociology. I have also tried to avoid another pitfall, which is to present a collection of chapters covering everything under the sun without any thematic unity. Instead I attempt to demonstrate the empirical basis of the subject and to present original arguments which serve to select and organise the material. This has proved difficult in places, because in a text which is intended in part to instruct students there is clearly a need for some basic information about the subject that might otherwise be omitted.

I would like to thank Nicholas Abercrombie, Keith Bradley, Betty Low, Donald MacRae, Ray Richardson, Keith Thurley and my publishers' anonymous reader for their perceptive and useful comments upon various drafts of the manuscript.

November 1980

1 Introduction: the competition of economic interests

The organisation of productive activity within enterprises has a peculiarly ambivalent quality in most modern economies. On the one hand co-operation is required for the production of goods and services. On the other hand the interests of the different parties concerned with production compete in certain fundamental respects. This is particularly so of management and labour. Employees need to collaborate with their employers if goods are to be produced and the firm is to survive, but otherwise their interests may not be the same. For a long time, however, the study of organisational life played down the oppositional element of economic activity within firms, particularly when this involved differences between management and labour. The 'human relations' movement, which was the major perspective in organisational analysis for the three decades up to the mid-1960s, appeared largely unconcerned with social conflict in industry, and when sociologists in this school did consider the issue they asserted the normality of co-operation and consensus and the abnormality of conflict. Social conflict was regarded as a sickness which would be cured by certain remedies drawn from Durkheimian sociology; namely, that a revitalised moral order would overcome any tendencies toward social conflict and create enough moral cohesion for co-operation to continue without threat (see Chapter 5).

It is a contention of this book that the analysis of economic interests and competition should have theoretical primacy in any modern organisational sociology. There has been a shift of opinion among sociologists, who now suggest that many of the issues addressed by 'human relations', for example the problems of low productivity, low morale and poor social relations at work, were the visible symptoms of deep-seated differences within the economy, even though they used not to be treated as such. Moreover, deteriorating industrial relations and increased employee unrest in Western Europe and America since the mid-1960s means that the issue of conflict is now of greater practical import. The concern with conflict in organisations should not be seen as a new development, however, because it is firmly grounded in the classical economic sociology of Marx and Weber, the work of modern sociologists within these traditions and in various assumptions of different schools within modern economics. The early part of this book addresses the problematic nature of co-operation in industrial and commercial organisations before discussion broadens to consider this against the background of social stratification and the political process. The major focus is on labour–management relations. Differences within the ranks of labour or management are regarded here as less central though they are treated fully where relevant.

This chapter presents the basis of the rest of the book by demonstrating that employees and employers are enmeshed in economic relations which by their very nature contain powerful oppositional elements. An appraisal of the assumptions which lie behind different accounts of employment reveals various sources of competition. These assumptions are theoretical and somewhat abstract, unlike the material presented in the rest of this book, but their discussion is necessary because these dimensions of industrial relations have not been tackled systematically before. There is a distinction to be made here between economic divisions which are the structural characteristics of economic organisation and actual social conflicts. The two are distinct, analytically and in fact. The competition of interests within the economy treated here does not inevitably produce social conflicts between people, so it is not possible directly to 'read off' the nature of social relations in industry from the nature of the economic system. The link between economic relations and competitive behaviour is mediated in various ways, some of which amplify while many others reduce the overt expression of conflict. A theoretical orientation which gives primacy to the forces of competition in the economy does not imply that manifestly conflictual social relations are always a feature of organisational life. A central task of the rest of this book is to elaborate just *how* differences of interest are reflected and managed in industrial relations and what are their broader manifestations beyond the economy.

A terminological issue must be clarified at the outset. Economists mainly use the term 'competition' while others including sociologists refer to 'conflict' to describe certain aspects of industrial relations. For the remainder of this chapter the two are used interchangeably. The justification of this is that competition is a word describing a conflict over the control of resources or advantages desired by others where actual physical violence is not employed (Weber, 1964, pp. 132–3) – in other words the form of social action or behaviour which specialists in the study of industrial relations usually have in mind when they talk of industrial conflict. One reason why some people have chosen to make a distinction between different forms of social action is that they have interpreted the idea of competitive behaviour to mean what Weber called a *regulated* competition which takes place within a framework of agreed rules and where the system itself is not in dispute, whereas they see conflict as unregulated competition where there is no basis of agreement. The fact that competition may carry this covert evaluation is reason not to distinguish it from peaceful conflict: one simply cannot take for granted as do those who use competition in this way that the expression of conflict is rule-bound and that people who struggle to control resources endorse the system, because non-violent industrial conflict does not necessarily have these characteristics. A major objection to the assumption of regulated competition is that it prejudges the results of scientific enquiry. The empirical evidence presented in this book demonstrates that there are wide variations in the extent to which industrial conflict is rule-bound or works within a framework which does not challenge the existing system. This chapter in any event deals with the structure or logic of economic interests and is not much concerned with competition and conflict as forms of social action: at this level of interests there seems little meaning in distinguishing a competition from a conflict of interests.

Utility, Production Factors, Exploitation

A common and straightforward way of looking at the conflict of interests in employment is as the result of each party maximising its own utility. Since wages are costs which affect profits and profits can be raised at the cost of wages, those whose interests lie in maximising wages are in competition with those concerned to raise profits. Both parties may be presumed to be acting in accordance with the dictates of rational economic action, but the rational appraisals of interests made by workers and managers pull in opposite directions. Thus the conception of employment as a relationship of co-operative exchange between parties who maximise their own utilities, which lies at the heart of much economic analysis and informs political doctrines that acclaim the pursuit of self-interest in economic life, also entails that competition is at the centre of this relationship. It may be pointed out that there are co-operative aspects involved in the parties to the employment contract maximising their own utilities. Clearly, because of the high degree of interdependence in modern economic organisation, firms could not survive without collaboration in the production of goods and services. A model of employment as exchange assumes that co-operation in production is voluntary and unconstrained. So, the maximisation of utility promotes both competition and co-operation. The majority of modern economic organisations by their nature contain this de-stabilising element. The task facing those who own or administer such organisations is to contain the potential of open struggle for they cannot rely on a harmony of interests to ensure stability.

This divergence of interests occurs in any economic system where those who work do not also retain the profits of their activity. To phrase the matter in another way, competition derives from the separation of the ownership of a firm from those who work for it and the consequent appropriation of anything remaining out of revenues after costs have been covered as profits for the owners. Modern capitalism is one economic system that is based on separation and this generates major differences of interest. But the same remarks can be made about a type of economy which in many ways differs: state socialism. Profits are taken by the state rather than appropriated privately and market mechanisms are not allowed to any great extent to determine levels of economic activity, both of which features distinguish this type of economy from the majority of capitalist ones. Nevertheless, in both systems those who produce do not own their means of production and the profits of their economic activity go elsewhere.

Other economic systems differ. Co-operative economic organisation based on co-ownership and profit-sharing does not lead to separation and the appropriation of profits and so avoids a form of divergent interests inherent in conventional capitalist and socialist organisations. A variant of the pure co-operative type occurs in Yugoslavia, where part of the enterprise's capital is publicly owned but, via self-management and profit-sharing, those who work in firms retain the fruits of what they produce. There is thus a wide range of economic forms, and opposition between owners or their agents and employees is not an inevitable feature of modern economic organisation.

The difference of economic interests may be treated in another and more complex manner, as 'exploitation', a concept which revives certain ideas from classical economics. This is a less familiar interpretation which should be explained at greater length.

Exploitation was at one time mainly associated with Marxism. The basis of Marx's own economic analysis was the labour theory of value, which assumed that a commodity had value in so far as human labour had been expended to create it. Labour theories of value also informed the work of other classical economists such as

Adam Smith and Ricardo. In the Marxist scheme this was linked with the idea of a 'surplus' product that embodied surplus labour value. Economic activity had first to cover the purchase of raw materials, replace tools, machinery and buildings worn out in the course of production and provide labour with the means of subsistence. What was left after these needs were met was the surplus product. To put this idea into concrete form, we can consider the working day: if the length of the working day is eight hours and if the worker produces in the first four hours enough value to pay for all the inputs, then the remaining four hours is surplus production. According to Marx, when surplus production was carried out within a capitalist economy the surplus went as profit to the owner of a firm and his financiers. Because value can only be created by labour in production, then by definition any surplus must result from the expenditure of that labour. Following this line of reasoning, the profits that went to capitalists were to be conceived as the appropriation of labour's surplus value and as exploitation. Exploitation followed from the separation of workers from ownership and the appropriation of their surplus value as profit.

This approach has largely been rejected in subsequent analysis. A commonly encountered view is that economic processes involve the interaction of several factors of production: land, labour, capital and enterprise. Labour does not necessarily have more weight than other factors. Therefore it follows that profits need not be exploitative if they are payment for the use of capital (interest) or are the rewards for risk-taking and enterprise on the part of owner-entrepreneurs and, by extension, professional managers. A further implication is that because economic activity depends on the interdependence of different factors rather than the exploitation of one, the relationship among factors may be described as essentially co-operative. There may be some competition amongst the factors over the distribution of the increased output because the different parties attempt to maximise their own separate returns, but the structure of economic relations is not mainly antagonistic. Of course, these arguments still leave open the issue whether in practice the labour factor shares in the rewards of economic activity in proportion to its contribution. For a long period exploitation and labour-value were regarded as irrelevant and discredited ideas.

A number of theoretical economists have rehabilitated certain neglected aspects of the classical tradition recently, however, and in particular they have re-appraised exploitation and labour-value (see especially Sraffa, 1960; Morishima, 1973; Meek, 1977). The claims about the contribution of capital to the productive process have been seriously challenged by Sraffa (1960), who contends that the value of capital is only a way of describing the distribution of net output between wages and profits. His position is that there can be no logical basis for the treatment of capital in economic theory as an independent factor of production which is equivalent to land or labour. Sraffa also questions the labour theory of value, not on the grounds of a factors of production approach but because of the insuperable technical difficulties that render the notion impossible to test (1960, pp. 58–9, 67–8). In place of labour-value he resurrects the appropriation of surplus in a different form, as a modern adaptation of the Ricardian economics dealing with the production of commodities. The details of this neo-Ricardianism need not concern us. What matters is that Sraffa's pioneering analysis has been influential in reviving the concerns of the classical economists.

The general orientation and a basic methodological principle of classical economics was that the conditions of economic exchange should be analysed in terms of the conditions of production (Meek, 1977, p. 124). These conditions were technological and social, the relations that existed among men as producers. One effect of the new perspective has been to restore the concept of exploitation to academic discourse. Meek has elaborated Sraffa's account of the production of commodities to demonstrate that exploitation is quite justified within a revived classical tradition, without linking it to the labour theory of value which has little scientific warrant (1977, p. 132). He suggests that the link between profit and exploitation starts with the monopoly of the means of production which capitalists possess. This monopoly position is used to compel a workforce to do more work than its own wants prescribe, thereby producing a net gain for the capitalist which reflects the amount of this extra work (1977, p. 126). This reformulation transforms the notion of exploitation from something which was discredited by association with labour-value theories into a concept whose intellectual legitimacy is established. Taken with the related idea of appropriation, it can also be a *useful* concept for economists and sociologists investigating productive activity.

The Sociological Tradition

The notion of 'appropriation' is deeply embedded in the history of economic sociology and forms common ground between the Marxist and Weberian traditions. Appropriation refers to the phenomenon that employees in most modern forms of economic organisation have no ownership or control of their means of production because these are possessed by others. The subordination of labour at work and in the labour market is one consequence of appropriation. A second is that employees are powerless to influence the decisions that determine their lives. Appropriation and exploitation refer to similar things but sociological discussion places more emphasis on issues to do with the control of labour and the means of production. For many years the only systematic accounts were to be found in Marx and Weber, though modern sociologists have resurrected some of the ideas recently. This section looks at the issue of appropriation within classical and modern sociology. In the course of this it will be demonstrated that there are grounds for seeing a greater unity in the accounts of economic organisation presented by the main schools of economic sociology than is usually acknowledged.

Marx and Weber

Writing in 1867, in volume I of *Capital*, Marx described how the growth of industrial capitalism in Britain dispossessed workers, individually and collectively, of their ownership of the means of production: they came to work in factories and to use machines and raw materials that belonged to capitalists rather than to themselves. The capitalist class emerged and managed to appropriate others' surplus products for itself, by dispossessing the direct producers of their means of production and using its monopoly ownership of capital to compel people to work 'gratis' during their superfluous time (the part of the working day which created surplus value in Marxist theory). Labour was formally free, because people were not compelled to work for any particular employer, but in reality there were constraints because people were deprived of their independence and the capability to work for themselves. They were obliged by their own subsistence needs to work for some employer.

Another form of appropriation followed from loss of ownership: namely, loss of control over the means of production. Workers could not decide what to make nor in what manner: owners or their managerial agents decided what would be made and how the job would be done. Loss of control was reinforced by the development of organisational techniques, which included an extended division of labour that subdivided jobs into their simplest component parts, and greater supervision of people as they worked, together with the development of production technologies which gave machines many of the skilled tasks previously performed by hand. One effect of lost control was to make work less human.

It has been customary to concentrate on the differences between Marx and Weber and to highlight the distinctiveness of the schools of economic sociology to which they gave birth, in particular to emphasise the anti-Marxist inspiration of Weber's sociology. One alleged difference is that Marx dealt with the realm of production relations whereas Weber, like neoclassical economists, was concerned with exchange and market relations. This is not so. Weber gave an important place to the conditions of production as well as exchange. He did not subscribe to a labour theory of value, but he did describe in *Economy and Society* (published in Germany in 1922) the same state of affairs as Marx when he dealt with the development of capitalism and appropriation. Weber claimed that workers, individually and collectively, had lost their former ownership of the means of production which passed to capitalists and their managers; that they had in turn lost control over the use of the means of production at work; and that workers had come to be regarded as 'hands' rather than people as the result of organisational and technical developments. Appropriation was central to his analysis of the social conditions of production.

Weber thought that appropriation of ownership and control and the subordination of the worker were necessary for the rational efficiency of any industrial economy and were not specific only to capitalism. The 'rationalising' tendency of modern life had two concrete forms: capitalism and bureaucracy. Capitalism, as a consequence of spiritual changes (the Protestant ethic) and new institutional developments (the market economy), embodied the qualities of impersonality, calculation and the purposive and rational pursuit of interests which constituted efficiency. Bureaucracy maximised rationality by means of the division of labour and specialisation, the hierarchical arrangement of tasks and authority, the impersonality and predictability of its operations, and its relentless, calculating search for productive efficiency. Both capitalism and bureaucracy depended on separating the individual from access to the means of control and placing him in a position of subordination. Weber predicted that even if a socialist revolution were to replace capitalism it would not halt the rationalising tendency, particularly in the form of bureaucratisation which he thought would transcend differences amongst economic systems.

On the contrary, Marx believed that the loss of ownership and control and the consequential subordination of workers were not to do with technical efficiency but were specific to the capitalist form of industrialism. This division has given rise to continuing debate about the logic of industrialism. A later chapter describes models of industrial organisation based on producer co-operation which combine a central characteristic of capitalism, that is profit maximisation within a market economy, with communal ownership and control. These indicate that conventional patterns of dispossession are not the necessary requirements of industrialism or even all forms of capitalism. The significance of Marx and Weber is of more than antiquarian interest. Both were concerned with what they saw as the enduring features of a particular form of economic organisation. Both helped to structure the concerns and conceptual apparatus of modern economic sociology. The subsequent polarisation of Marxist and Weberian sociologies has been unfortunate. An understanding of economic activity should draw more heavily on the areas of commonality and point out where the differences between the approaches have been exaggerated by defective arguments. The Marxist theory of labour value has been shown to have little scientific warrant. Equally, it can be shown that Weber did not satisfactorily establish his claim for the necessary requirements of a modern economy. This last assertion may be elaborated to throw light on economic processes and support a subsequent theme in this book, namely that existing patterns of exclusion from control and subordination are not technically required by industrialism.

In his empirical sociology of industrialism Weber devoted relatively little space to bureaucracy and dealt mainly with capitalism. But an examination of his evidence provides little support for his view that appropriation was technically required and was not simply a feature of exploitation. In an account of the forms of economic ownership he pointed out that workers individually must be dispossessed of the means of production, because the technical efficiency associated with large-scale production required centralised co-ordination of the people and commodities involved in production (Weber, 1964, p. 247). But he went on to say that this aspect of technical efficiency was quite compatible with the collective ownership and control found in producer co-operatives. The requirements of industrialism which Weber thought made collective dispossession necessary included only one element which at the time he might reasonably have associated with technical efficiency, which was the managerial direction of workers and production processes. Subsequent chapters of this book show that this element is now the subject of controversy. On his own evidence the other varieties of efficiency gain had more to do with a particular form of capitalism than industrialism. He suggested that financiers and investors looked more favourably on a firm when mangement possessed the means of production, because managers could offer better surety when they controlled the firm's physical assets. This assumed certain sorts of capital market. He also thought that when workers had no claim on the ownership and control of the means of production, they could more easily be subordinated within the labour market and the firm (1964, pp. 247–8). Subordination in the first area would weaken employees in the negotiation of employment contracts and enable managers to dictate the terms on which labour was bought, and in the second would make labour more amenable to discipline within the firm. Weber assumed a divergence of interest between employers and employees that was and remains meaningful only in the context of exploitation and collective dispossession.

He asserted that the equality of exchange supposedly enshrined in the contract of employment, and the voluntary nature of this contract, were fictions which concealed a reality of power and inequality, in which employers dominated the labour market (Weber, 1964, p. 248). Various directly and indirectly coercive measures were required to maximise output when labour could not be relied upon to work voluntarily. In addition to the direct compulsion of management on their employees there was the indirect and effective compulsion of their dependence on employment for their living standards. Historically, the conditions of this indirect compulsion were the rise of 'free' labour towards which employers had no obligation (unlike the unfree labour of slavery and patrimonialism which employers had to clothe, feed and house), the appropriation of the means of production so that workers depended on employment, and the state's support for dispossession against any challenge from below (Weber, 1964, pp. 262–5). This echoes Marx's celebrated description of the quality of economic life for people who, with no other means of livelihood than their labour, are obliged to work at the bidding of others and to defer to their commands, as the 'dull compulsion of economic relations' (1970, p. 737).

Weber also noted the inefficiencies that appropriation created in industrial organisations, a theme which is taken up elsewhere in this book. He described the difficulties facing managers in orthodox capitalism when they tried to make employees work hard and effectively. Collective dispossession required employees to carry out functions specifically designed to allow other people's objectives to be met, objectives in which they had no interest, and therefore they had to be compelled to work against their natural inclinations. In communally-owned industries there was little problem of motivation (1964, p. 261). Where production systems had a low division of labour and producers could see the completed products of their labours, motivation was also less of a problem (1964, p. 263). Weber believed that extreme specialisation and fragmentation were technically rather than organisationally required. This may perhaps have seemed reasonable when Weber was writing in the first two decades of the twentieth century, given the influence of the scientific management movement, though nowadays it is disputed as subsequent chapters show.

Modern research shows that bureaucratic organisation falls short of the rational efficiency attributed to it by Weber (see Chapter 4). It has often been rejected by modern corporations, though it still has a place in public administration which is less concerned with productive efficiency than impartiality and predictability. It is relevant to observe here that, where their analyses depended on appropriation, much of what Marx and Weber had to say about capitalism can be seen to apply to modern state socialism which also dispossesses labour.

Control and subordination

Modern sociologists have recast some of these ideas. Wright (1976) distinguishes the various modes of appropriation in a more precise and useful fashion which emphasises the importance of control. He suggests that the dispossession and exclusion of labour from control is meaningful in three dimensions. Direction of investments and resource allocation is one form. In modern capitalism this function is normally assumed by company directors, who effectively possess the power of economic ownership even if they do not themselves legally 'own' their companies. In state socialism appropriation is by the state. Control of labour power is a second form. This is achieved by managerial control, exercised through the hierarchy of supervision, of the people who are directly and indirectly involved in production. The third form is the appropriation of command of the physical apparatus of production, whereby employees are deprived of their autonomy in the immediate activity of production and of control of the instruments of production. In practice, this form of appropriation is achieved by organisational means such as increased division of labour and by new types of productive technique which replace men by machines. Workers, when excluded from the power of ownership, lose their influence over the means of production. This has consequences even for the smallest tasks that they perform in their work. Exclusion from control and its effect on industrial relations is a recurring issue in this book. To anticipate the evidence, it may be said here that when lack of control has become a source of industrial conflict the disagreements between employers and employees have centred principally on the second and third categories. Only in the last decade has industrial conflict openly shifted to the first dimension.

Dahrendorf (1959) focuses on opposition arising out of the

disparity of power and influence between employers and employees. In many social organisations some roles exercise control over others. This differential distribution of power 'invariably becomes the determining factor of systematic social conflicts' (Dahrendorf, 1959, p. 168). The structural source of such conflict lies in the particular arrangement of social roles of domination and subordination. Following Dahrendorf it is now accepted that opposing interests will be created by the possession of and exclusion from power. Whenever there are hierarchical structures of power and influence, as in most commercial organisations, there will be the potential of social conflict.

Conceptions of the Firm

The assumptions made about employment relate to differing views about the firm. A rough-and-ready distinction may be made amongst models that are unitary and harmonistic, pluralist and oppositional, dichotomous and oppositional. These parallel the divisions of opinion that exist among the Durkheimian school, the utility and factors of production approach, and neo-Ricardian economics and the sociological tradition outlined above. Unitary conceptions portray the firm as a homogeneous community based on shared interests, united by shared values and with a high moral density. Pluralism suggests that interests are not homogeneous and are usually in competition. These divisions are plural rather than dichotomous because labour and management contain sectional interests within themselves. But because the firm is an association which enables all parties acting collectively to do better than they would on their own, self-interest means that the pursuit of sectional interests is restrained. Competition occurs anyway over the distribution of the product while the actual process of production is a collaborative enterprise. Labour markets are free, the contract of employment is a voluntary undertaking and people choose whether or not to work for a firm, so it may be assumed that employees have endorsed and will abide by the rules which regulate the competition of interests. Some accounts of pluralism also assume a common framework of values uniting the various parties (see Chapter 7 for this sociological version). Dichotomous models assert that the major line of cleavage lies between the two sides of industry and that sectional differences within the ranks of labour or management are subsidiary to this other division. Co-operation is not entirely voluntary but is sustained by forces of compulsion within the labour market and the firm. Contracts may appear to be freely entered but the disparity of power and the absence of meaningful choice make this freedom illusory. Interests are opposed even in the realm of production and co-operation there must be enforced.

The distinction between the unitary model and the other two is clear-cut. But the differences between a pluralist and a dichotomous conception are not absolute. Both focus on competitive behaviour, which gives them something in common even though their explanations of this behaviour differ. They each adopt aspects of the other's framework. For example, pluralists acknowledge that there must be a hierarchical structure of power to overcome the recalcitrance of those who wish to maximise their own rewards but contribute as little as possible to the common good. Those who subscribe to a dichotomous model recognise that it is in employees' interests to co-operate with employers in the creation of wealth within existing forms of economic organisation, even though these contain basic conflicts of interest. There are real conceptual differences between the two approaches but the models blur at the edges.

Conclusion

The theoretical orientation here draws on the classical traditions in economics and sociology and the modern adaptations of these which emphasise the far-reaching differences in employment and the organisation of economic activity within firms. Labour markets, employment relations and hierarchy will be shown to contain elements of compulsion which reflect an asymmetrical distribution of economic power between employers and employees. These remain despite union organisation in the economy and popular political organisation in the state which have reduced but not eliminated the power disparity. Only a relatively few employees with skills that are in very short supply and are not yet capable of being performed by machines have anything approaching equality of power in the labour market. Profitability within conventional capitalist and socialist economics appears to depend on depriving employees of their independence and ensuring their subordination. Taken together, these points mean that the clash of financial interests which is often a source of competitive behaviour in industrial relations and which many commentators confine to the sphere of exchange because it concerns the share of the surplus, is intimately linked with the opposition of interests in the production sphere. The way a surplus is distributed should not be separated from the conditions under which production takes place. In most modern organisations these conditions embody forms of compulsion which indicate that the neo-Ricardian perspective is indeed a useful addition to the mainstream tradition in economic sociology.

An implication of the ideas presented in this chapter is that the commonly-drawn distinction between financial and control issues, the latter relating to the realm of production and the competition to establish who will dominate the productive organisation, is not useful. Even the explanation of competition in terms of a simple clash of utilities, which at first sight seems to confine conflict to the distribution of the product and to make no assumption that production need be a locus of struggle, in fact promotes an awareness that conflicts over financial and control issues are associated. As will be shown, when employees conflict with employers over financial issues they are not simply concerned with the amount of their pay but with the ratio between reward and the effort or time they expend in gaining it. This ratio may be altered in favour of employees if they gain control of the labour process. Conversely, management tries to control production organisation and labour in order to promote a balance between reward and effort which favours its interests.

The perspective that the nature of economic exchange and distribution is to be understood in conjunction with the conditions of production is one which informs what follows. It is worth reiterating that this book assumes the primacy of economic competition and will demonstrate that the main division of interests is dichotomous, rather than following the Durkheimian perspective, but does not suggest that overt social conflict is always a necessary feature of industrial life nor that peaceful production does not occur. The ways in which differences of interest affect the fabric of social and economic life are various and display no simple or universal manifestation in the conduct of industrial relations. The differences create the potential of industrial social conflict but do not have determinate outcomes. Some methods of organising commercial enterprises do promote real teamwork between the various parties in the firm and foster harmonious relations which successfully contain the forces of competition. The Japanese corporation is an outstanding example. Enlightened personnel policy may reduce the intensity of social conflicts in industry. Other methods directly express the competition of interests in ways that foster hostile industrial relations. One form of organisation even manages to abolish most differences of interest. The different parties within the industrial relations arena thus have many courses of action open to them, and there is evidence of a wide variety of strategies and outcomes historically and comparatively. These are dealt with in Chapters 2–6 as part of an analysis of the social relations involved in production. Specialised institutions exist to regulate the ways conflict is expressed in social relations and minimise its effect on firms and society, if the forces of opposition cannot be constrained directly. These attempts to 'institutionalise' conflict are treated in Chapters 7 and 8. Chapters 9 and 10 change focus from the earlier concentration on the relations of production within the economy and discuss the links between social stratification and economic organisation. Chapter 11 changes the emphasis again to look at the relationship between the state and economic organisation in the light of the issues raised in the previous chapters.

2 Structures of control

This chapter describes briefly the historical development of management and its role in production. It does so in order to illuminate two important social relations involved in production. The first is the control of labour by management, and the second is the employment relation linking a worker to a firm. Both are largely shaped by the competition of economic interests discussed in the previous chapter, and particular forms of control and employment are often associated.

Sociologists who study industrial organisation are concerned with various different aspects of management. Recently there has been considerable interest in management as a system of control. Managers are seen to perform technical functions connected with administration, which include the organisation of work and the integration of a complex division of labour. They direct the activities that occur within the firm. These technical functions also involve managers in the direction of subordinates who perform the various tasks associated with production. Thus management is both an economic resource concerned with technical, administrative issues and a structure of authority which ensures the compliance of subordinates, many of whom do not share the interests of management. Management clearly involves technical and labour control functions in the same instant. The notion of control refers to this simultaneous control of work processes and people.

Before moving to the substantive discussion, there is a distinction to be made between two dimensions of managerial control systems that are analysed separately. One is the structural dimension, the way a firm is organised in order to ensure the co-ordination of activities and the direction of employees. This leads to the study of managerial strategy. The other is the normative dimension. This includes the elements of the organisational value system which regulate the conduct and performance of the members. Sometimes the dominant values of an organisation transcend the interests of any particular group, as Weber claimed of the legal – rational values of bureaucracy, but more often they reflect the interests of those with power in the organisation. Thus the study of the normative dimension of control normally becomes a study of managerial ideology.

Management in the Early Factory System

In order to understand modern management, it helps to know how management has developed historically, for a historical perspective will give some idea of the inner dynamics of change. The most notable finding of historical study is that management as we know it is a comparatively *recent* phenomenon: industrialisation and factory production were well established in Great Britain and the United States long before the emergence of management as a distinct system of control and a separate occupational stratum. Indeed, the seeds of modern management were established only in the last two decades of the nineteenth century, and came to fruition in the early twentieth, first in the U.S. and more slowly in Britain.

The essential characteristic of work control systems and employment in many late-nineteenth century factories was the *delegation* of what are now regarded as managerial responsibilities to other groups. This created systems of indirect control and employment, and left factory owners or managers to concentrate on other aspects of the running of their enterprises, notably finance and marketing. As Hobsbawm has remarked,

> Capitalism in its early stages expands, and to some extent operates, not so much by directly subordinating large bodies of workers to employers, but by subcontracting exploitation and management.
>
> (1964, p. 297)

Subcontracting of management was the typical organisational form in British and American factories prior to 1900. In subcontracting, skilled men or foremen were responsible for the co-ordination of production activities and the direction of labour. This took several forms, though it is difficult to be precise about their distribution given the complexity of the nineteenth century factory system.

'Co-exploitation' was one of these systems of indirect control; workers (normally skilled) would assume managerial responsibility and became the co-employers of their mates and unskilled labourers. In its extreme form, factory owners subcontracted jobs at a fixed price to workers acting as piece-masters, who then employed and paid others to work on the job, while these in turn hired their own unskilled assistants. The factory owner provided the piece-masters and their employees with premises and plant, but production decisions, cost control and labour direction were the responsibility of the piece-master and not the person for whom the job was being undertaken.

Less extreme was the internal subcontract, whereby owners, managers or foremen subcontracted specific jobs to their own workmen, who in turn took complete control of all the activities involved in production. Internal subcontractors sometimes hired their own labour directly, and sometimes used the existing employees of a firm. In both types of subcontracting, the employing worker determined what, when, how and by whom production would be carried out, he alone knew the actual production costs, and he had complete control over the labour force. Contracting was not entirely confined to the skilled trades but was also found in unskilled gang work such as docking and navvying, where gang bosses organised teams of labourers.

How common was the 'co-exploitation' of labour in the form of subcontracting? Hobsbawm estimates that it was particularly widespread in England in shipbuilding, part of coal-mining, transport and construction, and in all trades based on small-scale workshops, but not in engineering and the building trades (1964, p. 299). Schloss went further and claimed that subcontracting was 'widely adopted throughout the length and breadth of British industry' (1898, p. 197). The available evidence does not permit a precise assessment of the extent. In the U.S. it was prevalent in the North East and Atlantic states, particularly in machinery factories (Nelson, 1975, pp. 36–8). In textiles, glass, pottery and iron, industrialisation in America led to a more decisive break with earlier practices than was the case elsewhere and more direct overseeing by foremen and owners was established.

'Co-exploitation' also took other forms, when skilled men hired their own helpers and paid them out of their own wages, or were themselves paid piece-rates and supervised unskilled labour on time-rates. Craftsmen had relatively fewer managerial functions in these circumstances: they worked under foremen, were given set amounts of raw materials, had a minor role in the cost-accounting system, and organised only a few helpers or apprentices. This form was widely spread throughout British and American industry and even continued into the early years of the twentieth century, by which time other forms of subcontracting were in rapid decline (Hobsbawm 1964, p. 300; Nelson, 1975, p. 39).

The other people who exercised managerial functions were foremen. Historically, in Great Britain at least, foremen's roles had contained elements of subcontracting when the foremen's pay had been based partly on results and they had assumed a financial interest in the men whom they supervised (Schloss, 1898). In the later years of the nineteenth century, both in Britain and America, foremen tended more often to be salaried employees rather than subcontractors, but the range of their duties was extensive and differed little from that of the subcontractors *per se*. In every firm there was always a large amount of less skilled work which was the direct responsibility of foremen rather than semi-independent craftsmen, while foremen were often responsible for the hiring of subcontractors and for the work these men produced.

The importance of foremen grew in the closing years of the nineteenth century, as subcontracting declined and all workers were brought more firmly under the foremen's control. Nelson has described the foremen's duties in American industry in the 1890s (and this description fits Britain as well) in the following terms:

> he made most of the decisions about how the job was to be done, the tools and often the materials to be used, the flow of work, the workers' methods and sequence of moves. In all fields he was held accountable for what, in fact, the workers did. Finally, in personnel matters – the hiring, training, supervising, motivating, and disciplining of factory workers – the foreman had virtually complete control.
>
> (1975, p. 40)

The delegation of the co-ordination and labour control functions to foremen and élite groups of workers, who thus directly controlled production processes and workers, was supplemented by more impersonal methods, notably by a particular type of payment scheme. Payment-by-results for all categories of worker spread throughout American and British industry and in Germany too (Hobsbawm, 1964). This placed workers in the position where they had to regulate their own effort, and gave them an incentive to make certain that production was properly co-ordinated. The personal control of the foremen was not eliminated, but payment schemes provided a useful extra source of control in addition to his task of supervision.

The average size of British and American factories in the 1870s was small by modern standards. In 1871 the average British cotton factory employed 180 people and the average machinery manufacturing plant only 85 (Hobsbawm, 1975, p. 213). The large-scale industrial enterprise was comparatively insignificant. The same was true of the U.S. at this time. The textile industry had the largest works in 1870, when the average number employed in cotton goods factories was 142 (Nelson, 1975, p. 4). The McCormick plant in

Chicago was one of the nation's largest with between 400 and 500 employees. The small size of the typical productive unit and its physical location in one plant helped to keep the scale and complexity of the managerial task within the bounds of the traditional system of internal management.

The scale and complexity of a very few undertakings, however, exceeded the capabilities of the traditional system. This was true of the railways and the postal services for example. These both employed many thousands of staff in a wide variety of locations, all of whom had to work in unison to produce the service. For these industries the only suitable existing models of large-scale organisation were the military and the bureaucracy. In Europe especially these undertakings were organised on pyramidal lines, with a hierarchy of posts of increasing responsibility, with codified rules and operating procedures and formal systems of labour management (Hobsbawm, 1975, p. 216), and developed a distinct managerial function that is more familiar to modern eyes than the typical administrative system of the period. These bureaucratic enterprises also had a distinctive system of employment which provided job security, promotion by seniority for all levels of employee, and sometimes even pensions. Surprisingly, when British and American industry began to substitute formalised, centralised controls and increase the influence of management over the factory in the early twentieth century, the military and bureaucratic models were largely ignored in favour of the 'scientific' management of the enterprise, as the next section demonstrates.

The employment relationship between workers and their firms in the typical undertaking was dominated by the market principles of what Marx termed the 'cash nexus', a phrase now widely used in industrial sociology. These principles were that employers had no obligation towards their employees other than the payment of wages in return for work done, while employees in turn merely sold their time or effort for an agreed price. Employees thus exchanged a cost (time or effort) for a benefit (wages), and had no other obligation towards their employers. The only nexus between the two sides of industry was naked self-interest (Marx and Engels, 1848, p. 52). Subcontracting and payment-by-results epitomised these principles. The cash nexus de-personalised employment relations by transforming them into market relations and economic exchanges pure and simple. Workers were regarded as commodities or factors of production rather than as individuals whose interests ought to be considered or protected. One historian of management has commented of the way workers were treated inside the factory, that 'the human element was merely to be manipulated as if it were an inert piece of machinery' (Pollard, 1965, p. 196). Even before they arrived in the factory, workers had assumed a commodity status: labour was a commodity to be purchased in the market place when required and at a price fixed by the market principles of supply and demand. These principles reinforced the cash nexus, with the effect that both sides treated employment relations as simple economic exchanges.

The delegation of managerial functions indeed meant that some employees may have regarded their 'employer' to be the person who had hired them rather than the firm. This was found to be the case in a recent study of one British industry (the docks) which preserved subcontracting and traditional foremanship until the late 1960s (S. Hill, 1976 b, p. 17). The informal nature of recruitment allowed those who hired labour to select whom they liked, including their friends and relatives, and modified the impersonality of the basic employment relationship (Bendix, 1966, p. 83; Nelson, 1975, pp. 80–1; S. Hill, 1976 b, pp. 16–29). But such bonds did not create the involvement of employees with the firm, nor did they modify the ways in which the owners of firms treated labour as a commodity in the workplace and in the labour market.

The ideology of management The ideology of self-help and *laissez-faire* supported this system of employment and the delegation of control. Bendix suggests that all managerial ideologies try to help the performance of the labour control function in two ways. They justify the authority of the few (managers) over the many (the labour force), thus suppressing conflict and maintaining co-operation between managers and workers. They also provide an internalised ethic of work performance which motivates workers to work well with a degree of steady intensity (Bendix, 1966, pp. 438–45). The contract of employment alone cannot provide sufficient control of labour. It is always incomplete and vague, and establishes the general principle that owners and managers have the right to command labour but not the concrete details of this command: it does not itself determine what tasks the worker shall do, what level of effort and skill he shall put into the job, what work rules he shall obey, and so on (Baldamus, 1961). These are all aspects of work that have to be determined *de facto* rather than *de jure*. Ideology is a managerial resource which supplements the authority contained in the contract.

Laissez-faire doctrines emphasised the principle of self-dependence, that is to say that people have to help themselves if they are to succeed. This principle had two consequences: those who possessed wealth and power in industry (factory owners and other entrepreneurs) were held to have justly earned their positions by virtue of their hard work and thrift; while any worker could succeed if he worked hard and effectively at his job. Samuel Smiles was the best-known exponent of this ideology: his gospel of work and self-help, summarised in a series of books evocatively named *Self-Help, Character, Thrift* and *Duty*, achieved immense popularity in the second half of the nineteenth century in Great Britain and, in conjunction with the Spencerian notion of the 'survival of the fittest', in the U.S.

A second principle emphasised that industrialists should not, and indeed could not, feel any obligation towards those whom they employed. Labour was a factor of production and an 'article of trade' (Bendix, 1966, p. 75), which was to be purchased when an employer needed it and at the prevailing market price. Thus employers were not obliged to provide stable and continuous employment, nor to pay wages that provided more than bare subsistence (nor even that if they could obtain labour more cheaply in the market place). Moreover, the popularity of Malthus's views that poverty was the result of the pressure of population growth on limited food supplies and that sexual abstinence was the only palliative within the scope of human control meant that any feelings of responsibility for employee welfare or attempts to mitigate the harshness of the market were held to be pointless and to run counter to the laws of nature.

Anthony has written of this nineteenth century ideology, that it 'depended for its motive force on self-interest or, more bluntly, on selfishness... it required self-interest to be seen as a moral principle' (1977, p. 67). It was, indeed, a *perverse* ideology, because the appeal to selfishness and the denial of any moral content to the employment relationship provided a fragile basis for managerial legitimacy and the internalisation of a work ethic. If workers pursued their *own* interests in an employment system which was based simply on the cash nexus and in which no effort was made to create some moral cohesion between employers and employees that would bind the two together, then they were hardly likely to pursue the interests of management or to accept the legitimacy of managerial authority when their interests failed to coincide. Because the cash nexus placed worker and employer interests in naked opposition, either party benefiting at the cost of the other, open conflict was inevitable. That workers tended to acquiesce to managerial authority and work effectively was nothing to do with the effectiveness of the ideology (Bendix, 1966, p. 203). Labour discipline followed from the pressures of the labour market when jobs were insecure and scarce, the use of 'driving', dictatorial methods of supervision by foremen, and the way in which the organisation of production under subcontracting and payment by results imposed the penalty of poor work on the worker himself.

Commodity status and the cash nexus have continued to describe the condition of labour long after the nineteenth century managerial ideology has declined. This type of employment relationship exacerbates the basic opposition of interests and makes manifest social conflict more likely. In the next chapter various modern attempts to improve the relationship between management and labour, workers and their firms, are described. These attempt to reduce the potential for social conflict which the dominant mode of employment in the United States and Great Britain contains. It is interesting to note here that in the nineteenth century some manufacturers bound workers to their firms in ways that provided control with less potential for overt conflict.

Paternalism in early factory villages and company towns was based on the principle that the owners had an obligation to provide for and protect their workers, and the employment relationship went beyond the simple, impersonal exchange of labour power for wages in the market place (Pollard, 1965, pp. 197–206; Abercrombie and Hill, 1976). Factory owners provided housing, welfare, education and health facilities, in addition to wages, and tried to guarantee employment regardless of fluctuations in the markets for their manufactured goods. The company town, which was organised on this basis and therefore hindered the transformation of employment into the pure market relationship of the cash nexus and preserved non-economic compulsions, was commonly found also in late-nineteenth century Europe, often on a much larger scale (Hobsbawm, 1975, pp. 213–4). Workers' lives were dominated by the factory-based community and they were far more dependent on their employers than was the case in other towns where workers were hired by the hour or day according to the needs of the factories for labour at particular times. Workers were protected therefore from the vicissitudes of the labour market, while employers gained an effective system of labour control in isolated areas where pressure for work did not provide its own controls. Paternalism is not found today in Britain in any meaningful way (Abercrombie and Hill, 1976), although it flourishes in certain sections of Japanese industry as Chapter 3 shows.

The Emergence of Modern Management

Several forces of change in the late nineteenth and early twentieth centuries led to the supersession of traditional management control systems and their replacement by management in roughly the form we know it today. In the first place, technical innovations in many manufacturing industries outstripped the capability of craftsmen trained in traditional techniques to organise production as they had done in the past. Secondly, in America, the enormous expansion of industrial output in the boom years between 1880 and 1920 led to a threefold increase in the size of the industrial labour force in forty years; this workforce was mainly recruited from immigrants without previous industrial experience. Traditional control mechanisms just could not be expanded quickly enough to cope with this increase and there were acute shortages of skilled men to organise subcontracting or to work as foremen. Moreover, the 'continued infusion of prefactory peoples' (Gutman, 1977, p. 69) into a mature industrial system created its own pressure for new forms of work organisation and control. Those internalised time and work disciplines which are necessary for effective work in industry and the manual skills of an established industrial population were both lacking in this new labour force, and scientific management provided an organisational substitute to compensate for their absence. There was also a great increase in the size of the enterprise in the U.S. and some plants had over 10 000 employees by 1920, which posed problems of organisation that traditional methods of organisation had not had to contend with. Finally, and most significantly, managers in America and elsewhere changed their views about delegation and came to regard the organisation of work processes and the direction of labour as functions which they had to control in the interests of maximum profitability. This change of philosophy was particularly associated with the rise of industrial engineers, who felt that the systematic application of engineering principles to factory organisation would create a more rational system. Rationalised organisation would find better ways of working and regulate labour more closely, thus raising its productivity. Because labour did not share the interests of business it could not be relied upon to produce the maximum output, despite the disciplines of incentive payments and job insecurity. Modern management techniques were developed primarily in America and were rapidly adopted there, and spread to Britain more slowly.

Taylorism The American shop management movement led to the transformation of work organisation and its control. This movement, better known as scientific management and associated with the name of F. W. Taylor (see the essays reprinted in 1964 in F. W. Taylor, *Scientific Management*), synthesised the work of industrial engineers and accountants in the 1880s and 1890s into a three-pronged attack on traditional delegated factory administration.

Taylor's scheme involved first the systematic analysis of the process of production and then its fragmentation by means of a greatly increased division of labour. Individual jobs were to be simplified to the performance of a single task wherever possible. The skill requirements of jobs were to be minimised by reducing operations to their component parts, many of which could then be undertaken by unskilled labour. The performance of jobs was to be carried out by workers, but all the elements of work planning which were traditionally done by workers were to be taken over by management, thus separating planning from doing. In this way, work tasks could be simplified, standardised and de-skilled. This in turn would increase efficiency and profitability: less skilled and therefore cheaper labour could be employed; labour productivity would increase once workers specialised on one endlessly repeated task; managers would have greater control of production costs through the fixing of standard times and the establishment of payment-by-results schemes geared to these.

The same principle of increased division of labour was to be applied to lower managers, foremen and subcontracting craftsmen: the multi-functional roles of traditional supervision were to be subdivided and de-skilled in order to give each role just one function. Taylor's scheme of functional management was not applied directly at the time, though the underlying principle of increasing specialism within management and reducing the scope of low-level managerial roles was slowly adopted over the following decades.

The second aspect of scientific management concerned the re-integration of the production process which had been fragmented by the increased division of labour: this was now to be co-ordinated and controlled by management. The principle of task control was that *managers* should plan and direct the organisation of production, which was an attack on the discretion enjoyed by foremen as well as the delegation of control to labour. Managers were to be the new masters of the work place:

> The work of every workman is fully planned out by the management...and each man receives written instructions, describing in detail the task which he is to accomplish, as well as the means to be used in doing the work.... This task specifies not only what is to be done, but how it is to be done and the exact time

> allowed for doing it.... Scientific Management consists very largely in preparing for and carrying out these tasks.
>
> (Taylor, quoted in Braverman, 1974, p. 118)

As Braverman has argued, this was a fundamental break with the traditional system of delegated control which brought production organisation and the work process under direct managerial control for the first time (1974, pp. 118–19). It simultaneously transformed the jobs of manual workers by removing the discretionary elements, and destroyed the autonomy of foremen and craftsmen by placing the responsibility for co-ordinating and directing further up the managerial hierarchy. It also firmly established management as a role distinct from that of ownership, with a distinct set of technical functions concerned with organisation: management was now defined as the resource which had responsibility for planning, organising, commanding, co-ordinating and controlling (Taylor, 1964, p. 6).

The simplification and standardisation of tasks, together with managerial intervention in work co-ordination, laid the foundations for the greater control of labour by management. Now managers knew what workers *ought* to be doing in their jobs because they had determined these. The third element, which was the development of an efficient cost-accounting system based on the systematic time and motion analysis of operations and the setting of standard times, for the first time provided the information necessary for managers to monitor the effectiveness of work. In practice, of course, labour control was achieved by a combination of several different approaches. The rationalisation of work organisation, which resulted from the fragmentation of operations and their re-integration by managerial co-ordination and scientific planning, meant that labour control was designed into the work organisation. Workers performed well-defined, simple tasks with few discretionary elements. The sequences of operations and the relations among tasks (and therefore people) were specified. Rationalisation also lessened the opportunities for worker resistance. Where jobs were de-skilled, this reduced the market power of men with skills over management. The simplification of tasks and the divorce of doing from planning turned the worker into something like a machine which could be closely controlled. Incentive payments, fixed by time and motion studies, established in addition monetary controls which placed the penalty of sub-standard performance onto the labour force. Both these controls were essentially impersonal. The third, the direct supervision of work effort and quality, was based on the role of the foreman as the overseer and 'driver' of labour.

The consequence of Taylorism was to raise productivity and profitability, partly by the *intensification* of labour and partly also by an increase in *efficiency*. Managerial control was used to increase the output of each worker directly, by making that person work harder and more effectively. Efficiency was increased by substituting cheap (less skilled) for expensive (skilled) labour. Scientific management thus improved labour productivity by organisational means, rather than technological means such as mechanisation and other forms of capital intensification (which is the purchase of more productive plant and a consequent change in the relationship between labour and capital costs).

Taylor, his disciples and certain imitators applied scientific management principles in about 250 American companies between 1900 and 1915, though most applications ignored the prescriptions about the functional specialisation of lower management and some neglected incentive wages (Nelson, 1975, pp. 68–78). One major firm of management consultants in Great Britain introduced a form of scientific management (without the functional specialisation of lower management) into at least 200 firms between the late 1920s and 1939 (Littler, 1980). These firms were mainly, though not entirely, in the new and expanding industries of that era which included food processing, light engineering, motor components (though not vehicles) and chemicals. ICI, Lucas and Joseph Lyons were among the most famous of these. The real significance of Taylorism was far wider than these examples suggest, however, because it established the basic philosophy of work organisation which has dominated the administration of work through to the present day: 'it may well be the most powerful as well as the most lasting contribution America has made to Western thought since the Federalist Papers' (Drucker, 1955, p. 247). The evidence does not exist that shows how many British and American firms over time adopted Taylorism in something like its full form, but this does not detract from the force of Drucker's statement that Taylor established the basic framework of assumptions which ultimately came to dominate managerial thinking about productive organisation. Developments in the *practice* of British and American management, as distinct from developments in managerial ideology, have largely represented the unacknowledged extension and application of Taylor's basic principles. Nor have the effects of Taylorism been confined to capitalist societies: Lenin, a fervent admirer of the ways in which scientific management increased productivity by intensifying labour and provided effective systems of work discipline and worker control, introduced Taylorism into Russian industry in the

1920s and established it as a major system of management by the end of the decade (Bendix, 1966, pp. 206–10).

There was another but less well-known development at about the same time as scientific management, which was also intended to extend managerial control over the labour force. This was the rationalisation of the personnel function in managing, which involved replacing the informal system dominated by foremen with more systematic techniques under the control of management (Nelson, 1975, pp. 79–112). Hiring, firing and training became managerial functions and the position of foremen in personnel matters was slowly eroded as a consequence. The rise of the personnel function was also associated in the 1920s with attempts by some large American corporations to improve the environment of work by means of welfare provisions such as improved plant safety, canteens, better sanitation, medical facilities and accident insurance. Personnel management became a distinct area of managerial expertise in American and British industry in the early years of this century though its subsequent development and growth in Britain was chequered until after the Second World War (T. Watson, 1977, p. 41).

The third strand in the development of modern management in the early twentieth century was the spread of the bureaucratic mode of organisation. Public service organisations such as the civil service led the field in the application of bureaucratic principles in Europe and America in the late nineteenth century, but these filtered through to private enterprises slowly. Bureaucracy to a certain extent parallelled scientific management as a method of work organisation in that it emphasised the division of labour and the establishment of integrative control systems. But the similarity should not be exaggerated, as the bureaucratic division of labour was concerned mainly with establishing specialised work roles, which might still require considerable expertise within a narrow task area, and was not a strategy of de-skilling by means of maximum task fragmentation. While in two other important respects it differed most markedly from scientific management.

Bureaucracy was more than a series of structural arrangements for work organisation; it also contained an over-arching, legal–rational value system. This was embodied in the bureaucratic rules, was internalised as the typical orientation of members, and provided a normative basis to, and justification of, managerial authority. Littler (1978) has emphasised that bureaucracy also created a different form of employment relationship which was based on employee commitment to the organisation. Bureaucracy attempted to ensure employee integration and involvement, partly by structural means such as the provision of careers and long-term contracts (often for life), and also by the internalisation of organisational rules that were felt to be rational and fair. In principle, bureaucracy provided a solution to some of the employee problems which taxed managers and led them to develop various managerial ideologies, because it served to make managerial authority legitimate and provided norms of effective work performance.

Scientific management was not directed to finding normative controls but concentrated on the structural level. Workers as individuals were thought to be concerned only with maximising their own wages. Collectively they were assumed to be intrinsically hostile to managers as their interests conflicted with those of the firm (Bendix, 1966, pp. 312–13). The philosophy of increasing the controls over work processes and workers embodied a perception that the way to cope with the difference of interests was by designing compulsion into the organisation of the workplace. The employment relationship implied by scientific management was a direct continuation of the cash nexus, based on both parties' pursuit of self-interest and the status of workers as interchangeable commodities. Davis has summarised the implications of this relationship as the 'minimum interaction model' in his discussion of Taylorism:

> there is a minimal connection between the individual and the organisation in terms of skill, training, involvement and the complexity of his contribution, in return for maximum flexibility and independence on the part of the organisation in using its manpower. In other words, the organisation strives for maximum interchangeability of personnel (with minimum training) to reduce its dependence on the availability, ability, or motivation of individuals.
>
> (1972, p. 302)

Until the second half of the twentieth century, managerial control systems developed differently for clerical and managerial staff than for manual employees: the former were governed by bureaucratic principles and the latter by those of scientific management. Fox has aptly distinguished between high and low trust positions in contemporary industry (Fox, 1974). He claims that managers do not trust their workers to work effectively and in the best interests of their firms and assume that workers' interests are in conflict with those of management. Consequently they manage the workplace in such a way as to reduce worker discretion, and subject workers to tight control and supervision. Thus the principles of managerial control and employment expressed in Taylorism are those of low trust.

Bureaucratic principles of work organisation, however, are based on a much greater degree of trust, and non-manual workers have normally been allowed far more responsibility and autonomy than the manual labour force. Rationalisation has indeed been introduced into the organisation of certain types of routine office work in the last twenty years, as will be discussed shortly. But the slowness with which firms have rationalised offices and the fact that even today rationalisation is largely confined to clerical work indicate that firms have long preferred to rely on the bureaucratic characteristics of structural integration and normative commitment to ensure effective task performance and compliance with authority among their non-manual employees.

This is obviously a somewhat schematic account of the major transformations in industrial organisation which laid the foundations of present day managerial control systems. In practice it has taken many years for the principles established in the early twentieth century to spread widely throughout industry, and even then the rationalisation of managerial control in production may fall short of Taylor's ideal in some cases. The reasons for this are considered more fully at various points in this book, but can briefly be stated here. In the first place, the resistance of labour, whether on an individual basis that is manifest in quitting or absenteeism, or on a collective basis that takes the form of workgroup or trade union action, may impede full-blooded rationalisation. Secondly, some operations and tasks have not proved amenable to complete standardisation, de-skilling and the separation of doing from planning, which may leave some workers with significant elements of discretion. This is particularly true of the most highly skilled jobs, though even some fairly unskilled tasks can retain discretionary elements. Now, however, modern technology allows the production technology itself to be designed with control purposes in mind in these cases. Finally, slowness of diffusion and the failure of managers to adopt rationalised procedures in place of more traditional forms of work organisation have also played a part, particularly in Britain. Nevertheless, it must be emphasised here that one often-encountered assertion, that scientific management was really just a managerial ideology which was later replaced by the beliefs associated with the human relations movement and other ideologies, is simply wrong. The underlying trend is quite clear. The principles of rationalised shop administration which destroyed systems of delegated production co-ordination and labour control were incorporated into the structure of work organisation and established the distinctiveness of the managerial function itself. Thus scientific management became institutionalised *as* the management of the production process.

Rationalised management in Britain

In Britain, rationalised control systems were first established in the 1920s and had spread quite widely by the time of the Second War. However, scientific management appears to have spread unevenly and rationalised administration did not entirely replace traditional methods: the delegation of managerial functions continued in a modified and attenuated form in many firms at least until the Second World War (and longer in a few cases). Subcontracting had largely died out in the early years of the century, but the assumptions on which it was based, namely that skilled men had sufficient grasp of how work was to be performed and organised, and that internalised standards of craftsmanship would ensure work of a certain quality, continued to influence work organisation in long-established industries. The term 'craft principles of administration' (Stinchcombe, 1959) describes a system of delegated control that relies on the occupational custom and practice of craft work to provide workers with the knowledge on which to take decisions about how a job is to be done, the sequence of operations, the speed of production, etc., and the standards of work quality and effort which reduce the need for close supervision. A more appropriate phrase for British industry would be 'occupational principles of administration', because occupational custom and practice of the sort Stinchcombe describes has been found in the past outside the ranks of craftsmen. Even in recent years, building workers, dockers, printers and certain highly skilled engineering workers have enjoyed a considerable influence over work organisation and a fair degree of self-regulation; while in docking and national newspaper printing, occupational control has even extended to labour recruitment, discipline and dismissal (Sisson, 1975; S. Hill, 1976 b). Managerial rationalisation, however, now slowly erodes even these remaining examples of delegated control.

Traditional patterns of foremanship survived on a large scale during the interwar years, and foremen appear to have occupied positions of central importance in the organisation of production and the control of labour (Goodrich, 1920; NIIP, 1951). Nelson's description of foremanship in late-nineteenth century America, quoted earlier, also describes the pivotal role of the foreman in twentieth-century British industry, a role which continued in a modified form until the 1950s and 1960s in a few firms.

It is not clear why British managers were so tardy in rationalising shop management outside the new industries of the interwar years and why so many continued for so long with modified forms of delegated control. Certainly, managerial conservatism in applying scientific principles of organisation was the subject of a considerable and hostile criticism from academic commentators such as J. A. Hobson and Sidney Webb, who were aware of what American and German manufacturers were doing at this time, and such criticisms became part of a more general attack on the overall ineffectiveness of British management (Levine, 1967, pp. 57–68). One possible line of argument, that occupational principles were so well-entrenched prior to the rise of modern, managerially-dominated industry that they could not be overthrown, is on its own unconvincing in the light of the American success in destroying a similar legacy and applying Taylorism. However, this success was won only after two decades of violent opposition from organised labour, characterised by massive strikes, gun battles and the murder of strike-breakers (Palmer, 1975).

The slowness of shop rationalisation should be set in the context of the industrial retardation which Britain experienced between 1880 and the 1920s. This period of stagnation was marked by a general unresponsiveness to technical and organisational innovation, during which British international competitiveness declined sharply. Economic historians have advanced a variety of explanations for this decline, which can broadly be divided into the social and the economic. Among the first category are a series of arguments that British manufacturers failed to act as rational capitalists, this because they were recruited from an upper class where amateurism, a distrust of professional competence, and an indifference to applied science and technology were dominant characteristics (Levine, 1967, pp. 57–78). One specific manifestation of this state of affairs was the shortage of trained engineers in industrial management, in contrast to the U.S. and Germany, and inadequate training for those people who did become professional engineers. In addition, so it is argued, British workers failed to act as rational economic men, because their wage expectations allowed them to be satisfied with wage levels which were low by international standards, with the result that lack of wage pressures provided managers with little stimulus to innovate (Levine, 1967, pp. 76–8).

In the second category, it is claimed that capitalist rationality itself probably did not decline, but that the economic environment did not place a premium on innovative behaviour (Hobsbawm, 1968, pp. 157–63). The imperial system and tariff protection at home sheltered British industry from the full thrust of international competition in many markets as well as providing cheap raw materials. As a result, managers faced relatively little external stimulus to increase labour efficiency. In addition, as the earliest industrialised nation, Britain had a technical and organisational base which, at least in the medium term, allowed individual firms to trade profitably, though at the cost of the long-term inefficiency of the economy as a whole: for example, old machinery whose costs were amortised continued to yield good profits while re-equipping appeared to be expensive and carried a risk of failure.

So far as rationalised shop administration was concerned, therefore, one may speculate that the socially-determined character of much British management was not conducive to this. In particular, the absence of a strong technical and engineering bias in management meant that scientific management, the application of engineering principles to social organisation, did not readily find favour. Nor were the economic pressures of market competition and wage costs felt sufficiently strongly in many industries to promote more cost-effective methods of administration. Nor indeed, in contrast to the experience of the U.S., did long-established British industry ever grow at such a rate that the influx of new workers swamped the capacity of occupational organisation and traditional foremanship. The one period of relative labour scarcity, the First World War, did see the dilution of skilled labour by new workers without significant industrial experience (mainly women workers), the introduction of new machines with lower skill requirements, and the collapse of traditional craft methods of control in the major industry, engineering (Hinton, 1973), but shop administration was not significantly rationalised and after the war an attenuated version of delegated control was re-established.

Friedman (1977) has made a distinction between two different managerial strategies for dealing with the labour problem on the basis of the British experience. He labels the continuation of the traditional practice of delegation on the basis of occupational principles as 'responsible autonomy'. This strategy entails conceding elements of control to workers so that they may use their discretion in the process of production. This strategy seeks to harness workers' own knowledge and abilities to managerial objectives. The other strategy, 'direct control', is the scientific management tradition in which management exercises its control directly to specify work methods and compel compliance. These two strategies, suggests Friedman, are tied to certain determinants: the stage of capitalist development, the production position of groups of workers – whether central or peripheral – and the position of particular industries on a centre-periphery dimension. Direct control is held to be more effective in less developed areas of capitalism and among peripheral workers and peripheral industries. One reason for 'responsible autonomy' is growing worker resistance to rationalisation which compels management to find other methods of managing. Friedman's distinction fits the one made here between delegated and rationalised control. The evidence does not support his particular set of determinants, however, because the long-run tendency toward direct control noted in this chapter has been fairly pronounced in developed capitalism and among central groups of workers and industries, though much slower in Britain than elsewhere. Chapters 3 and 5 suggest that when some contemporary firms reverse this trend, they do so because extreme rationalisation may have proven to be expensive and less than optimally efficient for their production systems, not only because labour resistance creates unanticipated dysfunctions.

Traditional structures of delegated control have now, of course, largely been replaced by managerial systems. This has coincided with the development of management as a distinct occupational stratum in industrial and commercial organisations and as a set of techniques of increasing sophistication and scope. Three developments stand out. The first is the growth of the size of management in Britain: between the censuses of 1911 and 1971 the number of managers and administrators increased by over 300 per cent and, as a proportion of the total employed population, this occupational category more than doubled in size (from 3.6 to 8.6 per cent; Price and Bain, 1976). Moreover, since many of the managerial specialists mentioned in the following paragraph are categorised in the census as technical or professional employees rather than as managers, these figures underestimate the real size of the increase. Over the last sixty years, management has become differentiated both from owner–entrepreneurs and from other categories of employee (Child, 1969, pp. 13–16). This has been parallelled by the foundation of specialist management institutes concerned with the technical problems of managing and the development of new managerial methods, and by the growth of a vast literature which treats management and administration as a distinct area of expertise based on a body of specialised knowledge (Child, 1969).

The second development is the increased differentiation within the managerial ranks which has resulted from the growth of functional specialisation. Management is neither a monolithic entity nor a single occupational role, but a range of separate specialisms, which deal with different aspects of the managerial function. Such differentiation has led to a distinction between line and specialist managerial roles, and to the proliferation of different departments concerned with aspects of work control. (Differentiation has in turn created problems of control within the managerial group itself, which are discussed later.) Production engineers, work-study practitioners, and experts in organisation and methods or systems analysis are concerned, *inter alia*, with the rational planning, co-ordination and monitoring of work activities, whether of those directly involved in production or those whose work is indirectly related to production. Specialists in personnel and industrial relations deal partly with labour control functions. These specialist services are based on systematic techniques and quasi-professional expertise, and greatly extend the knowledge-base and sophistication of managerial control. In this way, the multi-functional roles of craftsmen subcontractors and traditional foremen have not merely been taken over by managers but, as Taylor accurately anticipated, have then been subdivided on a functional basis within the managerial ranks.

The third development is the improved quality of the information with which managers work. Production processes and worker performance are now more closely monitored by production managers and the various managerial services, providing more accurate information of what happens on the shop floor or in the office than was previously available. More sophisticated cost-accounting systems and financial controls also play a vital part, as they produce rapid and centralised information about the state of the firm, which, prior to their development, was simply unavailable or too complex to be easily collected and assimilated. With the advent of computerised financial and production data over the last two decades, the most senior levels of management can now monitor what is happening among the lower levels of the organisation to the extent that such data translate social behaviour into units of financial and production accounting.

Modern management in the office

So far attention has been focused on the effects on manual workers of changes in managerial control systems, but these changes have had an impact on the white-collar labour force as well in recent years. First one should consider some of the changes which have occurred in the structure of the white-collar population.

The proportion of employees in non-manual jobs has risen

dramatically in Britain this century, from around 19 per cent in 1911 to 43 per cent in 1971 (Price and Bain, 1976). This has gone hand-in-hand with increased division of labour and specialisation. The result of these two processes has been to stratify and fragment the white-collar labour force, and to create more rigid occupational boundaries: a number of distinct, non-managerial groups of routine white-collar workers have emerged, such as clerks and technicians, along with quasi-managerial groups such as some of those functional specialists already mentioned, and managers *per se*. This marks a change in the composition and structure of management from the situation that prevailed in the late nineteenth and early twentieth centuries, when management was a homogeneous category and clerks performed managerial functions, had a social and financial status close to that of managers, and were frequently promoted into managerial positions (Lockwood, 1958; Clements, 1958).

The nature of employment has changed for many of the groups that are no longer part of management. Growing job insecurity has eroded the bureaucratic principle of lifetime employment, a trend noticeable in Britain over the last fifteen years. Career opportunities for most low-level, routine white-collar workers have declined as management has become differentiated from other levels of employment. Increasingly selective entrance requirements based on educational attainment mean that increasing proportions of managers are drawn from those with higher educational qualifications (and thus from the sons of higher social class parents, given the linkage between social class and educational attainment), rather than from the ranks of routine non-manual employees (Clarke, 1966; B.C. Roberts *et al.*, 1973, pp. 251–3; Stanworth and Giddens, 1974; Whitley, 1974). Indeed, the proportion of graduates among senior managers rose faster after the Second World War than the proportion of graduates in the population as a whole, both in Britain and America (Child, 1969, p. 14).

Changes away from the traditional characteristics of the bureaucratic mode of employment appear to have been accompanied by a decline in the commitment and normative integration of non-managerial, white-collar employees. B.C. Roberts *et al.* (1973) found that this was the case among a large group of technicians. Studies of clerical workers indicate that clerical involvement is not what bureaucratic models would suggest (Mercer and Weir, 1972; Bowen, 1976).

Many companies have attempted to rationalise office work along the same lines as manual work. Whether this is the result of the growing weakness of white-collar workers' internalised commitment, or simply because rationalisation is assumed to improve the efficiency of a category or workers whose increasing numbers have made them a more significant component of firms' costs, cannot be ascertained. Scientific management consultants applied the principle of task fragmentation and control to clerical work in a few American companies in the early twentieth century (Braverman, 1974, pp. 305–15), but managers did not pursue these principles on a large scale until the 1950s and 1960s. Until recently, most firms tolerated far more discretion and influence over the work process among their office workers than they did among manual workers. Bureaucratic principles may have emphasised the division of labour and the need for formalised rules to co-ordinate work processes, but these were never pushed to the extremes of task fragmentation and close managerial control.

The most dramatic application of scientific management principles in the office has occurred in clerical work. Clerks form the largest single, non-manual occupation (14 per cent of the total British labour force in 1971; 18 per cent of the total U.S. labour force in 1970). Rationalisation has followed the principles of decomposing multi-functional jobs with high discretion into simple and repetitive tasks, the introduction of time and motion study which establishes standardised work methods and times, and the removal of work planning from clerks to office managers. Indeed, management consultants over the last two decades have eroded the distinction between manual and clerical work, establishing the notion of the 'universal process' and the application of the same rules of work analysis in offices as on the shop floor (Braverman, 1974, p. 319).

Office rationalisation has coincided with the mechanisation and automation of office work, which further increases managerial direction of work processes and worker effort. The introduction of office machinery which simplifies tasks and makes them more routine also means that it is easier to subject them to a standard measure: thus managers are able more effectively to record and control the quality and quantity of worker output.

The advent of computers has had an even more startling impact, because their application has often involved structural change throughout the organisation. Weir (1977), in a discussion of office computerisation, shows how organisations tend to be re-structured into departments organised by function, rather than departments continuing to handle the multiple functions associated with, say, a particular product or geographical area. Departments emerge which specialise in data preparation, output handling and queries, and such specialisation encourages task fragmentation. The number of hierarchical levels tends to be reduced because many intermediate jobs are eliminated by the computer. Banks and insurance companies provide the most notable examples of this process, and computerisation produces something approaching a two-tier structure of senior managers, who deal with policy issues, and clerical workers, who prepare data for the computer and deal with customers – the computer assumes most of the functions of checking transactions and controlling the work which used to be performed by senior clerks and middle managers. Because all information about work activities within the firm is centralised, senior managers have the knowledge to direct and co-ordinate these activities far more thoroughly than before and to deal with a wider range of issues than before.

In computerised offices, lower level jobs become more routine and the required levels of skill and discretion are reduced, while higher level jobs become more interesting and responsible. The computer contains all the knowledge necessary for the satisfactory performance of work and can make its own decisions, so that the co-ordination of the work process is carried out inside the computer without human intervention. As the result, clerical work in computerised offices mainly involves feeding information into the computer and then acting on its instructions. Even the collection of information is highly routinised because clerks must follow strict procedures which allow no discretion, in order to prepare data in the appropriate form. Higher level jobs gain: computers provide the designers of office systems and senior managers with more scope for decision-making and more power to influence the activities carried out in their firms.

Attempts have also been made to apply the techniques of rationalised management into other spheres, notably technical work. Engineering design has traditionally been a skilled occupation and designers have been free to organise their own work with the minimum of intervention, because employers have generally been content to accept occupational principles of organisation. However, several cases have been recorded of firms with large design staffs attempting to rationalise design work in order to increase managerial control. In the early 1970s, Rolls-Royce in Britain wanted to impose work measurement techniques on design staff and divide jobs into their basic elements, in order to establish standard times which would then be used to control labour effort (Cooley, 1977). Union resistance prevented Rolls-Royce implementing this scheme. American firms have tried to break down design work into its elements, allocate these to different individuals, and use engineering managers to co-ordinate and integrate the work process (Braverman, 1974, p. 244). Such attempts are not yet widespread, but that they should occur at all indicates how managers are concerned to regulate all the activities carried out within their firms.

Managerial Ideology and Normative Control

Two important developments in the late nineteenth and early twentieth centuries constituted a 'managerial revolution'. One was the establishment of the managerial function as a distinct role separate from the ownership function, a process which Taylorism expedited. The other was the actual separation of the ownership of industrial capital from its control, a development manifested in the rise of managers who administered firms but did not own them. These two developments paved the way for the dramatic expansion of management this century. The precise nature of the separation of ownership and control, and its implications for managerial behaviour, are discussed in Chapter 4. Here we are concerned with the ideological and normative control aspects.

Traditional ideologies had assumed that managerial authority at work and the social standing of managers in the community were the consequences of property ownership: what required justification were the circumstances in which some people owned capital while others did not. Since ownership and management were largely synonymous, no separate justification of the right to manage was needed. However, the growth of large corporations administered by non-owning managers obviously made traditional ideologies an unsatisfactory base for the justification of the rights and status of managers. At the same time, the administration of large-scale bureaucracies appeared to need personal qualities which differed from the aggressive self-interest of owner-entrepreneurs making good in traditional small-scale enterprises (Bendix, 1966, pp. 297 f). Managerial ideology was transformed as the result of these developments.

A recurrent theme in British and American managerial thought since the 1920s has been the notion of professionalism (Bendix, 1966; Child, 1969). This has involved the idea that management is a highly technical function which requires appropriate levels of education, training and expertise, and that managers have earned their positions of authority and status because they have been recruited on the basis of widely accepted criteria of ability and then trained in a body of managerial knowledge. In addition professionalism has involved a second notion, derived from the advocates of the 'managerial revolution'. This is the idea that managers, because they are not the owners of capital, do not ruthlessly pursue profits like old-style owner–managers, but share the service and social responsibility ethics of the traditional professions. It is thus suggested that they care for their employees' material and other needs in a manner very different from that of the traditional business owners. This notion assumes that managers serve groups whose interests are complementary to their own (Child, 1969, p. 219).

By definition, business organisations involve some degree of co-operation between different individuals and groups or they would cease to exist. What is not obvious, of course, is how this co-operation is ensured in practice: the basis, the strength and the extent of co-operation may be explained in different ways. Notions of professionalism have fostered the belief among managerial theorists that managerial prerogatives to direct and control industry are accepted as legitimate, and that there is a sufficient degree of common purpose and normative consensus among all groups in the enterprise for conflict, should this occur, to be contained without disrupting this basic framework of consensus.

Professionalism thus fosters a unitary view of the firm: the development of managerial thought during the last half-century shows that there is a persistent tendency to regard the enterprise as a solidary community and to minimise the importance of conflicts of economic interests (Child, 1969, p. 219). Hence the appeal of the human relations movement. This emphasised, among other things, the need felt by employees for a high degree of personal involvement in their firms and the importance of managers for the creation of the appropriate climate. Human relations simultaneously provided a model of the firm in which managers could see themselves as representatives of shared aspirations, a body of professional knowledge and techniques – apparently grounded in scientific research – for dealing with the human aspects of the managerial control function (see Chapter 5), and a reason for employees to accept managerial authority provided managers were technically competent (Child, 1969, pp. 222–3).

Even when the reality of conflicting interests is acknowledged and it is recognised that firms comprise various groups that do not constitute a unitary community, which is usually now the case among practising managers and theorists concerned with industrial relations, this pluralistic model of the firm is normally defined in a way that performs the same kind of integrative function as a unitary model (Fox, 1974, pp. 273–4). In particular, this managerial perspective assumes that there is a strong framework of consensus which permits co-operation among groups to continue, and a moral commitment among employees to honour agreements with management. Chapter 7 considers in more detail the pluralist perspective on industrial relations.

Managers still feel the need of legitimating beliefs which justify voluntary co-operation and work effort standards, because the rationalisation of control may not be entirely successful for reasons already mentioned. These legitimatory beliefs are essentially ideological, because they distort the reality of management and managerial behaviour in a bid to win support for managerial interests. The aspect of managerial 'professonalism' which suggests that the overall goals of the management team are less influenced by the profit motive than other considerations is incorrect. The rest of this book, especially Chapter 4, makes this clear. Moreover, the actual behaviour of individual managers often belies the notion of a community of interest. A central, underlying philosophy of contemporary organisation is that the competition of interests in the economy means that workers cannot fully be trusted and a particular style of managerial intervention is thus called for. This adds the pressure of modern work organisation to that of the market place. One does not have to argue for any conscious or malevolent intention on the part of managers since it is the system which works in this way. The managers who apply techniques derived from this philosophy may genuinely believe in unitary conceptions of the firm, but their practical behaviour so often contradicts their beliefs. They appeal to employees on the basis of high trust theories but administer their firms according to low trust principles of control (Fox, 1974).

Employment relations reinforce the low trust principles embedded in work organisation. Employment based on the cash nexus, the commodity status of labour, and the play of market forces still magnifies the opposition between the interests of employers and employees. The worst effects of the operation of unrestrained market forces in the market for labour have been mitigated in most advanced capitalist economies. In Western Europe, union pressure on employers, and governmental legislation to protect employment, do to some extent restrict managers' ability to hire and fire at will, and guarantee some financial compensation from employers to redundant workers. Unionisation may also hamper the free play of market forces in fixing pay and levels of employment. In addition, full employment during the long period of sustained economic growth in the postwar era meant that employers had to attract and retain labour anyway, and market forces probably favoured labour.

Nor are the cash nexus and low trust work organisation confined to capitalism: socialism of the form such as that found in the USSR and satellite economies appears to operate on much the same lines. As was mentioned earlier, scientific management was imported into the Soviet Union as a way of increasing output and controlling labour. Great emphasis has subsequently been placed in the Soviet system on payment-by-results, as modified by the scientific management techniques of work measurement, standard times and output 'norms'. This appears to embody one of the principles of the cash nexus: namely that workers can be trusted to work only if they are given material incentives, since they have no other commitment to the goals of the organisation. This aspect of the cash nexus emerges strongly in an account of shopfloor life in a contemporary Hungarian factory (Haraszti, 1977). A second aspect also emerges: piece-rates in this factory are the locus of a conflict of economic interest between labour and management. Hungarian managers use a variety of rate-cutting techniques in order to raise output without raising wages, thus increasing the profitability of the enterprise and apparently also their own incomes.

Compliance

How far do employees accept modern management ideology? The answer must be that they do not, insofar as unitary conceptions of the firm are concerned: research into employee attitudes and behaviour shows how widespread is the view that workers and managers have conflicting interests (Goldthorpe *et al.*, 1968a; Beynon, 1973; S. Hill, 1976b; Nichols and Armstrong, 1976; see also Chapter 10). What does emerge, however, is the idea that managers and workers need to co-operate to some extent in order to protect their *own* interests: 'teamwork' is held to be essential in industry, in the sense that both sides need to work with each other if the firm is to survive and continue providing employment, despite the conditions under which teamwork takes place and the opposing claims on the way the profits of the teamwork are distributed. Co-existing with the awareness of inherent opposition between management and workers is 'an experience of (largely economic) interdependence with the employer at a factual, if not a normative level' (Mann, 1973b, p. 68).

With regard to the legitimacy of authority, the answer is more complicated. Goldthorpe (1974) claims that there has been little opposition to, and no loss of, managerial *authority*, but a distinct rejection of managerial *power*. He follows the conventional Weberian definition of authority as the 'legitimate exercise of command' and suggests that this is authority of a legal – rational kind: namely, it is the legitimacy of command that management derives from the performance of a specific function under the regulation of law. Managerial authority stems from the manager's status as the agent of the owner, and from the contract of employment in which workers have engaged. Adopting this perspective, Goldthorpe argues, leads one to the view that managerial authority is still intact, because workers have rarely rejected the principle that management has the right to perform its technical and labour control functions in the interests of the owners, and to issue orders to workers. He is largely correct when he says that management has not in fact ceded authority. But the growing interest of union confederations throughout Western Europe in new forms of management accountability and 'worker control' indicate that the very principle of managerial authority *is* now challenged (see Chapter 8), even if this challenge has as yet made little significant impact on the exercise of authority.

Of course, as was noted earlier, the contract of employment is incomplete and not explicit: it establishes the general principle that managers have the right to plan and command, but not the concrete details of this command. Since employment relations contain oppositional elements and workers cannot be relied upon to work in the interests of managers and owners, then the limited scope of managerial authority enshrined in the legal contract raises major practical problems of management. Because managerial authority is insufficient, it has of necessity to be supplemented by power: by the manipulation of various resources at the disposal of management in order to ensure worker compliance and discipline. One power resource is symbolic: namely ideology. But this has not been important in practice because there is no evidence that workers accept more than the minimal, legal definition of authority, such as the legitimation of managerial prerogative by reference to professionalism. Employees commonly dispute particular aspects of managerial prerogative, even if they accept the general principle that management has the right to manage. They resist the practical consequences of management's control. They may try to frustrate managerial objectives in a variety of ways, ranging from individual resistance to organised opposition against specific aspects of managerial control. The growth of collective action on the shopfloor in Great Britain and continental Europe is one significant indicator of how workers have questioned the manner in which managerial power is exercised (see Chapter 7).

There are other resources connected with the dominance of managers within the firm and their advantage within the rule of law. The strength that stems from organisational control and delegated ownership rights gives managers the capability to design and implement control systems which are intended to ensure employee compliance. Managers normally have more power in the labour market, which allows them more influence over the terms of the employment contract. The tendency of the law to support property rights, of which managers have the use, and to support a conception of the employment contract in which managers give orders and others obey, reinforces these organisational and labour market strengths. Managers can still rely on a fair degree of compliance, whatever the motivations of those who obey and despite a relative decline in the very high level of power which managers once had.

Acquiescent compliance is scarcely surprising given the indirect compulsion of employment that Weber and others have documented, the fact that people need to work to sustain reasonable living standards and so have to go along with those who control employment. Acquiescence is reinforced by the inertia of existing organisational forms, the sheer difficulty that employees acting on their own experience in changing anything but minor details of business without the agreement of those in command. Organisations have an apparent solidity which makes successful change initiated from below seem unlikely to those who work in them, which in itself is a deterrent against acting.

The ability of managers to supplement their legal authority has somewhat lessened and the passive compliance of workers has begun to give way to a more active pursuit of control in recent times. Subsequent chapters show how certain developments have strengthened the hand of workers in advanced European capitalist societies: the better market position of labour from the 1950s through at least to the recessions of the middle and late 1970s; more effective shopfloor organisation and greater aspirations for some degree of workplace control; the increased influence of organised labour on national governments. A result of these changes has been that management's success in ending delegated control has not always been matched by the totally successful application of rationalised control. These issues are elaborated in the subsequent discussions of technology, unionism and the state.

3 Alternative social relations of production

There has been a growing interest in the possibilities of alternative forms of control and employment. This interest has been shared by people of widely divergent philosophies and practical concerns. Management theorists and practising managers themselves have been concerned to find new ways of raising efficiency and profitability by minimising what are increasingly regarded as the dysfunctional consequences of the dominant forms of control and employment. Western socialists, learning from the experience of Soviet block societies that the abolition of the private ownership of capital does not necessarily lead to any change in 'capitalist' relations of production, since the forms of work organisation and employment in socialised economies have so far developed along lines similar to those of capitalist economies, have recently turned their attention to the possibility of running industrial enterprises on alternative lines. In so doing, they have raised once more the issue of whether there is any inevitable logic of industrial organisation, such that technical efficiency inevitably leads to the existing types of control and employment, or whether alternative social relations of production exist or can be visualised. Several of these alternatives will be discussed here and compared with the dominant patterns of control and employment.

The Managerial Response

Humanising work and employment

Work 'humanisation' techniques have gained considerable popularity with management theorists over the last decade and a small number of firms in the United States and Europe have introduced these techniques on a limited scale. Humanisation schemes have been designed to overcome two problems associated with the rigid application of scientific management. These are, first, the way in which extreme task fragmentation may sometimes lead to technical inefficiencies which increase costs rather than promoting more effective and cheaper methods of work organisation. Secondly, the way in which worker resistance to fragmented work and tight managerial control may reduce the effectiveness of scientific management principles in practice.

The technical inefficiencies of scientific management fall into three categories. First, the attempt to prevent workers exercising their own discretion leads to the underutilisation of worker resources and their costly duplication in the management control system, by creating numerous supervisory personnel with co-ordination and labour control functions who perform jobs which workers are able to do themselves. The same process of duplication results in excessive numbers of ancillary workers, for example maintenance workers, whose existence is justified by the principle of extreme specialisation and fragmentation, which overlooks the fact that many production operatives are able to perform these ancillary tasks themselves. Secondly, the increased organisational complexity which results from fragmentation and the need to co-ordinate production organisation via the managerial control system slows down problem-solving and the response both to emergencies and routine events. For example, production workers in many machine shops, when faced with simple machine malfunctions or the routine re-setting of tools, have to approach their foreman who then organises ancillary workers to perform a job which the operatives could do themselves with a little training. Paradoxically, Taylor himself *in practice* sometimes reversed fragmentation, when doing so produced more efficient organisation, even though he argued the theoretical need for maximum fragmentation.

Thirdly, scientific management produces rigidities in the face of change, particularly technical change, because long-established methods of working tend to become the subject of customary rules and protective or 'restrictive' practices among the workforce, which then resists change. This tendency occurs whenever workplace labour organisation is strong and is not confined to work organisations that have been rationalised along conventional lines, but the problem is more acute in fragmented organisations with multiplicities of different tasks.

The human problems of rationalised work organisation result from the frustration of what psychologists regard as the basic human need for work that fosters autonomy and self-expression. Faced with the expression of worker resistance in ways as diverse as sabotage, strikes, absenteeism and labour turnover, senior managers have adopted the psychologists' perspective, that these manifestations will disappear once work tasks are brought into line with human needs.

Companies have experimented with job redesign as a solution to both the technical and the human problems resulting from the rationalised control systems that fragment work and deny worker autonomy. Friedmann (1961) claimed that scientific management principles had been on the retreat since the early 1950s in America and Europe as the result of a spontaneous reaction among workers to restore their control and an appreciation among managers that 'humanised' work might be more efficient for technical and social reasons. Friedmann however anticipated the real movement against scientific management by many years and greatly exaggerated the significance of various small changes which he observed in work organisation. Jobs can be changed in two basic ways: job enlargement can be seen as a 'horizontal' process, which adds new tasks to a job but does not increase the levels of skill or responsibility required, so that an operator now performs several routine tasks instead of one; while job enrichment can be seen as a 'vertical' process which raises the level of responsibility or autonomy and sometimes increases the skill requirements of the job. These distinctions are mainly conceptual because job redesign in practice involves a mixture of both elements though one normally predominates.

Experiments in job redesign The best known example of work humanisation in Britain, and one of the most extensive anywhere in the world in terms of the number of employees covered, is to be found in Imperial Chemical Industries. Senior ICI managers in the late 1960s realised that, by the standards of the international competition in the chemical industry, their firm was overmanned and had insufficient flexibility of labour between jobs (Roeber, 1975, pp. 57–8). Long-established systems of fragmentation and control had ossified manning arrangements and fostered the growth of 'restrictive' practices: studies of the ideal manning arrangements for the sort of plant being operated in the early 1970s showed existing arrangements to be sub-optimal (Roeber, 1975, p. 260). At the same time, the old division of labour worked inefficiently, since decision-making was moved too far up the managerial hierarchy for a sufficiently rapid response to production problems, while the division between maintenance and production caused many production delays (Roeber, 1975, p. 259). In collaboration with shop stewards, managers embarked on an appraisal of every manual and supervisory job in the company, which resulted in substantial job redesign. This increased the scope of each job, partly by enrichment but mainly by enlargement which added together several routine and low-level tasks (Nichols and Beynon, 1977).

One of the programme's aims was to integrate maintenance

(engineering) and production (process) workers, and job enlargement typically took the form of some simple maintenance and adjustment tasks being added to production jobs. Elsewhere, enlargement took the form of reintegrating individual jobs which had a natural unity which preceding divisions of labour and union demarcation rules had disturbed. For example, the 'composite building worker' reintroduced a traditional method of working commonly found among small, unrationalised firms in the building industry, whereby one man did as much as possible and the job was no longer fragmented into various sub-tasks (bricklaying, plastering, painting, etc.) performed by separate people.

Enrichment was less common, but in one plant (the nylon works at Ardeer) workers were given more autonomy and responsibility: work teams were allowed to draw up their own work schedules and make many of the running decisions themselves, replacing a computer-controlled system of work scheduling and close supervision of worker activity. Machine utilisation increased by 5 per cent (because the men planned more efficiently than the computer), manning levels were reduced by 30 per cent, and worker morale increased (Roeber, 1975, pp. 264–5).

The results of the ICI scheme were to reduce direct and indirect labour costs, since fewer manual and supervisory employees were required. Supervisory functions were changed so that supervisors spent more time co-ordinating and less doing elements of manual work (for example, checking controls and machine speeds). In the Ardeer plant, one whole level of supervision was abolished and many co-ordination tasks were taken over by the men. Surveys of other schemes in Europe and America indicate that productivity and profitability increase as the result of reduced indirect labour costs and more efficient work organisation, and as the result of releasing worker creativity and improving morale (Pignon and Querzola, 1976).

Sweden has become the main centre of experimentation in new forms of work organisation since the late 1960s, and almost every major company has some sort of trial programme in progress in part of its organisation. The goal of management in initiating these schemes has been to find work forms which result in increased productivity and solve Swedish industry's acute difficulties in recruiting and keeping production personnel (Lindholm, 1978, p. 151). The prime emphasis has been on the individual and the work group. The individual's job content has been enriched and enlarged by means of job rotation, lengthening the work cycle, adding inspection to the operator's work load, and re-combining unnecessarily fragmentated tasks. 'Semi-autonomous' work groups have been created to give workers collectively limited responsibility for immediate production planning and provide a unit of organisation within which the individual's job rotation and task flexibility can best be arranged. These objectives have led managers to reorganise work directly by extending and redesigning individual and group responsibilities. They have also been implemented in the design of the new plant and equipment which have often accompanied new forms of organisation (see the description of Volvo's new technology in Chapter 6). Many of these changes are functional for management, particularly in assembly-line situations where they increase flexibility, for example making the manning of the line each day far easier (D. Wedderburn, 1978, p. 14). Where the production plant has been redesigned at the same time, there are instances of the assembly-line being scrapped in order to provide a more favourable environment for individual job satisfaction and group working, notably engine assembly in one of Saab–Scania's factories and the new Volvo car assembly plant at Kalmar. However new methods of organising work have not necessarily meant any real extension of control and managerial prerogative seems scarcely to have been challenged let alone altered in these experiments (D. Wedderburn, 1978, p. 15). Swedish labour in fact looks to the government for legislation to weaken the control of management at the workplace and within the firm (see Chapters 8 and 11).

Evaluation of work humanisation techniques suggests that managers no longer need the tight labour control and detailed co-ordination which scientific management introduced. The particular problems which faced managers in the early twentieth century, namely the traditional patterns of delegated control and the power of craftsmen, and the influx of masses of unskilled workers of rural origin who were unadapted to the time and work disciplines required for efficient work in industry (less of a problem in Britain than elsewhere, because the British economy did not experience the same rapid growth as the American and other European economies at that time), were solved by half a century of rationalisation. The restoration of some degree of worker discretion now appears to have become compatible with efficient operation. Indeed, it provides a solution to some of the technical inefficiencies of task fragmentation and to some extent counteracts the human problems arising from the low trust ethos of scientific management.

Job enlargement, which reduces task fragmentation by re-combining several tasks, has little effect on existing levels of managerial control because workers gain little extra responsibility. However, job enrichment does make a difference, since the role of lower level management (mainly supervisors) in the co-ordination and labour control areas is changed in a way that at first glance appears to reverse the trend of managerial development in this century. Some Marxists have even hailed job enrichment as proving the possibility of worker control of industry and the restoration of meaningful work divorced from the dictates of the profit motive, of a 'revolution' in the present forms of production which incorporate the 'domination' of capital over labour (Pignon and Querzola, 1976).

Arguments about the reversal of past trends or the transformation of the social relations of production must be treated with considerable caution, however. Job enrichment does indeed demonstrate how workers can exercise greater control over their immediate work environments, but it is clear that at the present time humanised work is still carried out within production systems which are planned and dominated by management, and in firms where hierarchical control is as strong as ever. The overall design of production processes and the design of individual jobs within these processes are still managerial functions which workers do not control, and the technical function of co-ordination resides with management. The labour control function is still exercised by managers, no longer perhaps by direct supervision and overseeing, but just as effectively by monitoring worker activity and intervening when necessary. In this context, it is worth noting the great significance of the development of computerised information-processing technology, which makes it possible for managers to plan, co-ordinate and monitor far more effectively than previously. As a consequence, the early twentieth century strategy, which was to increase the size and complexity of supervision in order to develop control systems, now has less relevance, because computers can perform certain of the activities which were previously done by supervisory staff. Managers may delegate to labour some limited responsibility for its own work behaviour, while still retaining their grip on the system as a whole. As is noted in Chapters 4 and 5, automated technology may even control production directly, without the intervention of workers.

Comparison of the restricted autonomy of workers in enriched jobs with the old system of delegated control shows how limited is the new control which managers have given over. This indeed is the crucial comparison to make, as those who merely compare enriched work with that degraded by scientific management miss the fact that these new jobs by no means reverse the logic of historical developments over the last fifty years. By creating space at the point of production for limited worker autonomy, normally by changing low-level supervisory tasks, managers above the level of foremen neither change nor renounce their own interest in control.

Some large corporations in the recent postwar period have attempted to change certain aspects of their employment practices as distinct from their control systems. They have done this in order to overcome the low trust dynamic of the cash nexus. Innovation has centred on building worker commitment to the company by developing a career structure for manual workers. 'Careers' normally involve a progression through a limited range of manual and supervisory positions of increasing responsibility, though these jobs may not require increasing skill. These career opportunities are selective: management chooses a few people who are to progress but it does not provide the automatic career advancement on a seniority basis which is characteristic of bureaucratic principles of organisation.

Trade unions attempt to routinise career advancement onto a seniority basis, which threatens managers' rights to reward selected employees. American evidence shows that unions have been particularly concerned to establish seniority rights and that a few corporations have gone along with this so far as the lower levels of the career hierarchy are concerned (Herding, 1972). Corporations can dismiss employees whom they find unsuitable and of course they monitor suitability closely at all stages. Where the seniority aspect applies, working-class careers resemble part of the bureaucratic employment system. The British evidence is that unions establish seniority criteria for lay-offs (the 'first in, last out' principle) but are less successful in replacing managerial discretion with seniority rights to a career (Blackburn and Mann, 1979).

Firms that pursue this method of building greater loyalty and commitment in fact create their own *internal* labour markets, selecting from their own pool of labour rather than hiring on the open market outside. Managers look for a diffuse set of attitudes including loyalty to the company and responsibility when promoting, rather than the possession of some specific skill, since people with the right attitudes can then be trained by the company to operate its plant. Such characteristics are difficult to assess and purchase on the external labour market, which is why managers select from people whom they already know. Co-operation and commitment are rewarded by improved pay, more interesting and less arduous work, and higher status. Those outside the selected group may be treated in much the same way as workers elsewhere.

Internal labour markets and working-class careers, whether on a selective or seniority basis are particularly noticeable in firms which employ capital-intensive and fairly advanced technology. High technology creates certain types of job which, though not especially skilled by the standards of craft work, are difficult to standardise and control in the same way as more routine and repetitive jobs, and thus require workers to act in the best interests of the firm when they exercise their own judgement. It is for this reason that workers with the right attitudes are needed in these key posts. Equally, labour stability is important in many advanced production processes, where absenteeism or turnover among key personnel can have disastrous effects on output and the physical condition of the plant. These developments are most frequently found in continuous-process firms (Mann, 1973a).

Enlightened personnel management techniques include various other ways of binding workers to supplement the cash nexus with more positive sources of commitment. Company pension schemes, improved working conditions, single-status employment which abolishes the most visible status differences between workers and staff (for instance, by aligning payment systems so that workers become salaried) and the promise of a greater degree of job security (economic conditions permitting) are aspects of the employment policies of a few large firms. The development of the personnel function may promote more formal and rule-bound procedures, for example when companies establish detailed job descriptions and criteria for assessing employees' performance and formalise the distribution of rewards or punishments. Such rules reduce the personal discretion of supervisors and lower managers and inhibit the arbitrary exercise of managerial power which used to be common. These modifications to traditional employment relations reduce the disruptive tendency of the simple cash nexus. The divergence of interests inherent in the economy remains, but employers hope to contain its expression by modern personnel techniques. The containment strategy has some limited success in promoting more harmonious social relations though the potential of industrial conflict remains (see Chapter 5).

In sum, the senior managers of a few large corporations have sought to modify the social relations of production which have been typical of European and American capitalism this century and before. The modification of work organisation by means of job redesign has broken with earlier twentieth century methods of increasing the impact of management. Nevertheless, managerial control of production and the separation of the worker from significant decisions concerning the production process are still maintained in 'humanised' work systems. Where the circumstances permit their introduction, computerised information and production control technologies have often made older forms of rationalisation obsolete. Employment relations have been changed as a result of introducing career structures for certain workers and adding new principles of employment which modify the cash nexus. Some of these developments represent the partial bureaucratisation of the employment relationship for manual workers. Modifications to the cash nexus are more widespread than changes in production control systems and managers obviously find this sort of change easier to make than the other. Changing the employment relation between the worker and the firm does not threaten managerial prerogative, is clearly necessary and beneficial to management in certain types of industry, and satisfies trade union objectives which are usually more concerned with the economic aspects of employment than the nature of work and authority in industry. The hope is that all of these modifications to the traditional social relations in industry will also modify the practical significance of conflicting economic interests. Management becomes less openly oppressive and exploitative in the organisation and conditions of work, and in the hiring and firing of labour. These developments allow managers to claim that conflicts of interest are now unimportant. Managers also endeavour to foster moral cohesion (in the form of sentiments of trust and belonging), in order to promote an image of shared interests and so to reduce the industrial relations' consequences of structural oppositions in the economy.

The Japanese corporation

The most far-reaching transformation of conventional employment relationships in modern capitalism can be found in large-scale Japanese corporations, which combine paternalism and bureaucracy in a unique synthesis. Following Dore (1973) and Okochi *et al.* (1973), the key elements of the employment system can be summarised as follows. Large corporations expect to employ people for life and provide security, rather than hiring and firing according to fluctuations in the demand for the corporations' products. Manual and non-manual employees are guaranteed career progression and wages that rise with age as well as 'merit' rather than careers for a selected few and wages based mainly on performance criteria. The principles of security, career and seniority are employment characteristics similar to those found in public service bureaucracies, for example the British Civil Service.

In addition, firms are committed to looking after the 'whole' man rather than his workaday self alone, and provide substantial non-wage benefits such as company housing and medical, educational and leisure facilities: this reflects a paternalistic view of employment responsibilities. The notion of the 'social' wage is important: firms provide wages and benefits which increase with an employee's age and social responsibility (for example his family commitments), rather than reflecting simply his work performance or the value of his skills as determined by supply and demand in the labour market. Paternalism is impersonal and bureaucratised, however, in that it is rule-bound and is not subject to the discretion of individual managers; indeed, the rules are frequently determined jointly by unions and the company.

Managers promote a company philosophy or ideology of community, identification of the individual with the collectivity, and loyalty to the paternalistic corporation. Collectivism and community are reinforced at all levels of the company by the creation of small work teams as the basic units of organisation.

Two arguments about the Japanese system are frequently encountered. One holds that employment relations merely continue certain cultural and organisational traditions peculiar to Japanese society: specifically, the historical legacy of feudalism which appears in the submissiveness of workers to authority and their willingness to subordinate themselves to collectivities, and the legacy of small-scale paternalistic firms. The other holds that Japanese industry is in a transitional phase and will move toward the patterns of employment that are found in other advanced industrial societies as the result of the logic of industrialism. Both arguments misunderstand the historical development of Japanese industry and underestimate the degree to which the present system reflects conscious managerial policy. They also fail to appreciate how managers outside Japan have followed not the dictates of an inevitable industrial evolution but deliberate choices from a range of possible types of industrial organisation.

So far as the significance of the Japanese social inheritance is concerned, it is undoubtedly true that Japanese managers have to some extent built on their pre-industrial legacy, but the inheritance argument misses two crucial points. First, in the late nineteenth century, Japanese industrialisation had already taken a path similar to that of Europe and America before Japanese managers deliberately restructured their employment policies. Second, modern, bureaucratised paternalism owes comparatively little to the traditional, personalised variety (Okochi *et al.*, 1973, pp. 505–6).

Labour markets, particularly in the engineering industry, had developed along western lines by the early twentieth century: workers possessed their own occupational skills which they sold on the market; employment was an economic exchange determined by the state of the supply and demand for skills; in periods of business prosperity, employees were mobile between firms and could dictate their own terms, but when the market turned against them they were exploited by employers. The state of industrial relations at the turn of the century was far from harmonious, with growing labour unrest manifest in strikes and the growth of occupational unionism, the latter spreading particularly among skilled engineering workers (Dore, 1973, pp. 389–90). At the same time, Japanese industrialists, like many of their European and American counterparts during periods of rapid industrialisation, faced two related problems in the market for unskilled labour: a relative shortage of suitable workers who would endure the new disciplines of industrial work and high labour turnover; and an inadequate industrial infrastructure, particularly with regard to health and housing, which added to the difficulties of recruiting and retaining labour.

The different employment patterns between Japan and the rest of the industrial world in the twentieth century represent different appraisals of what provides a workable basis for organisation, as much as different cultural and organisational legacies. It is worth recalling that European societies as well as Japan had pre-industrial legacies which fostered paternalism in the early phases of industrialisation (Giddens, 1973, p. 21; Abercrombie and Hill, 1976), but that manufacturers chose to pursue a different path as industrialisation advanced. Likewise, when faced with their dependence on craftsmen or others with occupational skills and the difficulties of maintaining adequate work performance from unskilled labour with little or no industrial experience, European and American employers chose to solve their problems by the new control techniques contained in the principles of scientific management.

Japanese industrialists chose another course of action in the period of rapid growth starting in the second decade of the twentieth century (Taira, 1970). This too led to heightened managerial control (Cole, 1979, p. 20). Their policy had three strands. These were to change production processes and replace skilled workers, as much by the introduction of capital-intensive technology as by organisational means; to destroy the existing labour market for people with skills and recruit from school-leavers with no previous work experience; and to incorporate workers into the companies by the material rewards and ideological appeal of paternalism. Thus, among a few firms after 1920 and on a wider scale in the late 1930s, employment policies began to create masses of unskilled and semi-skilled laboureres who were trained in processes specific to one firm, for whom there were few possibilities of moving elsewhere because firms mainly recruited from schools and not on an open market, but who came in any case to appreciate the benefits of working for large paternalistic companies. The majority of manual workers in large corporations were involved in this system only after the last war. The extension of the system owed much to trade unions, who saw it as being in the interests of labour. So employees are now dependent on and, both by necessity and choice, loyal to the corporation. Corporate paternalism is thus a modern creation. It has reversed the trend of the first half-century of industrial development prior to the 1920s, and owes little to the personal paternalism of traditional small firms. Traditional culture may perhaps be seen as a diffuse cultural resource on which the creators of the new institutions could draw, for example to justify seniority rather than ability rights (Cole, 1971, p. 114).

Only part of the labour force in the private sector of the economy is covered by these employment relations. Within big corporations, large numbers of people are outside the system: women, temporary workers, the employees of subcontractors, and sometimes late entrants (people who have not come directly from full-time education) do not benefit from permanent employment, careers and rising wages, and may be hired or fired according to market fluctuations. Outside the large-scale, modern sector, there are numerous small- and medium-sized firms, many directly dependent on the large corporations for work, where employment principles differ. The existence of employees outside the system and of smaller firms dependent on the large ones means that Japanese corporations have maintained a labour reserve which can be used or discarded according to fluctuations in economic activity. This in turn has helped make financially feasible permanent employment for part of the labour force. However, the long-run tendency in the postwar period has been for the new employment system to spread rather than contract with industrial development, mainly as the result of labour shortages between the mid-1960s and mid-1970s. In this period firms outside the modern sector found that they needed to imitate the policies of the large corporations if they were to attract and retain labour (Dore, 1973, p. 303); while large corporations themselves extended the system to previously excluded categories of worker for the same reason. In the later years of the 1970s a few corporations responded to the less stable economic environment of the times by increasing the amount of subcontracting again (Cole, 1979). But there is little evidence at present that Japan will move toward the model of other advanced industrial nations.

The employment relationship clearly differs from the western capitalist model. The cash nexus, commodity status of labour and free play of market forces do not exist for those within the permanent employment system. Security, incremental wage structures, real expectations of rising with age into supervisory and lower managerial positions and the custom that increased company prosperity results in bonus payments throughout the firm, reduce to a low level the manifest conflict of interests that the cash nexus aggravates. Outside observers occasionally describe the employment relationship as exploitative, because it is based on dependence and because company trade unions provide little countervailing power to that of the corporation. Dependence and weak unions are indeed both characteristic of the Japanese corporation. However, Japanese workers themselves appear to endorse the system (Dore, 1973; Clark, 1979; Cole, 1979). Far greater exploitation takes place among those excluded from the benefits of the large corporations, whether they are the marginal employees of these firms or the employees of their suppliers and subcontractors (Clark, 1979, p. 234). Two aspects of the capital market are significant. Shareholders are mainly other companies, often associates and business partners, whose primary interests are not necessarily maximising their returns in the form of dividends and profits; while much new working capital is raised in the form of long-term loans from financial institutions rather than as new equity (Clark, 1979, p. 221). As a consequence, corporations can pursue growth objectives rather than profit *per se* (Clark, 1979, p. 223). Expansion helps reduce conflict, because it provides the new jobs necessary for the career progression of existing employees and the prosperity to finance incremental wages. The absence of shareholder pressure for high returns on capital and the emphasis on growth goals mean that managers are not seen to be serving the interests of private profits against those of employees; this is a perception which fosters the sense of community.

There is a strong managerial presence in work organisation. Given the reasons for breaking with occupational power in the second quarter of the twentieth century, one would of course expect to find work organisation controlled by management and strong managerial authority at the point of production. However, this situation has not come about by the western technique of applying scientific management principles in order to weaken and control labour. Scientific management was imported in the 1930s to find technically efficient procedures, not as a means of labour control (Cole, 1979, pp. 109–10). Personnel policy inhibits the growth of either occupational identity or individual job consciousness because people are neither recruited nor promoted on the basis of their mastery of a particular job. Working practices reinforce this because tasks and responsibility are assigned to groups rather than the individual (Cole, 1979, pp. 196–214). Japanese employers have always tried to build on traditions of team work and collective responsibility characteristic of early industrial production and to ensure that these promote managerial goals (Dore, 1973, pp. 381–2). This is in contrast to the usual American and British practice of rationalising the shop floor in ways that have tended to fragment traditional collective organisation and promote individualism. Within the Japanese work team, members are expected to perform a wide range of jobs. Weak unions, employee dependence and the destruction of occupational principles, together with the positive identification of employees with their companies, mean that western techniques of control are unnecessary.

Some companies have recently begun to decentralise decision-making to work groups and to encourage worker participation (Cole, 1979, pp. 196–214). Managers believe that they can build more responsibility into jobs without groups acquiring power which might be used to frustrate managerial control. This managers can do because work groups are dominated by the foremen, who are both senior group members and enforce hierarchical authority. In effect, these schemes transfer power from higher in the hierarchy to foremen, while ordinary work-group members have a consultative and not a decision-making role. The idea is that foremen can better absorb the men's suggestions than remote managerial departments. The employers' 'mobilization and penetration of primary-group relationships among workers, while allowing these groups sufficient autonomy to assume meaningful roles, is critical to understanding the willingness of employees to identify with organizational goals' (Cole, 1979, p. 250).

Work organisation illustrates the ambiguity of the Japanese employment system. On the one hand it creates dependence which fosters compliance. On the other hand it generates feelings of identification and loyalty, with the effect that employees willingly support top management's goals. The absence of low trust controls in work organisation is to be explained both by the high trust employment relations that integrate employees into their companies, and by the systematic destruction of sources of countervailing strength within the labour force. Japanese corporations have not abolished the basic divergence of interests, but employment is undoubtedly far more harmonious than elsewhere and employees' perceptions of divergence and opposition are at present muted.

How long the system will continue in a stable form is impossible to predict, though certain potential sources of instability can be identified. The most obvious potential source of disruption is that a prolonged recession or the failure of individual firms to compete successfully in the market might lead managers to break with tradition, by reducing the level of benefits or even dismissing employees in order to maintain returns on capital. This would destroy the structure of welfare corporatism and consequently could lead to changes in employee perceptions of the business enterprise, to an awareness that a firm is not in fact a community based on shared interests.

The world-wide recession of the mid-1970s led to a reduction in business activity throughout the large-scale sector of the Japanese economy in the short term, and in the longer term led to the more permanent contraction of a few industries (for example, shipbuilding and steel). The reaction of large corporations, after first shedding temporary labour and squeezing their suppliers and subcontractors, was to maintain permanent employees despite the lack of work for them to do. As many as four million employees may have been kept on in this way at the bottom of the recession and have continued to receive full benefits, including annual, age-related increments. Japanese corporations certainly fulfilled their commitments to their employees for a considerable period until economic activity picked up. However, the longer-run decline of certain industries did lead to redundancies among permanent employees, which shows the fragility of paternalism in the face of adverse market conditions. Corporations involved in these industries managed to redeploy much labour into other areas of their business – Japanese corporations may straddle several industries – but industrial diversification and redeployment have not provided employment for all. Other corporations have chosen to rely on subcontractors to a greater extent and thus transfer the costs of future recessions onto the employees of other firms.

These considerations raise the related and broader issue, that industrial peace in Japan depends not just on avoiding recession and the collapse of paternalism, but on continuing rapid economic growth sufficient to provide career progression and raise the real wages of employees. Conflict over the distribution of profits and relative shares can be avoided while people each year continue to improve significantly their living standards. So far this economic growth has been maintained – indeed, the employment system is one cause of the labour productivity which is a component of growth – but the future is unpredictable. Other factors potentially threaten the system. Rapid industrialisation has created a relatively young labour force which will become progressively more expensive with each incremental rise. In addition, a declining birth-rate means that there is a shortage now of very young workers, who have a scarcity value which may result in a labour market strength.

As the result of cultural diffusion from other advanced capitalist societies, notably from America, Japanese workers may come to question their status as dependants in a corporation which sets itself up as their paternalistic protector, and also to resent the presence of managerial controls. This is a further potential source of disruption. There is already evidence that younger workers have become more mobile among firms, that many now subscribe to the belief that pay should be based more on skill and ability than other criteria, and that firms should become more egalitarian (Okochi *et al.*, 1973, p. 510). These phenomena suggest that individualism may have begun to supplant the traditional emphasis on collectivism and subordination, though commentators disagree about the extent to which new values will lead firms to modify the basic principles of paternalism or workers to oppose the system.

The Co-operative Alternative

The socialist critique of managerial control systems and employment relations starts with the assumption that the cash nexus and existing patterns of management in advanced industrial societies take their present form, indeed are only necessary at all, as the result of basing economic organisation on the expropriation of the wealth that workers communally produce, for the purpose of capital accumulation by private interests or the state. Two particular arguments have been advanced to explain the rise of existing patterns of management. The first holds that the conflict of interests which results from expropriation leads managers to reduce their dependence upon workers who are potentially unreliable and to develop methods of securing managerial objectives which do not depend on the willing compliance of labour. Though associated in recent years with Braverman's *Labor and Monopoly Capital*, this formulation is in fact an adaptation of a well-established viewpoint about economic conflict and labour's unreliability which has informed the philosophy and practice of management in this century from Taylor through to the present day.

A related but less conventional thesis is that the minute division of labour and centralised organisation, which characterise industrial work and which have been the two decisive developments in depriving workers of control over their products and work processes, are not technically required for productive efficiency. Marglin has claimed that the division of labour in early capitalism, using for illustration the early nineteenth century textile industry in Britain prior to factory production, was

> the result of a search not for a technologically superior organisation of work, but for an organisation which guaranteed the entrepreneur an essential role in the production process, as integrator of the separate efforts of his workers into a marketable product.
>
> (1976, pp. 14–15)

The essential task of the entrepreneur was to interpose himself between individual workers and the market, and to prevent his workers by-passing him to deal directly with consumers. The fragmentation of tasks and individual products gave him a crucial co-ordinating role and prevented individual workers from producing a completed product which could be sold independently.

In a similar vein, Marglin claims that the later development of factories was not initially due to any technological superiority but because factories made workers more dependent on the owners of the means of production and allowed owners to substitute their own control over work processes and quantity of output in place of that of the workers. The social function of the resulting system of centralised organisation and hierarchical authority was to increase the rate of capital accumulation, because owners were able both to raise the proportion of the surplus which they appropriated and to force workers to produce more in absolute terms by denying them the choice of how much to work and produce (Marglin, 1976).

These interpretations of why management has developed in the way it has serve a broader purpose: namely, to destroy the argument that there is an inherent logic of technical efficiency which leads to a particular form of specialisation and fragmentation, managerial co-ordination and direction. They claim that alternative social relations of production can be visualised, which are both morally preferable to existing relations and compatible with industrial progress and economic prosperity, that are based on communal ownership and worker control. A number of points can be made in support of this claim.

Specialisation is not incompatible with worker control: this principle has always been adopted by craftsmen and the self-employed in order to increase efficiency, either by specialisation between occupational roles or within a role. In the first case workers divide tasks between different occupations, while in the second an individual who makes a series of whole products produces batches of sub-components, in order to benefit from the economies of repetitive production, before assembling the final article (Braverman, 1974, pp. 75–8). Task fragmentation allied to job roles appears to be required for control purposes but not necessarily for productive efficiency. Indeed, the evidence presented earlier in this chapter suggests that fragmentation may often *decrease* efficiency. What often appears as increased efficiency resulting from the application of the principles of extreme division of labour and managerial control may well, according to Marglin, represent *no* efficiency gain in the technical sense of efficiency (a greater output without a corresponding increase in inputs), since the inputs of labour effort are also raised (1976). The apparent increase in economic efficiency is often no more than managers compelling workers to intensify their efforts without a corresponding increase in wages. Marglin ignores the possibility of some increased efficiency resulting from reduced wastage of effort and materials (a change in the quantity of outputs without increasing inputs) and the cost saving of simplifying work tasks and substituting cheap for expensive labour (a change in the quality of inputs). Historically, workers who had an overall view of the production process did perform what are now management functions, and it is believed that modern, socialised work organisation would allow such self-regulation to be restored once people work for themselves rather than to create profit for someone else. Concrete evidence of the feasibility of producing effectively without the dominant managerial control systems is to be found in the existing (though limited) experiments with autonomous work groups and work enrichment, and in the communal decision-making and control which are found in certain socialist economies, for example in Yugoslavia and China, and in producer co-operatives within capitalism.

How plausible is the claim about the feasibility of worker-controlled productive units? So far as economic efficiency is concerned, the answer must be that producer co-operatives can operate at reasonable levels of productivity and provide the sorts of progress and prosperity associated with traditional forms of ownership and organisation. Worker-controlled and worker-owned co-operatives already exist on a small scale in contemporary capitalist economies. In the service sector of the British economy, for example, the traditional learned professions and, to cite a more esoteric example, some symphony orchestras have long operated successfully as partnerships with communal ownership and control. More recently, a small number of manufacturing co-operatives has been established in America and Britain (see Sturmthal, 1975, on the U.S.; Chaplin and Cowe, 1977, on Britain). The largest communally-owned and -governed co-operative within a capitalist economy is the Mondragon group in Spain. This provides 18 000 jobs in over eighty industrial units. Members are required to invest a certain amount of capital on joining, which gives them an ownership stake. At the centre of the group is a co-operative savings bank which raises loan capital for the industrial units. On all important economic indicators, Mondragon's manufacturing units have outperformed the national capitalist economy (Oakeshott, 1978). Outside the capitalist world, Yugoslavia enjoyed rapid economic growth at least in the 1950s and 1960s on the basis of the co-operative organisation of enterprises within a market economy (Vanek, 1975).

Co-operatives are quite compatible with two central features of capitalism, namely market competition and accumulation. Indeed, when the members of the enterprise share the ownership of the assets or capital, then a co-operative is simply another form of capitalist organisation. In the socialist, Yugoslavian model producers manage the enterprise's assets, but these remain public property rather than being owned by the members directly (Vanek, 1975). There is nothing inherently socialistic about co-operation, despite the popularity of the notion in some socialist circles. Indeed, modern socialists divide into the advocates of co-operation who see it as a step along a road leading to the abolition of all capitalist forms, and those who regard it merely as workers' capitalism that perpetuates the coercion of markets and accumulation. Existing labour movements regard co-operation with great suspicion (Bradley and Gelb, 1979).

One can conceive of a market economy where the basic unit of ownership and organisation is a co-operative, in which the market disciplines of demand and supply, and of competition which weeds out less successful units, raise productive efficiency. The argument commonly put forward by the advocates of the particular form of privately-owned capitalism which exists today, that this leads to creative innovation, increased productivity, better and cheaper goods which benefit everyone, obscures a crucial fact: it is as much the competitive nature of the market place as the motivation of the individual owners of capital to make a private profit which has produced these beneficial consequences, and this would continue to be true even if capital ownership were to be in different hands. The present form of capitalism incorporates two distinct sources of compulsion: that of management on workers and that of the market on the firm. At present the two are linked, because managers have to be in command of labour which is potentially recalcitrant if they are to survive in the market place. But the internal structure of the firm could be changed, so as to transform employment relationships and resurrect worker control of production in place of managerial control, without thereby changing the wider discipline of the market on the firm.

Other things being equal, the co-operative organisation should match and even surpass the performance of the conventional business organisation. Co-operation is inherently more efficient because it avoids the cost of controlling recalcitrant employees, which is the considerable financial penalty paid by conventional capitalist and socialist organisation, and it benefits from the harnessing of members' energies to promote the prosperity of the enterprise in ways that are denied most other organisations. In a survey of co-operation in advanced Western economies, Jones (1980) finds that those co-operatives which require all their workforce to be full participants and where all control is vested in the members on an equal basis have the best performance when measured by the criteria of growth, income, efficiency and survival.

What is less clear is the practical viability of co-operative self-management of the enterprise as a whole and, at a more limited level, of the production system itself, given various organisational processes that appear to threaten democratic control. Studies of existing co-operative institutions focus primarily on the issues of overall organisational control and democracy, and rarely on the nature of the control system as it affects workers in their jobs. They produce ambiguous results about the possibilities of worker control at the management level. It is clear that in theory management should cease to operate as an independent structure of authority and become instead an economic resource performing technical functions, any authority that it possesses being delegated from the mass of members. Managerial functions cannot be expected to disappear, since producers require administrative back-up for effective production and there is, in addition, a range of non-producing functions (for example, accounting, marketing, product development) which have to be tackled.

In practice, many small co-operative organisations do indeed work on democratic lines. Overall policy is decided by the mass of members and managerial control of the production process is replaced by worker control of co-ordination and labour effort (Bellas, 1975; Hadley, 1975; Chaplin and Cowe, 1977). This is as one would expect, that both participative democracy and worker control of production are more easily achieved in small, undifferentiated communities with a high degree of social interaction and moral cohesion. However, size and increased differentiation, which usually go together in industrial organisations, create problems for self-management, in that the need for co-ordination increases while participative democracy becomes more difficult to organise.

Yugoslavian firms, which are self-managed and profit-sharing, attempt to maintain technical efficiency in complex and highly differentiated organisations without sacrificing member control of enterprises, by creating various levels of self-management (Vanek, 1975). Except in firms of fewer than seventy members, self-management takes place via elected workers' councils, which determine policy issues, and an executive management board (elected from the council), which jointly appoint and control higher management. Larger firms in addition have decentralised self-management bodies which are formed at the level of production units (three or four tiers being found in some cases), in order to preserve face-to-face interaction as an essential feature of self-management, and a variety of specialised committees. Vanek claims that

> all this amounts to an immensely complex decision-making process for which it is difficult to find an analogy or a precedent. According to most accepted management theories, it should paralyse all decisions, all action. Yet this conclusion is obviously incompatible with Yugoslav experience. There have certainly been cases where internal conflicts led to delays or inefficiency but, on the whole, there are few examples of actual paralysis of decision making within an enterprise.
>
> (1975, p. 260)

He further asserts that Yugoslavian enterprises combine this technical efficiency with active worker participation and truly democratic control, since 'the worker collectivity, in other words "labour", is thus in command of the entire decision-making process...' (Vanek, 1975, p. 263).

Detailed investigation of the reality rather than the appearance of self-management suggests that democratic control is in practice compromised. Two surveys of recent Yugoslavian research show that the effectiveness of democratic control varies between enterprises and according to the issues involved (L. Benson, 1974;

Ramondt, 1979). It is common for managers to assume dominant roles in decision-making and to usurp control of policy-formation and policy-execution. The extent to which democratic determination is relinquished depends partly on the immediate salience of the issues for co-operative members: wages policy, for example, is subject to greater democratic control than sales of financial policy. Managers are in a crucial position within the organisation, since they control the information on which the elected bodies make policy decisions, while their technical expertise is indispensable for day-to-day administration. Managers and technicians thus dominate the representative organs which deal with executive matters; both numerically, since they outnumber manual workers by two to one on management boards and committees, and in terms of their influence on the outcome of decision-making. In addition to the organisational process that increases managerial power, managerial prerogative is to some extent supported by outside agencies that have an influence over the enterprise, namely local communist parties (there is a close connection between managers and local political élites) and the law. The role of the law is two-edged. Self-management has been a legal obligation for more than a quarter of a century, and in the 1970s legislation was passed to check what appeared as the growing influence of management. However the law at the same time obliges chief executives to protect the assets invested in their enterprises. Depending on how they interpret this obligation, chief executives may be able to frustrate the council and management board on some occasions (L. Benson, 1974). Thus management emerges as something other than an economic resource and develops as a system of influence with some autonomy from the worker collectivity.

The Yugoslavian experience highlights several difficulties facing all self-managed work organisations. The first is the problem encountered in most large democratic bodies, of ensuring that participation is effective and that the power of the membership over officials is maintained in practice as well as in theory, a problem shared by political parties and trade unions as well as producer co-operatives, and best expressed in Michels' phrase 'the iron law of oligarchy'. It is the apathy of members and their failure to assert their rights that is crucial for the re-emergence of management as a system of influence rather than remaining as an economic resource, not the dictates of technical efficiency in industrial organisations. Put another way, the problem that worker co-operatives face is that of the tendency towards the oligarchic control of representative organisations rather than some putative logic of industrialism. There is evidence to suggest that where the membership of large, self-managed enterprises does assert its control, then the tendency for power to devolve to small groups is checked (Maccio, 1976). It is worth anticipating the discussion of oligarchy in trade union organisations, which appears in Chapter 7, to note that unions, once notorious for the extent of oligarchic rule, have managed to reverse Michels' iron law and make membership participation more effective. This suggests that co-operatives should also be able to resist oligarchic control.

Secondly, there is obviously a tension between the expertise of managers and their performance of essential technical functions, and the effective mobilisation of worker control, which is magnified in large, complex organisations where the technical functions are more important and the difficulties of organising participation are greater. The advocates of worker control correctly argue that workers normally have the capability to organise the immediate production process, but they frequently ignore the large areas of business activity which are not directly and immediately related to the production process, where the majority of members have little expertise and find it difficult to resist the re-emergence of groups which are not always effectively controlled by the collectivity.

However, the sort of managerial influence that can emerge in co-operatives is quite different from what is found when shareholders or the state delegate ownership power to managers, because ultimately it is the collectivity of members who control policy and managerial appointments. Managers may create a sphere of autonomous action, but this is circumscribed by their need to justify their actions to the collectivity or its elected representatives and the ever-present possibility that the collectivity may choose to exercise its sovereignty over management. The accountability of 'superordinates' to 'subordinates' means that subordination as such is unlikely to promote the conflicts Dahrendorf noted in conventional business. Yugoslavian experience shows that managers may succeed in implementing their policies, 'but they cannot find social legitimacy for the actual power which they exercise' (Ramondt, 1979, p. 90). Because managerial power is socially and legally defined as illegitimate, and workers have the institutional means to control managers, managerial control of the Yugoslavian self-managed enterprise is simply not the same as power and control in other types of business organisation. It is reasonable to assume that these conclusions about Yugoslavian self-management will apply *a fortiori* to self-managed enterprises elsewhere, which are not subject to the sort of support for management from extra-organisational sources that is found in Yugoslavia.

Conclusion

There is a growing interest in devising alternative systems of employment and management, thus modifying the social relations involved in production and superseding a system which alienates labour but does not totally suit management either. The range of alternatives reflects the different interests of labour and business. The variety of the new forms also marks the practical implementation of insights derived from a critical tradition which is as old as industrialisation itself. This tradition, moreover, contains liberal advocates of capitalism as well as socialist opponents: as long ago as 1848, J. S. Mill came close to anticipating some of the major features of recent developments when he suggested that industry should overcome the antagonism inherent in the cash nexus and repressive control by moving either towards paternalistic or co-operative organisation. In his celebrated chapter 'On the Probable Futurity of the Labouring Class' (1848, Book 4, Chapter 7), Mill claimed that since existing employment practices meant that workers worked only at the bidding and for the profits of capitalists, while their wages resulted from hostile competition with these owners, some alternative had to be found which would reconcile the need for the efficiency and economy of production on a large scale without dividing employers and workers into hostile camps.

Mill argued that his first solution, paternalism, would be unsatisfactory as a permanent policy, because in the end it would fail to bridge the fundamental opposition of interest between the two sides of industry and because workers would ultimately see through the rhetoric of paternalism to the reality of exploitation and the compulsion of dependence. The second, a form of co-operative organisation which gave workers a real stake in their firms and a share of the profits, appeared to be preferable. This would reconcile workers and capitalists (who would still retain a small part of the surplus as their own profits), increase worker involvement and therefore productive efficiency.

To date, Japanese company paternalism has surpassed Mill's pessimistic view of the potential of paternalistic organisation. 'Welfare corporatism' (Dore, 1973), which is rule-bound, subject to trade union negotiation, and provides real benefits for employees, has successfully held in check the clash of interests inherent in capitalism and certainly does not *appear* exploitative to the participants in the system. Some of its features, indeed, have been emulated by large corporations elsewhere in their attempts to modify their employment relations, though none has yet devised a fully-fledged system of welfare corporatism on Japanese lines. It is obviously difficult to predict how long the Japanese system will continue in a stable form and the potential of instability has already been commented upon.

Co-operative organisations overcome that opposition of interest between capital and labour which is manifest most concretely in the cash nexus and prevailing structures of managerial control. Co-operation changes the nature of the tie that links a worker to the enterprise, replacing the cash nexus by co-ownership or profit-sharing co-management. However, the evidence from existing organisations demonstrates that certain co-operative ideals, particularly self-management, may in practice be difficult to realise. In particular, there appear to be considerable, though not insuperable, difficulties in resisting tendencies toward control by minority groups and in mobilising participative democracy on a permanent basis. Of course, the existing evidence is far from conclusive since self-managed enterprises in Yugoslavia, which demonstrate the tendency for control to pass from the collectivity to smaller groups, are subject to external pressures which modify the internal structure of control and encourage the re-emergence of managerial influence. Co-operative ideals are more easily realised in the absence of such interference.

A number of developments suggest that conventional systems of control and employment are becoming less stable, partly as the result of the internal contradictions of such systems and partly as the result of outside pressures. The experience of many firms is that existing controls promote technical inefficiencies while reliance on the cash nexus creates poor industrial relations. Worker opposition to the denial of autonomy inherent in conventional work organisation and to the direction of business enterprises in the interests of outside capital is a further pressure for change. This is manifest in the varieties of shopfloor resistance to existing control systems, a growing number of experiments in communal ownership and self-management, and trade union demands for changes in work organisation and the control of firms (see Chapter 8). In a majority of the advanced Western European economies, trade unions have developed policies of 'industrial democracy' which, in the long run, are intended to give employees a major share in the control of business and place management in a subordinate position in the firm. The Swedish trade union movement goes further, and proposes that ownership as well as control should be transferred to employees (see Chapter 8). The response of a few large corporations to these pressures has been to change the structure of control on the shopfloor, so as to increase worker autonomy, along with somewhat modified employment practices. This response involves no change in the overall control of firms and some modification – though not the diminution – of managerial power at the point of production. However, as subsequent chapters show, the actions of organised labour and government have led to more extensive changes in managerial control in some cases than senior management would willingly implement.

4 Managerial goals and organisational structure

Ownership and Control

The separation of the ownership of a firm from its administration – 'the divorce of ownership from control' – has been one of the major structural changes in industry associated with the rise of management. Earlier generations of academic commentators argued that the 'managerial revolution' which resulted from the separation of ownership and management functions would lead to changes in the way firms were run (Berle and Means, 1932; Burnham, 1941; Dahrendorf, 1959). The essence of the argument was that because there was a trend toward giant corporations whose share-ownership appeared to be so fragmented that no single shareholder owned sufficient capital to impose his will on management, and because managers were salaried employees rather than owners of capital, then managers would no longer act to maximise profits in the way of old-style capitalists who owned and ran their own businesses. In particular, the separation of ownership and control would lead to a change in the basis of managerial authority and the nature of the firm, replacing the old conflict of interest between employers and employees and the low trust treatment of workers with a new state of shared interests and socially responsible management (Dahrendorf, 1959, p. 45).

It is now apparent that such arguments do not correctly interpret recent developments in the ownership and control of industry, are wrong about the attitudes and behaviour of managers, and simply ignore powerful constraints originating within the economic system. With regard to the first point, there are a number of facts about industrial ownership which show that shareholding has not become fragmented in the way once anticipated. Taking the *private* ownership of company equity, there is evidence that the family ownership of firms, whether complete ownership or ownership of the majority shareholding, is still not uncommon in advanced capitalist economies. This is the case even in America among some of the world's largest corporations (Burch, 1972). Among those firms which have apparently dispersed shareholdings, individual minority shareholders may potentially be able to influence company policy, either directly as the result of a substantial minority holding or indirectly by means of nominees or alliances with other shareholders. Nyman and Silberston (1978) estimate that more than a quarter of the largest 250 British firms are potentially controlled by private shareholder interests. This figure does not include nominee shareholdings nor alliances and so underestimates the total. Care is needed when interpreting this evidence, because the proportion of shares defined as creating the potential for control is as small as 5 per cent, and because there is less evidence of how this potential is used, if it is used at all. Francis (1980) suggests that the ability to appoint and remove the chairman is the crucial way in which control over a company may be exercised because chairmen are usually the most powerful members of boards of directors and dominate company policy and administration. How small a shareholding needs to be to create this ability depends on how fragmented other shareholdings are and what the mechanisms are that allow the generality of shareholders to influence the appointment or replacement of the chairman and chief executives. These are variable factors that render it impossible to define a certain proportion as necessarily giving control. In some cases 5 per cent is sufficient; in others more is required (Francis, 1980). Of course, being a professional manager does not necessarily preclude owning shares, and many do have stakes of varying sizes in the ownership of their firms.

Moreover, the postwar trend towards greater concentration of industry and the growing dominance of financial institutions in advanced capitalist economies has led to a decline in the private ownership of shares and a marked increase in *corporate* ownership. This reverses any previous tendency toward fragmentation because the institutions are few when compared with the multitude of private owners they replace. In Britain and America, the growth of 'monopoly' capitalism describes a process of industrial concentration which is largely based on corporations owning other firms, which they acquire by means of mergers and take-overs or by the creation of new subsidiaries (Zeitlin, 1974; Aaronovitch and Sawyer, 1975; Hannah and Kay, 1977). Such concentration consolidates the potential for control. Indeed, when a firm is the fully- or largely-owned subsidiary of another corporation, control is both consolidated and re-connected with ownership. A parallel development has been the concentration of share-ownership in the hands of financial institutions: large corporations themselves may be owned by various other corporate bodies. In America and Britain pension funds and insurance companies are major owners, while banks are more important in France, Germany and Japan. When private and corporate ownership are coupled, Zeitlin (1974) estimates that 60 per cent of big American firms are owner-controlled, while Nyman and Silberston (1978) place the British figure at 55 per cent.

Both 'monopoly' and 'finance' capitalism have grown massively in Britain since the early 1960s. Mergers and take-overs have made the British economy one of the most concentrated in the capitalist world (Aaronovitch and Sawyer, 1975). Over a twelve year period, from 1963 to 1975, personal shareholding dropped from 56 to 40 per cent of the total market value of shares, while the proportion owned by financial institutions alone increased from 30 to 48 per cent (Erritt and Alexander, 1977). There is a sense in which the final beneficiary holder of most stock is normally an individual: there are still personal shareholdings in corporations, including banks and insurance companies as well as industrial and commercial enterprises; pension funds act as trustees for groups of employees and mutually-owned insurance companies benefit their policy-holders. Indeed, in America several of the top fifty banks and trust companies are controlled and largely owned by wealthy families (Burch, 1972). But from the point of view of this chapter, what is important is that corporate bodies of one sort or another own large tracts of company equity. The effect of concentrated ownership on the management of firms remains an area about which not a great deal is known. The influence of outside directors, who represent shareholder interests such as pension funds, insurance companies and banks, is essentially covert but apparently increasing (Scott, 1979, p. 98). One visible indicator is the appointment of company chairmen: if this aspect of control is as crucial as Francis (1980) suggests, then the trend is for institutional shareholders increasingly to influence how firms are run. Apart from this area, influence is only visible when the covert system collapses. The most publicised cases of intervention by financial institutions in Britain have concerned mergers and take-overs when the institutions have opposed the policy of a company's executive directors. There is little sign of involvement in routine management.

Moreover, ownership is not the only source of influence over a company's affairs: banks which provide loan rather than equity capital may demand a say in company policy including board representation (Speigelberg, 1973). The proportion of investment funds raised as loans from financial institutions in Britain increased from 2 per cent in the 1950s to 32 per cent in the 1970s (NEDO, 1975). The upshot of these developments is that the independence of managers to pursue policies which are not acceptable to the owners and financiers of the company has been exaggerated by those who focus on shareholdings of individuals.

This leads to a consideration of the objectives and behaviour of the top corporate management, the board of directors. The concentration of the potential for control in other corporate bodies does not itself discredit one part of the thesis of the 'managerial revolution', because these other bodies are also run by professional managers who may be less concerned to maximise profits than were old-style capitalists. The evidence suggests, however, that top decision-makers throughout industry do not differ greatly from the traditional owner–controllers. If one examines the social connections of directors in Britain, one finds that they are integrated, both normatively and by means of social relationships, into a business community of financiers, capitalist–entrepreneurs and large share-owners. Senior managers of board level have a social background similar to those of other élite groups. This is reinforced by personal share-ownership and by the prevalence of interlocking directorships (Stanworth and Giddens, 1975). Interlocking directorships, normally held by non-executive directors, occur on a large scale and are a normal feature of business in advanced capitalist economies (Scott, 1979). There is little to suggest that the goals of board-level managers would be different from those of capitalists in general. A survey of managerial attitudes suggests that the profit motive is still central and has not been replaced by notions such as social responsibility (Nichols, 1969). Should managers' goals differ from those of shareholders as some have suggested, with managers aiming instead to maximise size and growth rates so as to promote their own special interests in security, power, prestige and personal income, these objectives would still require profit maximisation (Marris, 1964). Profits ultimately are the source of growth. Without them the internal financing of growth would not be possible nor would external finance be forthcoming. An analysis of the behaviour of firms with regard to mergers, an area of business activity which some believe demonstrates the difference between firms controlled by professional managers and firms run by their owners who are concerned with profit maximisation, shows no differences that can be attributed to ownership characteristics (Aaronovitch and Sawyer, 1975, pp. 157–94). Since it is board-level management which determines the goals of the management team, their commitment to profitability becomes enshrined as the firm's main objective.

The theorists of the 'managerial revolution' failed to appreciate that the issue of managerial behaviour is not in any case reducible to the personal preferences of managers. The policies and actions of top management are not unconstrained but are subject to certain external disciplines which operate regardless of their attitudes and motivations. Market competition is one obvious and well-understood device. Competition from domestic and foreign firms, if the market place is working effectively, means that managers are unable to ignore pressures which close off certain options if their firms are to survive. Another and less understood discipline on managerial discretion is what Marris (1964) aptly calls 'the market in corporate control' (the take-over mechanism). This maintains shareholder influence over the firm in an indirect manner, which those who regard ownership power as working directly through the voting power of shares often fail to consider. Managers who attempt to maximise corporate growth prefer to retain profits for internal financing, or to borrow or raise new equity in the external market against future profits, rather than distribute these profits as dividends. Existing shareholders, however, may sell their shares if dividends are too low, if borrowing is too high, or if new equity dilutes their earnings. In each case, selling leads to a fall in the market price of the shares. At the same time, profitability which first rises with growth may later decline, as expansion costs have a tendency to rise more than proportionately as the rate of growth increases. Thus the pursuit of growth after a certain point leads to falling profitability and market valuations. If the valuation ratio falls sufficiently, a take-over may occur when a buyer believes he can make more productive use of the existing assets than can existing management. If the market for corporate control is working effectively, the top management is compelled to take account of shareholder interests in order to protect themselves (top management positions are usually threatened in take-overs). Marris's argument about the market for corporate control applies should management for any reason neglect shareholder interests – should managers for instance 'satisfice' rather than maximise, aiming neither for wealth nor growth maximisation but opting for the quiet life by merely surviving within the market economy and not maximising profitability.

There appear to be differences between top corporate management and the rest of the managerial team. Lower level managers are not normally integrated into the broader business community, they do not experience the direct pressures of powerful shareholding interests, nor do they have as much reason to be concerned about market valuations as the board of directors. They may have little in common with top management in terms of their social backgrounds, their financial stakes in the company or in capital ownership generally. Case studies have indicated that some managers below the top executive level may adopt sub-optimal strategies regarding accumulation, aiming more for personal comfort and security than for entrepreneurial profit maximisation that involves some element of risk; they 'satisfice' rather than maximise in order to regulate their personal environments against the vagaries of the market system (Sayles, 1974, p. 260). For these managers the pursuit of profitability would not appear to be the major focus of their activity, which marks a disparity between their objectives and those of the top management. There are also other forms of divergence, resulting from the way different roles within a complex division of labour create different interests based on organisational position as is shown below. What matters of course is that these divergent objectives and interests are constrained and lower level managers are under pressure to act in ways that realise the objectives of senior management. Nor should the extent of the divergence be exaggerated, since managers in a firm do share a common framework of assumptions. One of these is the concern for managerial prerogative and authority. Another is the conviction that managers form a team with many common interests. The next section discusses the structure or internal organisation of the managerial team and looks at the nature of constraints.

What remains to be said here by way of conclusion is that nothing about the relationship of ownership to control indicates that developments in this area have been responsible for a significant shift in the objectives of economic activity in advanced capitalist societies. There is no evident reason why great changes in the ways firms are run and the ways employees are treated should have taken place simply because of the rise of professional management. Though an earlier chapter showed how the alleged separation of ownership and control has been used by managers to justify a new set of legitimatory beliefs.

Organisational Analysis

Organisational structure is both a technical and an administrative device which realises the organisational goals established by top corporate management and a means of influence or control over the behaviour of subordinates. In order to ensure that their objectives are realised, senior managers need to consider the most efficient administrative arrangements. These include issues such as the form that the division of labour is to take, the hierarchy of authority or chain of command, and the operating rules and procedures that people are to follow in their jobs. These arrangements constitute the organisation's structure. They also regulate employees' conduct; hence they have a control function. This control aspect is intimately bound up with the administrative efficiency with which organisational structure promotes top-level goals. The point of separating the two aspects here is simply to emphasise that organisation functions to keep managerial and other employees in line and is not a neutral set of administrative arrangements. The analysis of organisational structure and managerial behaviour has been dealt with by a specialised area of industrial sociology known as 'organisation theory'. The main outlines of this are sketched below.

Bureaucracy

One important strand in the analysis of organisational structure and managerial behaviour derives from Weber's model of bureaucracy and from the classical school of managerial theory associated with Fayol (Mouzelis, 1967). Both approaches developed principles of organisational management in the early twentieth century which suggested that there was a single best way of designing organisations. The most efficient model was based on a clear-cut hierarchy of authority of pyramid shape, with clearly-defined duties and responsibilities at each level, and command exercised down a vertical line. It was believed that generalisations could be made about the behaviour of individuals in organisations, particularly managers and administrators, because the principles of organisational structure applied universally. This in turn assumed that individuals acted according to the roles prescribed for them by the organisation's rules. The search for a universally applicable model is no longer regarded as a particularly fruitful enterprise, but the research conducted within this tradition, particularly that dealing with the Weberian bureaucratic model, has contributed significantly to the understanding of how organisational structure works in practice and how managers and other staff actually behave.

Weber's model of the ideal-type bureaucracy had several elements (Weber, 1946), five being of particular importance:

1. High degree of specialisation and a clear-cut division of labour, with tasks distributed as official duties.
2. Hierarchical authority structure with clearly delimited areas of command and responsibility.
3. A formal body of rules which governs the operation of the organisation; these rules ensure uniformity and, together with the authority system, also ensure co-ordination of activities.

4. Impersonality of relationships within the organisation.
5. Recruitment on the basis of ability, lifelong employment, promotion according to seniority.

These discrete elements were tied together into a coherent totality by one all-pervasive principle: the concept of rationality. This embraced two slightly different notions. In the simpler sense, rationality meant technical efficiency. The rules defined the most appropriate means to realise organisational ends, were based on up-to-date technical knowledge, and directed the behaviour of members along the most efficient path. In the other sense, bureaucracy was a system of social control or authority which was accepted by members because they saw the rules that guided authority as rational, impartial and just (a 'legal–rational' value system). Weber himself was mainly concerned with broad historical and comparative issues and with political administration and its effect on the political structure of society, and developed the model for this sort of macro-analysis. The use of the bureaucratic model in the micro-sociology of business organisation was taken up by his successors. The advantages of bureaucracy for firms were thought to include specialisation of people's competence, precision, speed, reliability, the removal of personal discretion and bias and the end of interpersonal conflicts (Sofer, 1972, pp. 235–6).

However subsequent research has shown that where bureaucratic principles were properly implemented organisations experienced many dysfunctions. Merton (1957) argued that Weberian-style bureaucracy became rigid and inflexible, because its primary objectives and principles produced secondary consequences that ran counter to these. This was particularly noticeable in the face of change but even under stable conditions bureaucracies developed inefficiencies. Organisational members tended to follow the rules slavishly, regardless of whether in fact these were the rational and efficient way of dealing with an issue, to become committed to the formal procedures in a ritualistic manner that ignored the goals the rules were intended to realise. Discipline, doing as one was told, might become more important than whether or not what one was told to do was the sensible thing. Specialisation could lead to a narrow and restricted outlook which would prove incapable of solving new problems. Finally, groups of colleagues developed loyalty to their own sections and to each other, and combined together to protect their own sections and colleagues, often by rigidly enforcing official procedures.

Crozier (1964) extended this analysis to show that bureaucracies have a vicious circle of decreasing efficiency and effectiveness. Impersonal and formal rules protect organisational members against their superiors and subordinates, because if people obey the letter of the law they are safe from penalties and dismissal, regardless of whether they in fact promote organisational goals. Centralisation of power at the top means that those who take decisions are usually people without first-hand knowledge of the issues. They rely on undistorted communication from below for the information necessary to deal with problems and to monitor the effectiveness with which their decisions are implemented. This is often not forthcoming, because the various managerial strata in large, impersonal and centralised bureaucracies tend to become isolated from each other, develop their own internal group solidarity, and withhold or distort information. In these circumstances a group can maximise its freedom of action to bend the rules to suit its own goals rather than those of top management, protect itself from outside interference and protect individuals who fail to do their jobs properly. The vicious circle effect arises when senior managers realise that they are losing control of what goes on below them and try to rectify this by proliferating more rules which attempt to regulate activity even more minutely, and reinforcing centralisation. This self-reinforcing rigidity is inversely related to technical efficiency and provides only limited social control, the two aspects of rationality that bureaucracy was supposed to maximise.

When a bureaucracy exists in the form described by classical organisation theory it produces the inefficiencies just mentioned. But commercial organisations have rarely met all the classical criteria because practising managers have usually been unwilling to tolerate the dysfunctions. It is no surprise that much of the research into bureaucracy was carried out in public service organisations which were largely unconcerned with profit-making within a competitive market and valued impartiality and predictability above all else. Businesses normally retain an element of personal discretion and arbitrary authority, unless obliged to do otherwise by legislation or trade union pressure. This is because firms require flexibility and adaptability that comprehensive, formal rules often inhibit. Senior managers also wish to avoid the ritualism and hiding behind the rules which replace a concern for results with an adherence to procedures, and limit top management's prerogative to reward and penalise subordinates. Promotion by seniority is another characteristic which has rarely found favour, for the same reason. The advent of new information systems and new technology allows senior managers to keep themselves more clearly informed of what goes on within their organisations and provides the capability for more effective control of subordinates. The communication failures of earlier bureaucracies can be overcome, and in principle it should be easier to make bureaucracy work. In practice firms may take advantage of the new techniques to run the managerial team on a looser rein without top management losing control thereby. Developments in some large firms such as divisionalisation, internal profit centres which are responsible for their own activities, and delegation of responsibility to lower levels of the hierarchy are forms of de-bureaucratisation that attempt to overcome the pitfalls of this method of organising and of large size in general.

Contingency

It is now recognised that there is a variety of organisational forms and managerial structures. In an influential study of the impact of technical and market changes on organisations, Burns and Stalker (1961) have distinguished between two extreme cases, a 'mechanistic' or bureaucratic organisation, which they regard as suitable for stable conditions such as uncompetitive markets and unchanging technology, and 'organic', non-bureaucratic forms which maximise personal discretion, de-centralise decision-making and avoid rule-bound behaviour where possible, which they see as optimal for conditions of rapid change. A major strand in recent analysis has been to focus on what are thought to be significant relationships between aspects of the formal structure of organisations and various contextual factors, notably environment, technology and size. Child (1972) provides a summary of the various explanations on which the following three paragraphs draw.

Environmental variability, for example unstable markets or changing patterns of competition, is thought to create the need for an adaptive organisation with roles open to frequent re-definition and with co-ordination achieved by frequent meetings and horizontal communication. It is also assumed that the more complex the environment the more need there is for specialist roles that deal with the environment, which may create new problems of co-ordination. While the harsher the environment the more the very survival of the firm is seen as problematic and the more structure is centralised and control tightened.

Technological influence has taken two main forms. Perrow (1970) looked at the nature of the physical and informational materials used in a variety of industries. He suggested that the stability of the materials used and the extent to which regular routines could be devised to deal with them determined the ways in which work roles could be defined. The greater the uncertainty or unpredictability of the materials, the less organisational roles would be structured. Woodward (1965; 1970) looked at the problems of administration in production technologies of varying degrees of complexity, ranging from craft through large-batch and mass production to automation. Together, Perrow and Woodward imply that highly structured managerial organisation and behaviour, involving task specification and rigid role definition by means of rules and paperwork, is most likely in conditions of standardised production such as mass assembly.

Organisational size appears to be related to the growth of the administrative component, greater formalisation of roles and procedures, and more complexity. One explanation of this apparent tendency is that size opens the way to the benefits of increased specialisation. Specialisation means greater differentiation between organisational sub-units, and this leads to a requirement for greater administrative co-ordination. Complexity also leads to more systematic controls and formal procedures. A second explanation is that large organisations find it difficult to operate with a personalised style of management and decision-making that rests with one person or a small group, and that impersonal mechanisms of control and delegation have to be adopted. This too leads to an increased administrative component.

The contingency approach is descriptive and establishes statistical associations between variables, however, rather than uncovering causal sequences and explaining the processes at work. Causal linkages have depended on researchers' hunches rather than scientific procedures. Nor are the associations between structural and contextual factors particularly close, and clearly a variety of structures is compatible with any particular environment. What is often ignored in this recent approach is the importance of human activity. There is a tendency to assume that for analytical purposes organisations may be viewed as abstractions which are somehow self-regulating, independently of the people who constitute them. Child (1972) rightly criticises the notion that the structure of management is causally related to contextual factors and that the pattern of associations can be interpreted as a rational or functional adjustment of the organisation and its sub-units. The adjustment of structure to contingencies is not automatic and is mediated through the agency of top corporate management who make the strategic choices.

Emergent behaviour and power

The research within the bureaucratic tradition has highlighted various unanticipated aspects of organisational structure and the 'emergent' nature of much managerial behaviour. The significance of interest groups is one finding which has been widely endorsed. The hierarchical division of managers into different strata and the horizontal division into different specialist functions (production, marketing, finance, personnel, etc.) create the conditions for distinct sub-groups to form. These develop their own goals which may conflict with those of other groups and top management. Some of these interests are work-related and result from goal-displacement, when managers pursue the objectives assigned to their own departments regardless of the overall efficiency of the firm. For example, production management may go for output regardless of its cost, making special pay deals with workers to ensure high output. This sectional goal conflicts with the aims of financial and personnel management, and ultimately of top management, which is to control costs and maintain uniform wage policies throughout the firm (S. Hill, 1974). There are other types of goal, as when groups of managers seek to reduce their subordination and increase their discretion, or look for a quiet life which lets them just tick over in their jobs, which bear no relation to organisational objectives and inhibit economic efficiency.

Chandler (1964) cites American case-study material which is relevant. She looked at the reaction of different groups of managers to the issue of hiring outside contractors for plant maintenance and construction. Economic pressures meant that subcontracting was the rational course of action. But there was no unanimity among management which divided along lines of group interest (1964, p. 63). Support for subcontracting came from top management and some middle-level groups, including plant engineering, industrial relations and purchasing. In opposition to the plan were the existing employees in the maintenance and construction departments. These included the departmental managers, who colluded with the workers and their unions in an attempt to frustrate the plans and supported the unions in a bid to call in outside arbitrators. Management placed more importance on its own job property rights and vested interests than on economic and technical efficiency or organisational goals.

The finding that managerial work groups have such significance shows in turn that role performance may be problematic. The officially-prescribed roles which appear as the formal organisation structure do not in fact determine behaviour. Every role must have some discretionary elements, because it is impossible to provide for all the contingencies that arise. In addition, a wide range of standards and levels of performance is normally tolerated before people cease to occupy a role. These two characteristics open the way to behaviour that is not role-determined, to an informal system of activity and the influence of colleagues. Communication is also crucial, because the relative freedom of managerial behaviour and the looseness of role constraints depend in part on how much top management knows of what is going on. Not that senior managers automatically disapprove of the informal system: if this activity is geared to realising organisational goals senior managers may welcome initiatives which find better ways of doing the job. Nevertheless, when communication is poor, role prescriptions are easier to break.

Sofer suggests that the most fruitful way of looking at managerial behaviour is to view organisations as networks of sub-groups (1972, p. 239). These groups contain members who adapt their roles and behaviour in ways that may not fit closely with what is asked of them, or may reflect compromises between what they are asked to do and what they want to do. This implies that group competition and conflict are normal within the managerial team.

In his appraisal of contingency theories, Child (1972) emphasised the importance of organisational power-holders in the determination of managerial structure. He maintained that patterns of organisation represent the outcome of political processes whereby the holders of power decided upon certain courses of action. These choices include both the sort of structure to establish and the sort of contextual factors or contingencies that are to surround the organisation. For example, power-holders make decisions regarding the centralisation or de-centralisation of the organisation; they also decide what markets to enter, what technology to use, and how large to allow the firm to grow. J. Benson (1977) observes that organisational forms change over time and the trajectory of these changes reflects a number of factors, including the power of different people to implement their ideas, the internal and external constraints on their actions, and the range of alternatives they conceive. Organisational structure is thus the product of processes which are as much political as economic.

The main power centre is at the top, where the powers of ownership are vested in the board of directors which includes the most senior corporate management. This centre controls the distribution of resources within the organisation. The power to allocate resources in one direction rather than another, to expand one area of the organisation while holding or even cutting back others, is one of top management's major sources of control over subordinates. Sub-groups need resources if they are to promote their own interests or even to survive. The major power centre also controls the distribution of resources and rewards to individuals, controlling the avenues of career advancement and dismissal. The capacity to commit resources in these ways provides a major lever of control. But subsidiary power centres do exist throughout the firm, as when subordinates are responsible for key areas or have skills that are indispensable. Given that management is a series of interest groups, it can be seen that particular managers' policies and actions do not depend solely on what is economically the efficient thing to do but also on the balance of power between sections of management and the ability of the people at the top to enforce their wills.

The traditional concern with the formal properties of organisations and simple causal sequences has thus given way to an approach that tackles the issues of power and interests and displays a sense of the ever-changing flux of organisational life. I suggest that explanations of managerial behaviour are best expressed in terms of interest groups, conflict, power and control, emergent behaviour and organisational politics. These reassert what empirical studies of organisations have always shown, namely that management is neither homogeneous nor completely united, but managers' freedom to act independently is circumscribed in varying degrees by the organisational control system and the power of those at the top.

The divisions within the managerial team need not obscure the fact than the top echelon sets the objectives of the firm and, as the major resource centre, has a greater capability than other interest groups to see that its decisions are implemented. These decisions are geared to the profitability of the enterprise and other considerations are taken into account only as far as they are compatible with profitability. In this respect modern capitalism differs little from earlier varieties. This is why one should expect to see control and employment strategies reversed only if alternatives appear more profitable for any reason. It should also be borne in mind that all levels of managers have an interest in the preservation of managerial prerogative, because this affects the scope of their own jobs. Even if middle managers do not necessarily have an identity of interests with directors this does not suggest any weakening of attachment to the principle of managerial control. The gap between directors and other levels is significant for the way the class hierarchy is conceived, as a later chapter dealing with social stratification makes clear. But so long as managers are under pressure to promote the economic interests of the board and their own positions and interests remain distinct from those of their employees, there is no reason to suggest any change in the relationship between management and labour.

5 Technology and the worker

The sociology of economic organisation has always been concerned with technology and many writers have used it as a major explanatory variable in the analysis of industrial behaviour. Technology, indeed, is a basic feature of the industrial sociologist's frame of reference. This continuing interest is oriented around two broad issues.

The first is the concern with worker morale, broadly defined as the satisfaction people have with their jobs and their companies. This was the main focus of attention for many decades and the problem of low morale was believed to be the cause of poor industrial relations. Within this perspective, technology is thought to have a major influence on morale in a number of ways: it determines the tasks which people have to perform; it determines the division of labour at work and thus influences the kinds of social interaction which are possible in the workplace and the likelihood of sociable groups being formed; it influences the occupational structure of a factory and thus the homogeneity or heterogeneity of the labour force; and it is associated with the size of the plant. The first of these assumed consequences of technology influences satisfaction with the work itself, while the rest influence satisfaction with the overall social system in which people find themselves in their place of employment and the likelihood that they feel they belong to a social community.

The second and more recent issue is an interest in technology and the industrial division of labour as aspects of the class structure of industrial society. Modern sociological class theory emphasises the differences that exist between the work situations of people in different classes: production technology is a significant determinant of these differences (see Chapter 9). Technology has also been described by some Marxists as the concrete manifestation of the class struggle that they see as resulting from the conflict between capital and labour (Braverman, 1974). This line of reasoning holds that new forms of productive technique are developed which control and coerce workers, deprive them of their skill, and thus reduce the threat to capital accumulation that results from the economic conflict of employment. The sorts of technology which are developed, it is claimed, show technology to be an aspect of the social relations between classes. Part of Braverman's thesis is discussed in the next chapter. Alienation, historically linked by Marxists to class exploitation, is often discussed by modern sociologists in terms of the effects and consequences of technology and the division of labour, as this chapter will demonstrate.

At this point, before proceeding to discuss the effect of technology on employees or their industrial behaviour, it is worth elaborating briefly on how technology is defined. Many people regard technology as being synonymous with machinery, but this is a limited definition which does not capture the full meaning of the term in recent sociological discussion. In the first place, technology embraces all forms of productive technique, including hand work which may not involve the use of mechanical implements. Secondly, it embraces the physical organisation of production, the way in which the hardware of production has been laid out in a factory or other place of work. The term therefore implies the division of labour and work organisation which is built into, or required for efficient operation by the productive technique. Thirdly, machinery and the organisation of production are human products, in the sense that they have been consciously designed, which should be an obvious point but which is unfortunately obscured when people refer to technology as if it were something with a separate existence, with its own laws of development and its own logic in use on the shopfloor. Thus, in sociological debates about the consequences of technology for worker satisfaction or the social organisation of factories, it should be remembered that the constraints of any particular technology result from engineering and managerial decisions about how work is to be performed and how the division of labour is to operate on the shopfloor; while the decision to use one technology rather than another is a decision taken by managers and is not the consequence of any inevitable or inescapable logic of technology.

The Human Relations Tradition

Sociologists in the human relations tradition have primarily been interested in the effect of production techniques on social relations at work, and to a lesser extent with the intrinsic satisfaction which work tasks provide for the individual. The assumptions of the human relations perspective in its classic form are that workers need to be members of cohesive and supportive communities at work and that these 'social' needs are of paramount importance in determining workers' attitudes and behaviour. Sociologists working within this framework embarked on investigations into the nature and determinants of factory social systems, with a view to developing knowledge which would allow managers to harness these 'social' needs to company ends. The assumption was that social conflict in industrial relations would effectively disappear if people could be made to feel members of a company community.

The most celebrated studies were conducted in the 1950s into the effects of assembly-line technologies, mainly in the American automobile industry, where technology seemed to have a dominant influence on work tasks and social organisation (Walker and Guest, 1952; Chinoy, 1955). The results showed that work tasks were fragmented and repetitive as the result of the extreme specialisation and subdivision of work operations, operatives had no control over their methods or pace of work, and social interaction on the job was negligible because people were strung out along the assembly line and could not move from their work stations nor talk to those near them on account of the noise. The consequences, as reported in these studies at least, were severe problems of adjustment and low morale. The role of management in these conditions was seen to be one of countering the pressures and tensions inherent in the technological environment, by creating a community feeling which the work did not foster: Walker *et al.* (1956), for example, argued that a foreman could establish personal relationships with the operatives, treat them as a team and establish himself as their group leader, and so try to harness their social needs to managerial ends.

Sociologists studying the effects of assembly-line technology decried the dissatisfying and even inhuman nature of the tasks which operatives had to perform, and Chinoy (1955) and Friedmann (1961) suggested that job rotation and job enlargement might relieve the monotony to some extent, though the scope for improving tasks is not great in many assembly lines. But the central prescription of all studies was that managers ought to create workplace social communities which embraced both workers and managements. It was assumed that managers were powerless to modify the work tasks or the system of social interaction which resulted from technical constraints, except in relatively minor ways: they might compensate for the deprivation of people's needs by manipulating the human relations 'climate', but could not change the underlying constraints on tasks and interaction.

This pessimistic view of technology, with its emphasis on the frustration of social needs and the belief that technology is beyond human control, has been influential in industrial sociology, particularly in America. It does, indeed, have a certain amount of plausibility when assembly lines in automobile factories are the subject of investigation, but most industrial production systems are not of this character. Highly developed assembly-line technologies are feasible only where firms make fairly simple products with standardised designs and few variations, and have very large markets for these products, so there is a limit to their numbers. Nor is there evidence that such technologies are becoming more common. Investigation of other types of production system has shown that technology may often structure work in ways that facilitate the formation of work groups, particularly when production methods require team-work or co-ordination between different individuals (Meissner, 1969). Even when the production requirements of a particular technology establish certain patterns of interaction these requirements are rarely totally constraining, and there is a tendency towards sociability in excess of what is required. Homans has expressed this view most succinctly in his axiom that, 'if interaction between members is frequent in the external [the technical] system, sentiments of liking will grow up between them, and these sentiments will lead in turn to further interactions, over and above the interactions of the external system' (1950, p. 112). A considerable amount of empirical research has shown the truth of this statement, and it is normal in most factories to find informal groupings which transcend the requirements of production. Production technology helps to structure social relations on the shopfloor, but it is rarely the determinant.

The Tavistock Institute The Tavistock Institute of Human Relations in Britain has shown that the constraints of the production hardware may in fact be considerably less coercive than many sociologists and practising managers have believed. Members of the Tavistock have demonstrated how work organisation, which is the way in which people on the shopfloor are related to each other in order to carry out production tasks, can be varied in different ways while still retaining the same machines (Emery and Trist, 1960). They claim that a firm's profitability can be improved by designing work organisation in a way which optimises the satisfaction of human needs within the limits of what is possible in a given technology. Specifically, they believe that people will work more productively and with less grievance activity (manifest in reduced absenteeism and work stoppages) if their work tasks are satisfying and their social environment is supportive. They recommend that work tasks be reorganised to reduce fragmentation and specialisation, so that individuals perform 'whole' tasks which are more interesting and are felt to be more meaningful, in that a person completes the whole of an operation rather than just one part. They also suggest that production be organised on a group basis, so that a small team can do all the jobs, and that these groups be given discretion to work with the minimum amount of managerial intervention. This means creating partly autonomous work groups. In this way, production technology can be manipulated so that human needs for interesting tasks and social community are fulfilled. The Tavistock Institute used the label 'socio-technical system' to describe the notion that both technical and social needs have to be met if production is to be organised efficiently (Emery and Trist, 1960).

The Tavistock Institute's best-known study is of change in the work organisation of a coal mine from a 'conventional' method, where management distributed the miners into seven separate units performing fragmented and specialised tasks, to a 'composite' method, where all the miners formed one team and allocated work among themselves, thus allowing individuals to perform a variety of tasks and work with different people (Trist and Bamforth, 1951). The technology, partially-mechanised hand work, was not altered with the change in work organisation. Productivity and morale increased, managers were less involved in the details of production, and conflicts between the small groups of miners in the old units disappeared when all were in one team.

The real significance of this and numerous other case studies lies in the clear demonstration that, in many situations, work organisation and the types of social relationship it facilitates are influenced but not determined by the production machinery, and that operating managers may have considerable discretion as to how they arrange the division of labour. The claimed relationship between human needs, the satisfaction of these by socio-technical design, and improvements in productivity and grievance behaviour is less clearly established, however, because other variables were often changed at the same time as the work organisation. A survey of all the recorded Tavistock experiments claims that most of those that succeeded in boosting productivity and reducing grievance activity were the ones in which workers received higher earnings as the result: the beneficial effects may well be the result of more *money* rather than work which is more satisfying (Carey, n.d.).

The view of technology which dominated industrial sociology of the 1950s and 1960s had a distinctive theoretical underpinning, which shaped both the problems of research and the practical prescriptions arising from empirical investigations. Elton Mayo, the pioneer and most influential exponent of human relations in America, drew heavily on psychology and anthropology for the intellectual basis of his ideas. The assumptions and prescriptions of the human relations tradition have proved to be highly congruent with those of Durkheimian sociology, and the two theoretical traditions have merged in the sociological analysis of work and technology. Both perspectives have emphasised the 'pathological' state of industry as the result of the division of labour, which in its 'anomic' form has provided the worker with little sense of belonging to a community and few socially defined norms to guide his or her behaviour. The symptoms of this discontent have been thought to include low morale and productivity, and sometimes hostility to management. Both Durkheim and the later industrial sociologists argued that a new form of moral order, based on the sense of belonging to an industrial social community, would provide a solution to this normative disorder and the frustration of needs.

With the notable exception of the Tavistock Institute in Britain, industrial sociologists for long fatalistically accepted the division of labour on the shopfloor – which, in its extreme forms, isolates individuals from each other and makes work tasks meaningless – and scarcely considered the possibilities of changing the work organisation itself. Rather, they suggested that the consequences of existing productive techniques could be made more tolerable by the creation of a normative system which fostered sentiments of community membership and identification with a firm and its goals. The solution proposed to the problems of technology was to create a moral order and social collectivity oriented to managerial ends.

Robert Blauner

The most famous and influential synthesis of the Durkheimian and human relations traditions, and the most sophisticated and extended analysis of technology within this particular framework of analysis, is to be found in Robert Blauner's book *Alienation and Freedom,* published in 1964. This will be discussed here in some detail. Blauner takes as given 'the Marxian premise that there are powerful alienating tendencies in modern factory technology and organisations' (p. 4), and argues that the problem sociologists now have to solve is to determine 'under what conditions these tendencies are intensified in modern industry, what situations give rise to different forms of alienation, and what consequences develop for workers and for productive systems' (p. 4). He assumes that variations in industrial conflict reflect variations in the incidence of alienation. He defines his own view of alienation as 'the notion of fragmentation in man's existence and consciousness which impedes the wholeness of experience and activity' (p. 32), and argues that there are four different principles of fragmentation which create four separate dimensions of alienation.

The first dimension is powerlessness: 'A person is powerless when he is an object controlled and manipulated by other persons or by an impersonal system (such as technology)' (p. 16). The opposite of this form of alienation is control and freedom. Industrial workers can experience powerlessness at a number of levels, including their lack of control which results from the separation of the ownership of the means of production and productive labour, failure to control managerial policy and decision-making, failure to control conditions of employment, and failure to control the immediate work process. Blauner claims that workers do not feel the first two levels of powerlessness to be meaningful, so he excludes this pair from discussion, and further argues that, as trade unions have regained control of the third level for workers, it is only the level of the immediate work process which is important. He therefore breaks decisively with Marxist premises, despite his express indebtedness to Marx, because he drops the notion that alienation is linked with the exploitation inherent in the economic system of capitalism. (The Marxist conception of alienation is discussed at the end of this section.) Indeed, his decision to confine powerlessness to people's experience of work tasks is in direct continuity with the traditional themes of industrial sociology, despite his use of the language of alienation.

The second dimension, meaninglessness, refers to the familiar argument that the division of labour subdivides work into minute tasks, with the consequence that workers see no overall purpose to their work and have no conception of their part in the making of the final product. The third dimension is isolation, which Blauner also calls social alienation, and describes the feeling a person has that he or she does not belong to a social community: it refers to a lack of social integration with its consequent anomie, and is taken over directly from Durkheim. Blauner links isolation or social alienation from a work-based community with the failure to identify with the firm: 'Isolation...means that the worker feels no sense of belonging in the work situation and is unable to identify or uninterested in identifying with the organisation and its goals' (p. 24). Isolation refers both to the lack of social relationships and to the absence of a normative system. The last dimension, self-estrangement, refers to activity which is not self-expressive or creative, and which damages self-esteem.

These dimensions are systematically related to technology. Blauner defines technology as 'a complex of physical objects and technical operations (both manual and machine)...primarily the machine system' (p. 6), and sets this up as the major independent variable in the explanation of alienation. Technology determines powerlessness directly, because the nature of the machinery determines the amount of control an operator can have over his or her work process. Meaninglessness is the consequence of the division of labour or work organisation in a factory. Because he defines technology as production hardware, Blauner does not regard the division of labour as part of technology and treats it as an intervening variable in his theoretical discussions. However, in his subsequent analysis of empirical material, he normally treats the division of labour as being determined by technology, even if the two are conceptually distinct. Isolation or social alienation is indirectly influenced by technology, which 'determines a number of aspects of industrial structure that affect cohesion and integration: the occupational distribution of the blue-collar labour force, the economic cost structure of the enterprise, the typical size of the plant, and the existence and structure of work groups' (p. 25). Blauner views self-estrangement as the consequence of powerlessness and meaninglessness, though not necessarily of social alienation, and thus determined by technology.

On the basis of some case studies of different factories and the re-interpretation of an early national survey of workers' attitudes, Blauner argues that empirical evidence shows how four distinct patterns of alienation exist and how these are related to four different types of technology. (In practice, however, the character of two of the technological categories – large-batch and mass-production – is so similar that it is often more useful to compress these categories than to separate them in discussion of Blauner's argument.)

Craft work in the printing industry minimises alienation by allowing workers control over work processes, providing 'whole' tasks which are meaningful, creating the conditions for a social community based on the feelings of occupational identification of skilled craftsmen, and fostering self-esteem.

Machine-minding or assembly work in large-batch and mass-production industries, such as textiles and automobiles, maximises alienation, because workers are powerless in the face of machines, they have meaningless work, they are isolated in large and anonymous factories which have occupationally undifferentiated masses of unskilled workers who feel no sense of occupational community, they have little chance of forming sociable groupings on the shopfloor, while their work tasks deny them any sense of self-esteem at work.

Automated work in continuous-process oil-refineries and chemical plants reduces alienation virtually to the craft level. The work is routine for much of the time, but periodically demands the use of skill and initiative during emergencies, when workers control the plant, and, even during routine working, provides a greater variety of tasks and responsibilities and more personal involvement than machine-minding in other industries. Continuous-process plant provides workers with an overall view of the production process and allows them to understand their contribution to the final product. Workers are organised into teams which provide them with supportive social relationships. Managers can use the cohesive groups which result to integrate the individual into the company and foster a sense of identification with the firm. Jobs are arranged in a hierarchy of skill which allows people to develop their abilities and supports a normative structure favourable to the firm, for those in higher positions have internalised the goals of the enterprise and express its values.

The final strand in Blauner's argument is the claim that his four technologies, a cross-section of technological types in American industry at one moment in time, in fact represent stages in the progressive development of technology itself. Technology, he claims, evolves historically from craft work, where products are unstandardised, mechanisation is low and hand work predominates; through intermediate machine-tending and assembly-line stages, where products are more standardised, mechanisation is higher and operators either 'mind' machines or assemble parts on a moving line; to automated work, where products are highly standardised, mechanisation is so complete that operators largely monitor instruments, unless the process develops faults in which case it requires operator initiative, and work tasks are done by teams of workers. Thus the long-term trend is for craft work to decline and automation to grow, ultimately replacing even the intermediate stages of technology. Because alienation is low in the technological extremes of craft and automated, continuous-process work, but high in machine-tending and assembly-line, Blauner concludes that alienation can be visualised as an inverted U-curve: alienation grows with the shift from craft to intermediate technologies but declines with automation, which is the technique of the future.

Any evaluation of Blauner's thesis must make a number of critical points which undermine the credibility of his argument as a whole, though some sections survive scrutiny. The critique of Blauner's thesis made by Eldridge in *Sociology and Industrial Life* (1971) is the most complete and penetrating, and the rest of this section draws heavily on it. Criticism can be made both from within his own framework and from outside. The former concerns us here while the latter, which in effect constitutes a critique of traditional approaches to technology as a whole, is dealt with in Chapter 6.

The interpretation of the empirical evidence used in support of the conceptual scheme of *Alienation and Freedom* is contentious. Blauner takes an old opinion poll survey of attitudes, breaks down the responses to this survey industry by industry, classifies industries by their (presumed) dominant forms of technology, and argues that workers' expressed attitudes vary according to the technology. There is no direct evidence of the type of technology which individual respondents encounter nor of the actual jobs which they perform. Yet, as Blauner himself recognises, there is no self-evident association between industry and type of technology which allows one to assume that workers in an industry are working on a particular type of job: for example, Blauner notes that official figures on the U.S. automobile industry in 1959 indicated how *only* 18 per cent of employees in that industry worked on the assembly line itself. Attitudinal data show differences among *industries*, therefore, but provide no reliable or convincing evidence that these variations in expressed alienation are attributable to differences in technology rather than to other phenomena. Thus, acceptance of Blauner's argument must rest on its plausibility rather than its empirical validation.

Blauner's description of the direct effect of technology on the individual's work tasks is indeed plausible and has been documented in other studies already mentioned. He does not consider why production machinery and work organisation are so designed that they lead to powerlessness and meaninglessness, which has taxed sociologists working within different frameworks, though such an analysis of the dependent nature of technology would of course reduce the explanatory power of technology as the major independent variable. With this reservation, that one would like to know more about why existing techniques and work organisations have the forms they do – what determines the technology and the division of labour in specific factories – one can accept Blauner's account of the interaction between individuals and their work.

It is much more difficult, however, to accept Blauner's claim that technology determines social alienation via the social structure of the factory, a belief in technological determinism which surpasses anything in previous industrial sociology. This constitutes the second area of criticism. It is obviously true to say that technology helps to structure social relations on the shopfloor, although we have seen that it by no means determines them. But the rest of Blauner's case is highly contentious: indeed, his own account shows the difficulty of maintaining such a position. He states that technology determines the occupational distribution of a factory, its size and its cost structure (the relative proportions of total costs accountable to wages or capital investment), and the existence of work groups, and that these intervening variables then determine the degree of cohesion and sense of community, and the modes of social control and managerial authority (1964, p. 75). However, he then presents evidence from the textile industry which shows in fact that social cohesion and managerial authority in this industry are determined by factors *unrelated* to technology, namely the extent of social cohesion in the community outside work and a submissive attitude towards authority which is characteristic of this community.

Other evidence suggests that two of the intervening variables, occupational distribution and size of plant, are not necessarily related to technology. Recent experience shows how the occupational compositions of firms, which historically may have been determined by technology, have often survived changes in productive technique. Printing and docking are both examples of industries where organised labour has succeeded in preserving traditional occupational divisions and rights to certain jobs, despite technological changes which should have changed those occupational distributions if Blauner's argument were correct. Compositors in Britain who work on modern type-setting machines perform tasks which are indistinguishable from those performed by secretaries elsewhere, while longshoremen in the U.S. have certain rights to handle cargo within fifty miles of the coasts and perform tasks which include driving fork-lift trucks, container carriers and lorries. In these examples, feelings of occupational community and solidarity, which exist *before* the introduction of new technologies, shape the occupational structures of firms without reference to productive technique.

The size of individual factories clearly depends on factors other than technology: for instance, the size of a firm's markets and the quantity of goods it therefore produces, and managerial decisions which determine the size and disposition of its factories. The first point is obvious and well documented (George and Ward, 1975, p. 3). The second point refers to managerial decisions about the merits of decentralisation versus centralisation, and decisions about the merits of subcontracting certain parts of the firm's business to other concerns. Within the British automobile industry, for example, British Leyland produces cars and components in numerous factories throughout the country whereas Ford mainly centralises production in three sites. However the British industry as a whole uses outside suppliers far more extensively than does, say, the German, where firms make a greater proportion of the final product 'in-house'.

The third area of ciritcism concerns Blauner's typology of technical stages and the evolutionary schema which links these. In the late 1950s and early 1960s, there was a remarkable convergence between Alain Touraine in France (1955), Joan Woodward in Britain (1958) and Robert Blauner in the U.S., when all three sociologists arrived at broadly similar conclusions about the stages and course of technological change, and their conclusions have been accepted widely. Thus discussion of Blauner must also involve these other authors. All three distinguish between handwork in craft industries, mechanised and fully automated work.

Woodward distinguishes unit and small batch production, large batch and mass production, and process production (which is high volume), based on differences in technical complexity and the extent to which managements can control the uncertainty of the manufacturing process. Touraine's three stages are based on the progressive subdivision of 'whole' tasks into component parts, a division of labour which de-skills traditional craft work, and the subsequent mechanisation of these simplified tasks, which results ultimately in automated and integrated production. He claims that technology evolves from machinery that is universal and flexible, which can be used to produce a wide variety of products, through single-purpose machines and assembly operations which produce single, standardised products and require unskilled, machine-minding or assembly work, to automation where products again are fairly standardised and produced in high volume, and production is self-regulating, leaving operatives with only a superintending role. Blauner argues for the long-run mechanisation and subsequent automation of tasks, the change from universal, flexible machines to single-process ones, and the standardisation of products. He claims that the nature of the product manufactured is the most important determinant of technology.

There are two problems with these formulations. The first is the emphasis they place on the product which is being manufactured, because the description of technology is couched partly in terms of the physical characteristics of the raw materials and end products (variability or standardisation, liquids or solids) and the volume of production. If there is indeed a close fit between different productive techniques and the products manufactured, this conflation of technology and product is unobjectionable. However, technical developments since the period of these studies show that there is no necessary fit between the two phenomena, which means that the conflation is incorrect as a description and, furthermore, may be misleading if it impedes a fuller understanding of the course and dynamic of technical change.

The second is that the stages and evolution of technology are based on the description of previous events, which are then extrapolated into the future without a full explanation of the underlying tendency of change or with insufficient consideration of the consequences of such a tendency. Blauner argues, wrongly as the next paragraph suggests, that products determine development and thus the differences between stages. Both he and Touraine *describe* technical differences in terms of the progressive elimination of human skill and effort from production, but do not extend the analysis to argue that this tendency is in fact the dynamic of change; namely, that the people who commission and design new techniques have this as their aim. More recent theorists of technical development, notably Braverman, hold that this is indeed the motive force behind particular changes in technique, as will be discussed later.

Recent developments in automated technology have highlighted the inadequacy of these approaches. The techniques now exist that automate craft work directly, making a nonsense of suggestions that there are necessarily 'intermediate' stages between craft and automated production or that unit production cannot be automated. Moreover, many of the automatic machines appropriate to craft work are relatively cheap to install and economic for low production volumes. Thus automation spreads to industries where the scale of production, the nature of the products and the level of capital resources would have ruled out even mechanisation, let alone automation, two decades ago. Nor is it so easy to find benign consequences for workers in automation. A survey of automated technology in the early 1970s (Cooper, 1972) showed that the problem-solving and teamwork characteristics of Blauner's process technology were rapidly disappearing as the reliability and sophistication of process plant increased. Blauner was describing a primitive form of automation which was neither completely reliable nor truly automatic. The logic of automation is to abolish human intervention in production. These points are elaborated in Chapter 6.

Other evidence suggests that Blauner may have associated certain aspects of the work environment with technology which were in fact the product of *non*-technical factors: notably the employment policies of firms which were massively capitalised, profitable, and large enough to have developed strong personnel functions within management. Blauner's examples of automation were of firms in which labour costs were relatively insignificant to management, with the result that managers were not under pressure to control the use of labour and could afford to exercise their authority in a relaxed, non-interventionist manner, and were able in addition to tolerate generous manning levels which allowed workers free time on the job to mix with their mates. However, in the 1960s, just at the time when machinery was becoming more sophisticated and needed less human control, competitive pressures in the industry intensified and wage costs became more significant to managers. Two recent studies of oil refineries show how managers have become more concerned to control their labour costs and have attempted to reduce manning levels, with a consequent reduction in the possibility of teamwork (one refinery, for instance, abolished mates and made operatives work individually) and an increased possibility of conflict between men and managers (Flanders, 1964; Gallie, 1978).

Michael Mann's study (1973a) of a large and profitable food-processing firm which had a continuous-flow technology, found that workers felt they belonged to a company community because of management's policy of being a 'good employer', and that this evaluation spilled over into their perceptions of their work tasks. Thus, Mann concluded that technology was relatively unimportant for worker satisfaction with either the social system of the firm or intrinsic job content. The managerial policy of paying high wages, maintaining secure employment and providing some prospects of career advancement was the principal determinant of employee attitudes.

Wedderburn and Crompton (1972) reported the findings of an investigation of workers' attitudes carried out on one site of a large English chemical company in the mid-1960s. A few of the variations in perceptions of work tasks lent some support to Blauner's thesis because workers on automated processes reported more autonomy and discretion than those on more traditional technologies within the same site. However, variations in the control structure imposed by management which were largely independent of technology also accounted for part of the difference. Technology had nothing to do with the overall positive feelings towards the employer which characterised all workers, whether on advanced or intermediate technologies. These derived from the level of pay, the security of the job, the good welfare provisions and good working conditions available in the company. Despite these positive evaluations most workers also had direct experience of 'conflicts of interests between themselves and their employers which had to be bargained about' (1972, p. 151).

In view of these arguments, it seems unlikely that the spread of relatively cheap automated devices into smaller and less capitalised firms will necessarily have benign consequences for employees. Managerial policy rather than technology is the crucial variable, and it may be supposed that not all managements deciding to use new automated techniques will either be willing or able to afford the sorts of employment practice just described.

Alienation

A final criticism is that Blauner does not deal with what is normally meant by 'alienation', despite his claim that he accepts Marxist premises (Eldridge, 1971, p. 190). Alienation is a somewhat metaphysical concept, though Marx regards it as the inevitable consequence of the economic structure of capitalism. Marx distinguishes objectification from alienation. Objectification is the process of production, whereby men make material objects which embody human creativity yet stand as entities separate from the men who created them. Alienation occurs when, once objectified, man no longer recognises himself in his product, which has become alien to him and 'is no longer his own' and 'stands opposed to him as an autonomous power' (Bottomore, 1964, pp. 122–3). Objectification, however, only becomes alienation in the specific historical circumstances of capitalism. What is significant about these circumstances is that one group of people, capitalists, accumulate the surplus products of others who produce: capital itself represents the embodiment of creative human activity into an object which is then appropriated by others and becomes a force uncontrolled by its producers. This is why capital is described as the alienated product of human activity. The Marxist discussion is couched in terms of the labour theory of value, in which capital is the appropriation of part of the value (the 'surplus value') created by men labouring together, but using the notion of a surplus product still catches the spirit of this line of reasoning. Alienation and exploitation are aspects of one process because capitalists use their monopoly of the means of production to compel their employees to create surpluses which go as private profit and capital accumulation. It is also claimed within Marxism that the class division between capitalists and workers stems from this process. Appropriation is the basis of the division and class relations are oppositional because of alienation and exploitation.

In Marxist theory capital is the source of further alienation within the developed capitalist economy. This is because capital accumulation generates its own 'needs' which reduce people to the level of commodities. Workers become factors in the operation of capital and their activities are dominated by the requirements of profitability rather than their own human needs. Within a market economy, the rules that govern accumulation are those of the market place. These rules constitute a set of impersonal mechanisms which dominate all economic actors, capitalists as well as workers, and the market has a coercive force. Marx notes that, although the needs of profit and capital accumulation seem to take on a life of their own, these impersonal mechanisms in fact disguise the human origins of capital and the exploitation that allows one class to appropriate what another has produced.

In his early writings, where he most clearly identifies the alienated state and the various components that make up its totality (Bottomore, 1964), Marx identifies four particular aspects of alienation:

1. The worker is alienated from the product of his labour, since what he produces is appropriated by others and he has no control over its fate. The disposition of his products follows the dictates of seemingly impersonal market mechanisms, which in reality work to promote the interests of capitalists against those of workers.
2. The worker is alienated from the act of production. Working becomes an alien activity which offers no intrinsic satisfaction, that is forced on the worker by external constraints and ceases to be an end in itself, and that involves working at someone else's bidding as forced labour. Work thus becomes a commodity that is sold and its only value to the worker is its saleability. In his later writings, Marx suggests that alienation from the act of

production is intensified by a further process of work dehumanisation: in response to increasing market competition, capitalists introduce an elaborate division of labour and new machinery which, in combination, create de-skilled and machine-like labour, lead to the domination of machinery over people's lives, and ultimately even place workers in competition with machines. Workers are thus regarded as commodities on a level with physical objects, are ultimately interchangeable with these objects, and are subject to the same market forces as other commodities.

3. The worker is alienated from his human nature or his 'species being', because the first two aspects of alienation deprive his productive activity of those specifically *human* qualities which distinguish it from the activity of animals and thus define human nature.
4. The worker is alienated from other men, since capitalism transforms social relations into market relations, and people are judged by their position in the market rather than their human qualities. People come to regard each other as reifications – as worker or as capitalist – rather as individuals.

Blauner's treatment of alienation fails to touch on most of the central issues in Marx's usage. The assumption that control issues are significant only in the immediate work situation, where workers come into contact with production technology, clearly ignores the more fundamental loss of control that workers experience by virtue of the logic of capital accumulation and the power of the employer. Alienation in the face of technology is merely one manifestation of the general tendency of the capitalist system of production and the market economy. Indeed, Eldridge has commented of Blauner's position; that 'to restrict his attention to factors affecting control over the immediate work situation is simply to operate within the framework of alienation' (1971, p. 190). Industrial sociology has long been concerned with the interaction between men and machines, but has preferred to use the terminology of job satisfaction or dissatisfaction to describe the subjective feelings which result from this interaction. Blauner works firmly within this framework and his 'alienation' is indistinguishable from the concerns of the human relations tradition.

The same is true of what Blauner terms 'social' alienation, where his theoretical assumptions and practical prescriptions clearly derive from the Durkheimian or human relations perspective. What Blauner is really talking about is *anomie*, a state of normative disintegration which results from the division of labour, which can be 'cured' by re-establishing the feelings of belonging to a community and the development of a new normative system or moral order. This would bind together workers with each other and with managers, and contain any feeling of sectional interest. No such solution appears possible outside the Durkheimian tradition. The conflict of interests built into the economy cannot be overcome by the remedies for anomie. Alienation is inherent in the character of capital accumulation and is manifest in the relationship between management and workers. Unless the underlying economic basis of alienation is removed, the attempt to bind management and labour into a unitary community is unlikely to promote industrial harmony for any length of time.

6 Technology, control and orientations

The interest in the role of technology has changed over the past decade, with the result that there is no longer one dominant and clearly defined focus of concern. The treatment of technology has fragmented into a number of different strands, though one can discern two basic themes beneath this diversity of approaches. Both tackle the problems noted in the previous chapter and develop analytical frameworks which differ considerably from those of the older tradition. On the one hand, there are those who acknowledge the effect of technology on the worker and the significance of this in the analysis of industrial life, but who regard the traditional treatment of technology as a reification which disguises the social processes underlying the phenomenon. On the other, there is a body of opinion that suggests the effect of technology has been overstated at the cost of a real understanding of industrial attitudes and behaviour, and implies, indeed, that technology should no longer be of central interest to sociologists.

Choice and Control

A central issue in any analysis of the effect of technology must be the socially determined character of productive techniques, in particular the way in which managers choose certain types of technique and use these to influence the social organisations of their factories and offices. The key notion here is managerial choice. Accepting that productive technique has a major effect on the tasks that an individual performs and the social organisation in which he works, it is still correct to argue that the type of technical environment is determined by management. The Tavistock studies demonstrated that in many existing technologies managers can choose how the social organisation of production is to be arranged within the limits of what is feasible, given the nature of production hardware. The research was carried out in fairly 'primitive' technical conditions with low levels of mechanisation and little mechanical integration of the various components of production hardware, and the scope for such a re-arrangement of existing plant would appear to be more limited in mechanically integrated plants such as automobile assembly lines.

However, choice is exercised at an earlier stage as well, as the people who run organisations choose what sorts of technique are to be used in their factories. This point has rarely been expressed in academic discussion of work, presumably because most research has been conducted in plants where a given technology is already operating and because strategic decisions about future techniques have not been open to research workers, but also because many sociologists and practising managers have made two important assumptions about technical choice. The first is that there is some inherent logic of technical evolution that leaves little room for managerial choice, while the second is that new techniques are utilised in specific firms as the result of market pressures in a competitive economy.

Leaving aside any discussion of the logic of technical evolution for the moment, it is obvious that market pressures do not determine managerial choice as closely as might be assumed: it is not true that managers' freedom of choice is totally constrained by the need to adopt certain technical arrangements in order to survive against competition. In the first place, senior managers choose the markets in which their firms operate and any technological 'imperatives' which may follow from market pressures are in fact the result of this prior managerial choice. Secondly, there is evidence to suggest that within any given market, competitive pressures may permit choice among a wider range of productive techniques than economists and engineers have previously believed.

One notable example of this can be found in the Swedish motor industry where Volvo and Saab-Scania have recently experimented with new production methods in order to break with the assembly-line techniques which have dominated automobile manufacture since the 1920s and which for a long time appeared to be the only economically efficient technique. The design of these production methods has been based on the principle that work organisation ought to foster autonomous work groups and individual task satisfaction, echoing the prescriptions of the Tavistock Institute. At Volvo's Kalma plant, the most sophisticated example of these new methods, the central technical innovation has been the design of a new transfer mechanism, which permits greater flexibility than the traditional line in the scheduling of work flow, particularly with regard to the routing and speed of production. Cars are moved on individual battery powered carriers which can be guided anywhere in the factory on magnetic strips embedded in the floor and controlled by a central computer. Advantage has been taken of this flexibility to organise workers into teams of between 15 and 20 people, who work in small workshops and are assigned a wide range of tasks which cover a whole operation. Team members arrange working methods between themselves, in consultation with management specialists. Assembly is carried out on cars which are stationary rather than moving along a line, and a facility for stockpiling work allows workers some degree of control over their speed of working rather than being tied to that of the line.

Kalma therefore represents a radical change in production techniques, based on the conscious decision to organise work in ways which workers might find more satisfying. Evaluations of the new methods indicate that competitive efficiency in the market place has not been sacrificed by the new technology (Aguren *et al.*, 1976). Moreover, because these methods are still at an early stage of refinement, further development is expected to increase the economic efficiency of the system, just as various developments have refined the conventional assembly line since Henry Ford began his experiments before 1914.

Volvo workers appear to prefer Kalma to other motor assembly lines, and the methods and conditions of working are certainly less coercive and degraded than elsewhere in the automobile industry. Volvo claims that the lower than normal rates of labour turnover and absenteeism reflect increased job satisfaction. But one should hesitate before hailing Kalma as a revolution in work humanisation, as some people are prone to do, because in certain respects Volvo has not done a great deal to improve the quality of industrial work. The content of individual work tasks differs little from other assembly operations, and workers merely perform a greater variety of simple tasks than before. Nor is worker control of production particularly high because working methods are largely prescribed by the layout of the workshops and the supervision of management specialists, while work scheduling and speed are partly determined by the centralised control of the vehicle carriers.

It has now become clear that technology is one of the means by which managers control the activities that occur within their firms, which, by implication, suggests that when managers choose a particular technology they also choose how their firms are to be controlled. It can be argued that different technologies incorporate managerial policies regarding the appropriate organisation of activities within the firm and thus are designed with particular control systems in mind, which is the reverse of Blauner's claim that technology determines authority and control. Joan Woodward has defined managerial control systems as containing the four elements of objective setting, planning, execution and control (monitoring and enforcing the outcome of activities), and her empirical research into technology and organisation suggests that control systems can be classified along a scale according to the degree control is exercised personally or by impersonal and mechanical mechanisms. In personal systems,

> control was exercised through the personal authority pyramid, work was largely unprogrammed, and end results were difficult to predict.
>
> (Reeves and Woodward, 1970, p. 39)

In impersonal systems, mainly in continuous-flow process firms,

> a framework of control was created when the plant was built or automated equipment installed. The setting of objectives, in respect of time, quality and cost, the sequencing of manufacturing activities and even in some cases the mechanisms for taking corrective action were specified and built into the plant design.
>
> (Reeves and Woodward, 1970, p. 39)

Woodward was mainly concerned to show how control systems varied along her original unit-batch-process classification of technology, but what is significant for our purpose is her evidence that managers can in many cases choose whether to move towards personal or mechanical control systems and her suggestion that technology can be viewed as a *means* by which managers implement their notions about control. It thus becomes clear that attempts to use technology as an independent explanatory variable risk mystifying its nature by their failure to analyse the social processes that lie behind productive technique.

Harry Braverman

In 1974 Harry Braverman published *Labor and Monopoly Capital*, subtitled *The Degradation of Work in the Twentieth Century*. This is an important attempt within the Marxist perspective to explain *why* production technology has developed in the way it has, and is oriented around the notion of control. The argument will be treated here in some detail.

Braverman starts with the basic Marxist assumption that labour power under capitalism is geared to the creation of profit, rather than the satisfaction of man's needs, with the consequence that the very nature of work 'is dominated and shaped by the accumulation of capital' (1974, p. 53). A historical survey of the development of capitalism in America shows how it progressively transformed the nature of work, first by re-structuring work organisation along scientific management lines, and secondly by the application of science to production. The transformation of work, however, created major problems of control, which, Braverman argues, were specific to the capitalist organisation of production.

The gearing of labour power to the accumulation of capital, which Braverman defines as the expropriated surplus of communal activity, creates a fundamental conflict of interest between workers and capitalists, and workers cannot be relied upon to work in the best interests of capital in a setting of antagonistic relations of production. Thus control is necessary in order that capital should realise the full potential of the labour it employs (p. 57). In a discussion of scientific management, Braverman argues that Taylor was the first management theorist to recognise the need for a new system of control, the essence of this philosophy being the realisation that,

> Workers who are controlled only by general orders and discipline are not adequately controlled, because they retain their grip on the actual processes of labour. So long as they control the labour process itself, they will thwart efforts to realise the full potential inherent in their labour power. To change this situation, control over the labour process must pass into the hands of management,...by the control and dictation of each step of the process, including its mode of performance.
>
> (p. 100)

This view, that it is the inherent opposition of interests in capitalism which leads to new needs for control, underpins Braverman's treatment of technology: he argues that the effect of productive technique on the worker is a manifestation of the conflict between labour and capital, that it is not an extraneous factor which disturbs the natural harmony of industry and which enlightened human relations policy can overcome.

Braverman claims that three of Taylor's principles have guided the application of production technologies on the shopfloor and determined the development of new technologies. The first is that the work or labour process should be divorced from the skill and autonomy of the individual worker. Secondly, that manual and mental labour should be dissociated, separating conception from execution and removing 'brain work' from the shopfloor. Thirdly, that managers should have a monopoly of knowledge to control every step of the labour process and its manner of execution.

Together these principles reflect the need to control labour and to reduce managerial dependence on worker co-operation.

As a consequence, work has been progressively 'degraded': there has been a continuing process of de-skilling which removes all elements of knowledge, responsibility and discretion, and leaves only the most simple tasks for operatives to perform. Machines are designed which incorporate the manual skills and intellectual knowledge that previously belonged to workers, and people are subordinated to these machines which come to dominate them. The tendency of modern industry is to de-humanise work: the performance of tasks requires the exercise of few human faculties, people become appendages of machines and are controlled by these, and ultimately machines even replace workers and deny them the right to work at all. Viewed from this perspective, the traditional accounts of work on assembly lines describe the results of managerial control strategies which work through the design of production systems.

Braverman shares with a number of other commentators a view that the crucial significance of production technology is the effect that it has on workers' tasks and that the relationship between men and machines should be the primary focus of interest, rather than the traditional concern with the effects of technology on the wider social system at work (Bright, 1966; Meissner, 1969; Cooper, 1972). Taken as a group, these authors argue that the evolution of production technology is based on the principle that those who design or utilise new production methods are concerned to replace direct human effort and control skills by mechanical devices. They suggest that technology can be classified by the extent to which the components of human work performance are built into machines. This is more precise and provides a more useful developmental scheme than those analyses mentioned in Chapter 5, which were too broadly based and contained numerous variables which were not particularly relevant to technology.

Different authors produce different numbers of stages of technical development, reflecting the varying degrees of precision with which they classify the basic scheme, but the following classification is a convenient summary of the basic levels of mechanisation and automation:

1. *Mechanised manual production* (the simplest form of mechanisation). Manual labour is used to perform the work with the assistance of tools or machinery, powered manually, electrically, hydraulically, or by compressed air. Some manual labour may be needed to place machines or instruments in position.

2. *Mechanised production.* The work is performed by machines powered electrically, hydraulically, or by compressed air. The operation of the machines and the performance of ancillary operations are partly manual.
3. *Integrated mechanised production.* The whole cycle of the production process is performed by machinery. Basic and ancillary processes are linked and carried out at a co-ordinated speed. Control, adjustment and regulation of the machines is manual.
4. *Automated production.* Certain basic and ancillary operations are performed by machines and mechanical devices without human intervention. The worker is only needed to regulate machinery, to watch it and to make adjustments during production.
5. *Integrated automated production.* This system covers a complete production process, in which the basic or ancillary regulatory operations are carried out by machines or mechanical devices, so that the desired quality and output are achieved without human intervention. The only functions of the workers are to watch the operations and manipulate the control apparatus. Integrated automated production excludes any form of mechanised or manual work, except in the case of operations in which, for technical or economic reasons, automation is considered inappropriate.

(ILO, 1966)

This sort of developmental scheme recognises that different levels may coexist at any moment, as different industries and different parts of the same industry operate with a variety of techniques, but assumes that the long-term trend throughout industry is to replace direct human intervention in production. 'Mixed' systems which use men and machines can be regarded as technical stop-gaps, in which men are used to patch up imperfect technical designs. Thus intermediate technologies such as the assembly line represent techniques which will eventually be replaced. It should also be noted that, while mechanisation has long replaced human effort and devalued traditional control skills, it is the recent development of information processing technologies which has led to the most significant erosion of human control, with the growth of 'closed loop' processes which create *self*-regulating production systems.

Concrete examples of the effects of the latest stage of technical development can be cited in metal-working and the continuous processing of fluid products. Automation now transforms traditional craft jobs in the engineering industry. The invention and development of 'numerically-controlled' machine tools, which are increasingly computer-controlled, mean that low volume, unstandardised metal products can now be manufactured automatically on metal-forming machines which work without human intervention once a programme has been inserted in the control unit. These machines, moreover, are universal and flexible: simple programming changes mean that one machine may perform all the tasks of a craftsman working by hand on his multi-purpose implements. In continuous processing the primitive technology described by Blauner was neither reliable nor completely automatic, which is why there was a requirement for continuous monitoring by teams of skilled operatives who had a view of the total production system and intervened in emergencies. Nowadays the equipment is more reliable and contains *automatic* monitoring and fault-correcting devices which dispose with most human intellectual and control skills. Process workers have little responsibility and little opportunity to work in teams.

Braverman, along with other socialist critics of technology (for example, Dickson,1974; Elliott and Elliott, 1976), extends the ideas current among commentators on technology to suggest that there is no necessary logic of industrialism which creates one particular form of the division of labour or the trend of replacing human control by machines. He argues that the specific need to maximise control and reduce reliance on worker co-operation, in order to increase capital accumulation in an economic system based on opposed interests, is what has led to contemporary developments. In an economic system based on co-operation and trust rather than hostility, technological progress could have a liberating rather than a degrading effect, because new technologies remove the drudgery from work and in principle allow workers to concentrate on the more enjoyable tasks. For example, skilled engineering workers could easily be trained to program and operate numerically-controlled machine tools, which would raise the skill level of their tasks, preserve their control over the work process, and remove some of the more tedious manual tasks (1974, p. 199). Other commentators note that developments in computer technology, particularly the mini-computer, now make it technically feasible to reverse bureaucratic trends towards centralisation and to create autonomous clerical work groups using their own autonomous computer systems (Weir, 1977).

The claim that most socialist economies have followed the same path of technical development, and therefore that technology transcends the frontiers of different economic systems because of some logic of industrialism, is countered by Braverman with the assertion that the brand of socialism found in the Soviet Union and associated societies is also directed toward capital accumulation, with the state rather than a private individual or corporation assuming the role of the capitalist agent (1974, pp. 22–3). In other words, these societies appear to have a mode of production which is basically similar to that of capitalism, even though their other social institutions may differ from those of capitalist societies. Thus the logic of industrialism turns out to be merely the logic of capitalism.

Finally, *Labor and Monopoly Capital* extends the traditional concern with technology by demonstrating that work and productive technique are significant for the analysis of class structure. The linkage of class and productive technique has several aspects. For Braverman, the nature of work and production technology are the *products* of class relations: managers, who represent the interest of capital in an exploitative relationship, transform and degrade work in order to maintain this relationship as the source of profit. At the same time he suggests that the transformation of the labour process has *consequences* for the structure and composition of the working class: the degradation of work homogenises the traditional manual working class by removing old skill differences, and proletarianises white-collar and low-level managerial groups whose work has been transformed by the routinisation and mechanisation of office work in recent years. Developments in productive technique would thus appear to create a more uniform and proletarian work situation. Modern, non-Marxist class theory also takes up this point, that transformations of work have important consequences for class structure (see Chapter 9).

Braverman thus contributes significantly to the development of the traditional concerns of industrial sociology. He consolidates and extends various critical reactions to the human relations treatment of technology, by incorporating into a coherent analytical framework the growing interest in managerial control systems and the somewhat neglected concern with the nature of the work that people have to do in their jobs. Productive techniques are no longer reified and regarded as determining worker activity, because their use reflects managerial policy concerning the organisation of work. Technology obviously has an effect on workers, and Braverman shows how an understanding of the consequences of technology must consider *why* it is designed to have this effect. Moreover, technology has a broader relevance for the analysis of class relationships in modern societies if it can be viewed in part as a product of antagonistic social relations of production and/or as a force which structures working-class experience of the labour process. It has become an important intervening variable in recent accounts of the class structure.

However, various criticisms may be levelled at Braverman's analysis. The first is that it is too single-minded in the emphasis it places on the conflict of interests between labour and capital as the source of managerial control needs and on these needs as the determinants of productive technique. Capitalism is concerned with the making of profit, and to this end it has increasingly transformed the forces of production. One way of improving profitability is to create a production process which prevents the conflicts of interest in industry from hindering accumulation. But this is by no means the only impetus towards new techniques. The second is that it over-estimates the extent to which control is in fact achieved through the design of new methods, at least in the short and medium terms. Thirdly, it is too concerned with the consciously-intended effects of managerial activity. Braverman's description of the tendencies of modern technology is useful, but the origins and outcomes of these tendencies are more complex than he states.

There are alternative explanations of why managers have transformed the work process which are more appropriate in most instances than Braverman's. Senior managers are obviously concerned to use resources in the most efficient manner in order to create profit and increase the rate of capital accumulation. But economic efficiency does not result only from the reduced discretion of potentially recalcitrant labour, and new production techniques are frequently developed because they raise profits directly and with little reference to this form of control. New processes may improve product quality by working to tolerances beyond human capability or simply by reducing unavoidable human errors; they may produce goods in greater volume and at lower unit costs; they may permit the manufacture of new products which just could not be made prior to the discovery of these processes; or they may be the answer to labour shortages on existing production methods. The urge to extend managerial domination of the production process is significant as one source of the impetus to formulate and adopt new techniques. But such control is significant only inasmuch as it enhances accumulation and profitability, and it is this over-arching concern that accounts for capitalism's incessant transformations of the productive apparatus within industry.

However, Braverman is quite correct when he argues that the common *outcome* of new technology is to abolish worker control.

Managers may be inspired to introduce new techniques for reasons apparently unconnected with control, but the techniques themselves *do* embody the principle that profitability depends greatly on reduced employee discretion and greater managerial domination of production. What is significant, as other studies have shown, is that engineers and managers share a design philosophy of producing machinery which eliminates as far as possible the 'human factor', in order to achieve the regularity and predictability that managers regard as necessary for profitable operation (Cherns, 1973). In this sense, increased control is often the consequence of technical development, rather than its primary cause. The end result for the worker is the same in either case, but the causal mechanisms differ.

Braverman also exaggerates the inevitability of the transformation of the work process and underestimates the potential resistance of workers to work degradation. The experience of the United States suggests that work may have been transformed successfully over the last sixty years as workers have become acclimatised to their loss of control (this though at the cost of two decades of bitter conflict and violence early in the century which Braverman ignores in his argument). But other evidence suggests that labour resistance may be sufficiently serious to stimulate managers to reconsider the nature of their production processes.

The European motor industry, for example, found increasing worker resistance to its production methods during the mid-1960s and early 1970s; this was manifested in recruitment difficulties and high rates of labour turnover and absenteeism. Rising aspirations concerning the quality of working life, in combination with conditions of full employment, meant that many workers refused to work in car plants. One solution adopted in France and Germany was to recruit unskilled labour from less-developed nations with high unemployment rates, where workers had low aspirations for work satisfaction, to do the jobs which the native population rejected, without modifying production methods. Where jobs required more skill than was readily available in the migrant population, then managers introduced automation to dispense with people altogether: the rapid spread of robot welding, for example, was stimulated by the difficulties of recruiting trained welders for repetitive and arduous work in conditions of heavy fume, high heat and loud noise. Automation was thus a second solution to the human problems which previous transformations of the work process had presented.

But where automation was technically difficult or just too expensive, as for example in the majority of car assembly jobs, and where there was no reserve pool of unemployed or migrants willing to do degraded work, managers found themselves obliged to modify working methods in ways which ran against the previous trend of production technology. This essentially was what happened in the Swedish motor industry: resistance among the available labour force to conventional assembly-line methods at a time when public opinion was hostile to increasing the numbers of migrant workers required manufacturers to re-design production in order to increase the variety of jobs tasks and restore some limited degree of control to operatives. Future developments in production technology may succeed in automating car assembly but, at least in the medium term, it appears that worker resistance can sometimes modify the inevitability of work degradiation.

Some managers, aware of the difficulty of successfully implementing many types of production technique in the face of worker resistance, have made a virtue of necessity and argue that the design philosophy which creates degraded work must now be overturned. The head of personnel development at Shell International, for example, has written that the 'socially responsible company' must re-examine its assumptions about technology 'for social reasons as well as considerations of efficiency' (J. Watson, 1977, p. 145). In rejecting technological determinism as a myth, he adopts a line of argument akin to Braverman's, that advanced technology *should* be able to create jobs which are compatible with worker needs for more autonomy and greater control. It is clear that productive techniques can be designed to enhance as well as degrade work, and that what determines the effect of technology on workers are the ends which production systems are designed to achieve. Indeed, Shell provides an interesting example of a production system where the design criteria differ from those normally associated with automated processes. When designing a new, computerised, plant control system, which required an operator to supervise its working and could not be left to run entirely automatically, engineers and systems analysts deliberately refrained from automating a number of information and control loops. They planned the process on the premise that the operator should be given some challenge and stimulus in his work tasks, so that he could exert his influence and become part of the control process (P. Hill, 1971).

However, the evidence to date suggests neither that very many companies have re-appraised their control strategies, nor that those firms in the vanguard of work 'humanisation' have yet fundamentally changed their approach. The humanised work that has resulted from changing the structure of managerial control systems, as outlined in Chapter 3, and from the examples of technical change cited here, is confined to a handful of companies and restores only a limited degree of worker control even in these firms. Where technologists have not yet developed totally automatic processes that require *no* human intervention, then the resistance of individual workers and, in some countries, the pressure of organised labour for more human work would appear to limit the full-blooded application of traditional managerial strategy, but not fundamentally to transform it.

Braverman also interprets the tendency of production technology to give management responsibility for the organisation of the work process to mean that technology determines worker control in its broadest sense. This is an exaggerated and overly deterministic view which ignores the significance of other aspects of workplace control which are not determined by technique, particularly in non-automated technical systems. In Britain, for example, where organised labour has rarely disputed the *principle* of management's right to extend its direction of work processes and rationalise production, there have been challenges to managerial control over other aspects of work. Workers have sometimes successfully prevented managers from exercising unilateral control over manning levels, operator effort and the quantity of production. There has thus been little opposition to the transformation of production methods *per se*, but more resistance to the consequential changes which follow new production techniques and which concern the rights of managers to organise production as they see fit.

For Braverman, the application of numerically-controlled machine tools is the most extreme, indeed the *classic* case of de-skilling and control. These new machines separate skilled craft work into two components, the highly skilled job of programme design and the unskilled job of machine supervision, thus splitting the cognitive-planning and manual execution elements of what was once a single process. Computer control automates categories of work that were previously thought incapable of being mechanised, let alone automated. Braverman argues that managers have the choice of allowing craftsmen to continue to perform both operations, because they are capable of programming the machines with some extra training, but in practice always choose to allocate the programming to technicians and to deprive craftsmen of their control of the whole process.

Yet there is empirical evidence which suggests that the application of these new techniques does not always have the effect which Braverman believes. A recent case study of the British toolmaking industry shows how managers have in fact chosen to upgrade their craftsmen into programmers, on the grounds that men who understand the whole process make better programmers that technicians with programming expertise but no craft knowledge (Senker *et al.*, 1976). Occupational principles of administration have been preserved in this industry through to the present day, and at least some managers appear fairly content with a situation of delegated control. New machines are introduced to combat labour scarcity and managers are unconcerned about the control potential of the new technology. Some firms suggest that in future they might recruit specialised technicians and degrade existing manual workers, but others reckon that they will continue to add the higher skills to their craftsmen. Thus managerial policy in this industry is by no means as clear-cut as Braverman would suggest.

Moreover, numerically-controlled machine tools raise the wider question whether management necessarily benefits in the way Braverman suggests from the transformations which automation produces. Control over the work process has obviously been taken away from manual workers who perform all production operations. But many control functions now reside with a new group of indirect workers, the technicians (whether upgraded craftsmen or new specialists) responsible for programming the work process, rather than with managers. These workers do not necessarily identify with the interests of management and capital and thus co-operate harmoniously with senior management: the unionisation of technical workers in Britain indicates that many are aware of at least a potential conflict of interest between themselves and their employers, while the theory of the 'new working class' suggests that technicians are a major source of opposition to those who control industry in France and Italy (see Chapter 10).

In the long run, of course, Braverman is probably correct about the likely consequences of present trends in productive technique. At any one moment, technical development creates new groups whose work gives them some degree of control over the work process. But then there are subsequent developments which remove control even from these groups. Machine tools again provide an interesting example of this. The cost to the user of having numerically-controlled machines standing idle while re-programming is carried out even on relatively straightforward jobs prompts equipment suppliers to install more powerful computers into the control units. These have a greater range of pre-packaged programs and the ability to adapt these, and so provide a 'self-programming' capability for numerically-controlled machines. These computing devices, which are based on recent developments in micro-electronics (notably the advent of cheap microprocessors), reduce the idle time between batches to a matter of minutes in the typical installation. They entirely remove the element of human skill – even from the programming of the control units. Thus the cognitive-planning element of craft work is now increasingly to be given to machines and not even to technicians. The most highly skilled manual trades, such as patternmaking and toolmaking, have yet to undergo this further stage of automation, but the logic of development is clear. Indeed, skilled intellectual work is increasingly affected in the same way as skilled manual work, since information and control technology has begun to automate many technicians' jobs. Designing, for example, is now heavily automated in large engineering firms, with a consequent loss in the draughtman's control and the opportunity he has to use his skills, to say nothing of his increased prospects of unemployment. The search for profitability which results in the continual transformation of the instruments of production implies the abolition of human intervention and control.

It is sometimes claimed that technological change produces shifts in skills rather than de-skilling, and that the present development of micro-electronic, information-processing technology will merely change the skills of the working population rather than eliminate skilled work. This claim is likely to prove misguided for two reasons. As the automated machine tools illustration shows, during its primitive stage the new technology did create new skills such as those involved in programming the control units of automated machine tools. But as it becomes more developed, information-processing will in turn destroy many of these new skills. Just as continuous process plants advanced from the primitive systems which Blauner described in the early 1960s, so other applications of control automation can be expected to develop in ways that transform the very jobs that they have created.

Secondly, some new and permanent skills undoubtedly will be created but they will provide employment for relatively few people, many of whom will be concentrated in the upper reaches of the occupational hierarchy. Automated machine tools can once again be used as an example. A 'self-programming' capability involves the manufacturers of equipment and programs in new varieties of skilled work. The cognitive-planning functions were originally performed by every single craftsman who used a machine tool, then they were taken over by technicians in every workshop where an automatic tool was installed, and now they may at last be centralised into the design offices of the equipment manufacturers. Such centralisation dramatically reduces the number of people who need to be conversant with the cognitive-planning functions. Moreover, the skills involved in the design of the programs and equipment are of a higher order than before; they require graduate-level, professionally qualified manpower rather than manual craftsmen or lower-level technicians. Thus the 're-skilling' effect of new technological developments is likely to be very skewed: a few professional engineers and programmers will practise new and arcane skills, while the mass of people who use the artefacts of new technologies will neither need real skill nor have the opportunity to learn those skills involved in the performance of cognitive-planning functions.

Orientations

In the late 1960s there was a second type of reaction against the traditional interest in technology, which was concerned with the same issues of worker morale and the integration of workers in their firms, but claimed that these were not influenced by technology in the ways previously assumed. As part of a general shift of theoretical interest in British sociology at that time towards a more phenomenological approach, it was argued in industrial sociology that workers' *orientations* and definitions of the situation were more useful for explaining what went on at work than technology. In their celebrated study of factory workers in Luton, *The Affluent Worker*, Goldthorpe *et al.* (1968a) argued that the expectations people brought with them to employment, which were moulded by their social experiences outside work, determined their reactions to the structural attributes of the workplace such as technology.

Goldthorpe, Lockwood, Bechhofer and Platt distinguished *solidaristic* workers, who fitted the human relations stereotype in that they sought work which was both intrinsically satisfying and provided the chance to participate in a social community, and *instrumental* workers who sought only economic rewards such as high pay and security. The people they studied fell into this latter category and were unconcerned that work on assembly lines was intrinsically unsatisfying and provided no social community. Instrumental orientations were found to be associated with life-cycle factors: Luton workers were young and middle-aged men with dependent families and heavy financial obligations; they experienced geographical mobility which severed their ties to traditional working-class communities and work values; and they were more concerned for social relations within the family rather than outside the home. The authors thus questioned the universality and salience of the desire for community at work and the desire for intrinsically satisfying work. A belief that workers seek community underpinned the human relations movement, while a belief in the need for job satisfaction is more widely shared by other perspectives. As long as people's wants could be treated as fixed and universal, then it could be argued that technology working through these might produce significant and fairly predictable industrial consequences. Once wants were held to be variable and dependent on non-work processes which created different orientations, then these orientations became the independent variable in the analysis of attitudes and behaviour at work.

It is obviously correct to argue that what people want and expect from work determines their reaction to what they experience. But it is by no means clear that *The Affluent Worker* correctly identified the origin, content and consequences of these expectations in such a way as to make the interest in technology or other aspects of workplace structure less relevant. The emphasis placed on social processes outside work obscures the way work experience teaches people what it is realistic to expect and want. It is a fact that, with the exception of certain highly skilled craft workers, the great majority of manual workers use less manual and intellectual skill in their jobs than they do in driving their cars to work (Blackburn and Mann, 1979, p. 280). Given the constraints of the environment in which orientations exist, orientations are moulded to fit the possibilities that employment has to offer. For example, the frequently observed phenomenon that satisfaction with employment increases with age clearly shows how people adjust to the realities of work: younger workers tend to have higher aspirations regarding work content and to experience greater dissatifaction than do older workers who have fitted their expectations to what work actually offers. Thus part of the explanation of instrumentality must be that it represents an *adjustment* to work which offers very limited non-economic rewards. The degradation of work, therefore, to some extent fosters expectations that are congruent with the nature of work tasks. Whatever the source of instrumentality, if the cash nexus is what binds workers to their jobs then instrumentality is the appropriate response to the alienated work of modern industry: as Marx argued, work becomes the means to an end rather than an end in itself.

Research conducted since *The Affluent Worker* has greatly modified the conclusions reached there. Blackburn and Mann investigated the orientations of a thousand workers in a variety of industries in an English city (Peterborough), and found that 'the support for the existence of orientations of any sort was not impressive' (1979, p. 281). They defined orientation as a central organising principle that lies behind people's attempts to make sense of their lives, so linking work and non-work in the way suggested by Goldthorpe, Lockwood and their colleagues. This tended to exclude people whose work expectations had no wider implications. Even with regard simply to preferences in work, only about half the sample had any recognisable and consistent priorities (1979, p. 136). These findings clearly throw doubt on the usefulness of the concept of orientation for the analysis of industrial organisation.

Blackburn and Mann also found that those who did have orientations normally had multi-stranded rather than single-stranded priorities (1979, p. 281). In these multi-stranded forms, orientations covered factors relating to both extrinsic and intrinsic aspects of work. Goldthorpe *et al.*'s classification of orientations into dichotomies of economic and non-economic factors ignores the fact that even among workers with predominantly instrumental orientations, there may be important subsidiary wants. The Luton workers expressed considerable dissatisfaction with the level of non-economic rewards and wanted to see these improved (Goldthorpe *et al.*, 1968a, pp. 23–42). Other studies of largely instrumental workers have found a greater concern with the non-economic aspects of work which has made it difficult to find straightforward relationships between the dominant orientation and workers' reactions to the work situation (Beynon and Blackburn, 1972; S. Hill, 1976b). Of the non-economic rewards, intrinsic work content appears to be somewhat more salient than the set of 'social' needs emphasised by the human relations tradition. Case studies and attitude surveys in Britain and the United States indicate that male workers are more concerned with the nature of work tasks than with the quality of social relations, though the latter are not altogether unimportant, and that it is a mistake to join together into one category all non-economic rewards in the manner of Goldthorpe, Lockwood and colleagues and writers in the human relations tradition (Beynon and Blackburn, 1972; Sheppard and Herrick, 1972; S. Hill, 1976b). Pay, security and work content appear to be three dominant concerns which the majority of workers share.

Not a lot is known about the orientations of women workers as distinct from men, because only a few industrial sociologists have distinguished between the genders (Baldamus, 1961; Lupton, 1963; Cunnison, 1966; Beynon and Blackburn, 1972). What is known suggests that women share much the same concerns as men, but that companionship may feature more prominently as a source of compensation for unsatisfying work. This is particularly so with women workers whose incomes are not essential for the support of themselves or their families, as is sometimes the case with married women working part-time.

Because of the mixture of economic and intrinsic rewards which people seek from work, one would not anticipate that an individual's orientations would be static over time, for different circumstances would make some aspects of work more salient than others. Life-cycle factors, such as those identified in *The Affluent Worker*, obviously play a part in this process, as do external economic conditions such as high rates of inflation and unemployment which threaten financial rewards and job security: there are obviously times when having a job and a decent wage are all which anyone asks of their work. However concern with the nature of work never entirely disappears and continues to play an important part in people's perceptions of technology and their reactions to work.

There is indeed other evidence to suggest that many people are now more concerned with the content of their work. Attitude surveys in the U.S. show heightened aspirations for jobs that contain elements of skill, control and variety, and reduced tolerance of existing tasks, particularly among white workers (Sheppard and Herrick, 1972). Two processes appear to be at work: the ever-increasing degradation of work as the result of organisational and technical change and a shift in values among young workers which leads them to resist domination by managers or machines. In the U.S., during the relatively full employment conditions of the early 1970s, the consequences of these changes were sabotage, increased absenteeism and labour turnover, and even a major strike over the control issue at one General Motors factory. Government recognised the extent and significance of the malaise of industrial work, when the Health, Education and Welfare Department issued a report on *Work in America* (1973), which noted that absenteeism, wildcat strikes, turnover and industrial sabotage had become an increasingly significant part of the cost of doing business. The concern for work content had a significant impact in Scandinavia throughout the 1970s, prompting the rash of experiments in job redesign in Sweden and Norway and a demand from the Swedish manual union confederation (LO), subsequently reinforced by government, that companies should restore to workers some of their lost control over the work process. In Germany too, trade unions and government are publicly committed to humanising work that has been degraded by organisational and technical change.

Control versus Co-operation

This is an appropriate place to tie together some of the points raised in the last five chapters concerning managerial control systems, technology and the social relations arising out of production. In an economic system containing real conflicts of interest managers use a variety of techniques to reduce the extent to which profitable operation depends upon the discretion of lower level employees. One technique is to extend managerial control by organisational means. Another is to use technology. Thus the development of organisational structures and production technologies represent a distinct line of evolution and reflect a particular strategy. One does not have to argue, however, for a conscious and intentional managerial policy, for some identifiable 'conspiracy', particularly regarding technology. Managers introduce new production techniques in order to maintain or increase profitability and their assessments of new methods may contain no conscious evaluation of the control potential. What are important are the internalised design values and unconscious assumptions about what constitutes 'progress' which managers and engineers bring to bear when they apply scientific and technical knowledge to industry. These embody a central feature of conventional capitalist production, that control is one condition of profitability.

Of the existing forms of economic organisation, worker-owned and co-operatively managed systems in principle appear to provide the most appropriate means of re-structuring ownership and control in order to remove the opposition which lies at the heart of conventional capitalism and state socialism, while at the same time preserving the vital market mechanism which has largely constituted the wealth-producing dynamic of capitalism. The creation of common ownership and democratic control ends the various forms of appropriation, abolishes exploitation, and ensures that workers collectively are free to dispose of the profits of their collective activity as they choose. There are consequential changes in the nature of the social relations involved in production; namely, the end of control based on opposed interests which is also the end of 'class' relations at work. The manifestations of alienation which Blauner located in productive technique are consequences of the road down which modern economic systems have travelled. Within a co-operative rather than an antagonistic economy the particular manifestations of alienation that are found in productive technique should in theory disappear, since scientific progress can be used to enhance rather than degrade work and technology is no longer required to perform control functons.

Co-operatives operating within the framework of a market economy pose problems, however, for the analysis of alienation. The difficulty is that ending appropriation and class domination does not remove those other sources of compulsion which derive from the *market* rather than the nature of economic relations within conventional capitalism. 'Worker capitalism' is still dominated by the need to survive within a system of commodity production and market forces. Thus, following a strict interpretation of the alienation concept, producers would still appear to be dominated by the needs of capital accumulation if the dynamism of the market is retained. It seems a matter of common sense that people would *feel* less alienated and more in control of their own lives were one major component of alienation to disappear with the ending of the basis of opposition between workers and the agents of private or state capital. But abolishing the domination of capitalists and their agents, so transforming social relations in industry and society, and reasserting the control of people over their working environment, thus heightening job satisfaction, would not remove that other constraint – the power of the market.

7 Trade unionism and the regulation of conflict

The Institutionalisation of Conflict

There is a fundamental and continuing competition of interests within the economic system. However the expression of this opposition in social conflicts within industry has moderated, at the same time that such conflicts have become less threatening to the wider social fabric, in comparison with early capitalist industrialism. Sociologists explain the dramatic decline in social conflict as the result of the institutionalisation of conflict. This term describes the development of institutions that arise out of conflict, providing the means to regulate it without further recourse to violence or coercion.

The institutionalisation of conflict thesis

This has various strands. It assumes that one reason why industrial and political violence marked early capitalism was the destruction of traditional social bonds and normative regulation, which was a temporary and transitional phenomenon. With the growing maturity of capitalism, new regulatory and integrative institutions and values developed. Institutionalisation in mature capitalism results from the separation and autonomy of political and industrial conflict, so that one is no longer superimposed upon the other. The rise of social democracy, universal suffrage, and working-class political organisations, mean that the interests which dominate industry no longer control politics (Dahrendorf, 1959, pp. 267–79). Indeed, there is a 'fundamental separation of economy and polity' in *all* spheres (Giddens, 1973, p. 202). Workers also become more integrated into society when they possess citizenship rights in the political arena (Bendix, 1964, p. 101). Institutionalisation depends on a further process, the development of specialised institutions for regulating conflict within the industrial arena, once industrial conflict has been separated from political. Trade unions, together with collective bargaining between employers and trade unions, are institutions which reconcile the differences between workers and employers, labour and capital. In C.W. Mill's famous phrase, the union acts as the 'manager of discontent' and channels a potentially disruptive antagonism into a relationship of employee accommodation with management (1948, p. 8). These regulatory institutions in turn create agreed frameworks of rules for dealing with conflict, and so provide normative as well as institutional regulation.

The early exponents of the institutionalisation thesis, in the 1950s and early 1960s, had a pluralistic view of capitalist society and the industrial enterprise. Hyman (1978a) has discussed pluralism at length and he identifies three essential elements of the particular brand of pluralism common to the institutionalisation of conflict school in sociology and academics concerned with industrial relations. It was assumed that there were no undue concentrations of economic power. Economic power was either so widely diffused that no large accumulations existed, or where they did exist the power of large firms was evenly balanced by that of organised labour. This diffusion and the structure of checks and balances went with the rise of political and industrial interest groups organised into political parties and unions of employers and employees, so that political and industrial conflict became struggles between groups of roughly similar power. Indeed, some people suggested that social classes had ceased to have any importance, because interest groups were not the components of class movements or organisations (Kerr *et al.*, 1960, pp. 290–2). A second assumption was that of the public interest: despite the acknowledged plurality of sectional interests within modern society there was still believed to be common to all groups a single 'public' or 'national' interest (though this remained undefined and the idea contained major conceptual and practical difficulties). Thirdly, the state was regarded as the guarantor of this public interest. According to this view the state remained independent of any particular group, was not influenced excessively by the economically powerful (either because no such group existed or because competing groups rivalled its power), and thus pursued a neutral, mediating role in any social conflict. There was also a fourth assumption which lay behind and informed these three elements. This was the belief that conflict between interest groups in industry and society was confined to narrow issues and relatively minor details, that there existed a widespread consensus about, and endorsement of, the basic features of the polity and economy and the rules for regulating conflict (Kerr *et al.*, 1960, p. 292; Fox, 1974, p. 197).

The pluralistic approach to industrial relations within the firm pursued similar themes. In 1958 the American pluralist Ross claimed that power was evenly balanced between management and unionised labour, and that it was a necessary condition of stable industrial relations that this should remain so. Moreover, labour was not to be treated as a single homogeneous entity because in fact it was divided into many smaller sectional groups. Thus the lines of conflict were as much between employees themselves as between labour and management. Indeed, labour–management conflicts seemed to be less significant than sectional conflicts amongst employees. He claimed there was an over-arching general interest within the firm and that it was management's task to promote this collective interest by balancing the claims of rival groups: by implication, management's role was analogous to that of the state in society, rather than management standing as one of the two antagonists in the competition between the interests of labour and business. Many of these ideas entered the mainstream of thinking about industrial relations in Britain and America. Fox was typical of a number of commentators in the 1960s when he suggested that the firm should be seen as a 'coalition of stakeholders' with a multiplicity of sectional interests (1971, p. 61), though he later renounced this conception of the firm in favour of a dichotomous view (1974). Labour – management conflict in the pluralist perspective was treated as the outcome of functional differences and there was little conception of any sort of fundamental opposition of interests (Hyman, 1978a). There were assumed to be corporate goals to which all the sectional groups could subscribe. Finally, normative consensus on the rules regulating competition between management and labour was thought both desirable and possible: agreement on these allowed the institutions of conflict regulation to perform their role of promoting industrial peace.

Many of these traditional views have subsequently been questioned. Marxists by and large *have* accepted one basic notion of the pluralist view of society, that conflict has been contained within the polity and economy by structural and normative elements; in particular they place weight on the perceived role of trade unionism and collective bargaining for channelling the social conflicts arising out of economic opposition into forms which can be accommodated. Trade unionism and collective bargaining are hailed as integrating workers into capitalism (Marcuse, 1968, p. 21).

On the other hand, the extent of the separation between economy and polity and the autonomy of industrial and political conflict are subjects of debate among sociologists of all persuasions. What is not disputed is the achievement of capitalism in *convincing* people that there is a real divorce (Mann, 1973b, p. 19). Indeed, it is commonly claimed that capitalist ideology is in turn the source of whatever normative consensus can be found in industry or society. We have already seen that the continuing importance of real differences within the economy means that conflicts, when they occur, are not about the minor issues that pluralists assume. An implication of this is that labour shares a common interest in these conflicts which transcends any internal sectionalism. The neutral role of management in some pluralist accounts cannot of course be sustained. Modern industrial sociology rejects the pluralist conception of industry and society, demonstrating that there is still a real and substantial imbalance of power in both realms, that normative consensus may be low and provide little basis for effective regulation, and that industrial conflict often has a political expression.

In this chapter it is argued that the successful institutionalisation of conflict within industry is by no means assured and competition now increasingly bursts the bounds of the regulatory framework. An analysis of trade unionism reveals no inherent reason why unions should regulate conflict in ways that managers find acceptable. A careful look at the actual conduct of workplace industrial relations in advanced capitalist economies shows that institutional regulation may fall far short of what the different sociological perspectives have suggested. Normative regulation is marked by its ineffectiveness and dissension over values is commonly found. The chapter concludes with an appraisal of various arguments supporting the view that trade unionism segments labour and weakens its capability to reform industrial and social organisation. The focus here is mainly on the regulation of conflict within the industrial arena. The nature of economic interests and managerial strategy in response to these have been looked at in previous chapters. Subsequent chapters will consider in more detail the broader issues, such as how effectively unions pursue their goals, the threat that unionism poses to the existing economic order, what is the nature of normative consensus in society, to what extent the economy and polity can really be separated and the role of the state.

Trade unionism

Conflict between workers and employers is manifest in various ways:

> The strike is the most common and most visible expression. But conflict with the employer may also take the form of peaceful bargaining and grievance handling, of boycotts, of political action, of restriction of output, of sabotage, of absenteeism, or of personnel turnover. Several of these forms, such as sabotage, restriction of output, absenteeism, and turnover, may take place on an individual as well as on an organised basis and constitute alternatives to collective action.
>
> (Kerr, 1964, p. 171)

Industrial sociology, however, is concerned primarily with collective rather than individual expression, and with organised rather than unorganised methods of conducting conflict.

Trade unionism is founded on a striking paradox, that it arises out of the antagonism inherent in the economic order yet at the same time works to contain this conflict within bounds which preserve the basic features of this order. As long ago as 1902, Lenin (1961) identified what has become an important feature of modern trade unionism, when he claimed that unions tend to be *reformist* institutions. They promote a reformist rather than a revolutionary outlook among workers and persuade them to accept capitalism, despite the real conflict of interests that exists between capital and labour (Lenin, 1961). The typical economic and political demands of trade unions, such as the improvement of pay and conditions of work and actions by government on social welfare and labour law, can easily be met within the existing system. However, against Lenin's argument, it should be noted that, under certain conditions, even reformism may be more than the system can cope with. For example, the cumulative effect of pay bargaining backed by the collective organisation of labour may be harmful to capitalist profitability at certain moments. Other demands of union members, in the area of job control for example, are threatening at any time.

The *imbalance* of power between unions and employers is basic to the analysis of unionism. Individual workers have little power *vis-à-vis* their employers because the economic strength of the two parties is vastly different. Thus collective organisation in trade unions provides workers with some collective strength to offset their individual powerlessness. This collective strength, however, is only occasionally a countervailing power equivalent to that of the employer, if for no other reason than that employers can normally cope for longer without workers than workers can without jobs. The economic climate affects the extent of the power imbalance between capital and organised labour. Labour market conditions, whether unemployment is high and jobs are scarce or whether employment is full and there are numerous alternative jobs, influence the strength of the unions' countervailing power. The market for a firm's products and the size of its fixed costs (such as capital tied up in production machinery) influence the power disparity, because they partly determine the cost to the firm of labour withdrawal.

However, unions do at least have enough power to persuade owners and managers to negotiate with them. The accommodation between trade unionism and business has never emerged spontaneously, but has arisen as the reaction of government and business to the threat that unregulated trade unionism poses to the economic system. Collective strength is sufficient to ensure recognition of trade unions, if not to determine the outcome of bargaining. There has never been anything inevitable about the institutionalisation of conflict, but, as Ingham suggests, all too often social scientists have ignored the importance of workers' struggles against employers and taken institutionalisation for granted (1974, pp. 8–9). For example, the two periods earlier in this century when British governments most readily recognised the unionisation of their own employees, and most actively put pressure on private business to follow suit, coincided with the major wars, when governments reacted to the capacity of organised labour to weaken the war effort, rather than for any other reason (Adams, 1975). The history of the institutional regulation of conflict has in fact been one of mutual adaptation as the result of struggle. Owners and managers have compromised on issues which do not fundamentally threaten their interests while meeting some of the aims of unions. In their turn, unions have emphasised those areas where they *can* win something and have ignored more radical objectives. In modern social democracies, the political power of labour over government is sometimes greater than its economic power over business, and in these circumstances organised labour may use the political arena to wrest more extensive concessions from employers (see Chapters 8 and 11).

Trade unionism has not advanced at the same pace in all advanced industrial societies. Table 1.1 shows the wide variation that exists in the proportion of employees unionised in different countries. Britain is moderately well-organised by international standards, while the U.S. has only a small proportion of union members and moreover is the only country where union density is declining yearly. American unionism is mainly concentrated in a limited range of industries, where densities are somewhat higher than national figures would suggest. The Anglo – American pattern of industrial relations is the inspiration for those parts of the institutionalisation of conflict thesis which deal with unionism and collective bargaining. It remains an unremarked paradox, that American social scientists have for so long emphasised the contribution of trade unionism to the process of conflict institutionalisation, when the spread of unionism and collective bargaining in industry, and the political influence of organised labour on government, are both so *small* in America in comparison with social democracies of Western Europe.

Table 1.1 Degree of Unionisation in 1977

Country	*Density (%)*
Belgium	68
Denmark	64
France	20[a]
Germany	32
Italy	43
Japan	24
Netherlands	39
Norway	66
Sweden	80
United Kingdom	51
United States	20[b]

Notes: Density is trade union membership expressed as a proportion of the total employed population (including agricultural workers). Figures courtesy of C. J. Crouch, based on ILO Year Book and national statistical yearbooks.

[a]No accurate statistics are available for France and the reported density is an estimate.

[b]United States government statistics distinguish between trade unions and employee associations. If professional and state employee associations which bargain collectively with employers in more than one state or in two cities in one state are included in the table, the density rises to 26 per cent. Joining together unions and autonomous employee associations in this way, places the U.S. figures on a more similar footing to those in the rest of the table.

Economism, Control and Trade Unions

Trade unionism expresses the two major concerns of industrial and commercial employees. The first is the interest which they have in improving their market capacity, and to this end the collective strength of organised labour enables them to secure scarce economic rewards which individually they would be unable to obtain. Collective rather than individual bargaining may indeed produce some change in the way in which surpluses would otherwise be distributed, away from profits and into wages. Trade union action in this area concerns workers' economic interests. The second is the interest which subordinates have in offsetting the domination and control of owners and managers in the workplace, and in maintaining or regaining some measure of creativity and control at work. This is the issue of job control.

In a broad sense, control is a 'political' issue because it concerns the distribution of power within the enterprise and the economy as a whole, and raises the question of who 'rules' in industry. The concern to restore creativity and control is a reaction against those managerial strategies described earlier, and it places workers and employers in opposition because the nature of control means that one party can normally gain only at the cost of another. This is why managers have usually resisted so fiercely encroachments on their control. Although, as was noted in a previous chapter, some companies have learned that an *acceptable* degree of managerial control can now be maintained without totally denying shopfloor discretion. More significantly, the control issue raises questions about the logic of the economic system: it brings into the open the fact that profitability has depended on denying autonomy and creativity.

Collective bargaining

'Economic' and 'political' issues have largely been separated within the industrial realm, at least until recently (Mann, 1973b). Union leaders have mainly pursued their members' demands for improved pay and working conditions, rather than their control demands, while collective bargaining between union and management has centred on economism and excluded the more political issues. The crucial thing here is that owners and managers will strike bargains on financial issues and conditions of employment, whereas they will resist concessions on control, while unions react to this state of affairs by negotiating where they know that they have some chance of success. Unions contest those issues which they can realistically expect to influence, and these rarely include essential props of the economic structure (Fox, 1974, p. 276). The separation of economic and control issues, and the subordination of the latter to the former, are essential pre-conditions of the institutionalisation of conflict. Wage bargaining can be accommodated because it is not a zero-sum game with fixed resources where one side can only benefit at the cost of the other. But conflict over control cannot be moderated and regulated in the same way. Should control issues come to the fore, institutionalisation would become less effective as the later discussion shows.

Two conditions are necessary for satisfactory accommodation on economic issues. The first is that workers should be able to negotiate increases in real wages without compromising the financial interests of capital. The economy must therefore produce sufficient wealth to satisfy workers' economic demands. Simultaneously, labour productivity must also be increased or, alternatively, firms must be able to pass on wage rises as higher prices to customers in order to prevent an unacceptable decline in profits. In the three decades following the

Second World War, capitalism was sufficiently dynamic to create the economic conditions that were necessary to reconcile union demands with its own continuing viability. Diminishing rates of economic growth after the mid-1960s meant that trade unions' economic aspirations were less easily accommodated. Consequently, industrial conflict became more intense in most capitalist economies and, in a few, profitability declined (see Chapter 8). The second condition is that labour should not dispute the overall shape of the existing reward system, the basic framework within which surpluses are distributed, and should not make demands that threaten this. British trade unions appear to accept the present *structure* of income distribution, though there is less agreement that the actual amount of the existing differentials is fair (Hyman and Brough, 1975, pp. 74–92). Trade union economism may thus be a profoundly conservative force, however aggressively unions may pursue their members' financial interests.

Collective bargaining in America, Britain and most continental European nations in the postwar era has normally covered a restricted range of issues (see Herding, 1972, pp. 122–78 on America; Stewart, 1974, on various European nations; and Elliott, 1978, pp. 127–8 on Britain). Bargaining for most of this era has dealt mainly with pay, hours of work and other basic conditions of employment such as disciplinary and dismissal procedures. The trend now is for a widening of the range of employment conditions which are bargained, though these do not touch much on the issues of control and managerial prerogative in work organisation. For example, collective bargaining in Sweden between the major manual confederation (LO) and the employers (SAF) was extended from basic conditions to issues such as safety, training, the status of shop stewards and the experiments in work humanisation in the 1960s and 1970s. During the 1970s the British TUC urged its constituent unions with some success to extend bargaining to cover conditions such as job and income security, which includes guaranteed wages, pensions, sick and injury pay; manpower planning issues such as training, recruitment levels and redeployment agreements; and union and shop steward facilities at the workplace. There is still a wide variation among nations. On the one hand, British and Swedish unions have largely brought the full range of these employment conditions within the scope of bargaining. On the other hand, in France, where the development of institutions of conflict regulation has lagged far behind other northern European nations, bargaining in the 1970s for the first time produced real results even in such basic areas as pay, hours of work and provisions for retirement.

Control issues have been bargained over less often. The unrestricted rights of managers to manage have been accepted by unions and managerial prerogative has been endorsed even by large and powerful union movements. Prior to the 1970s when rank-and-file pressure brought control issues to the fore (see Chapter 8), Swedish unions wanted no share in the way work was managed, despite their successful influence over a wide range of employment conditions through collective bargaining, and every collective agreement had a clause reserving to the employer the right to hire and fire and direct labour at will (Forsebäck, 1976). The British engineering union for years endorsed managers' right to manage in its collective agreements. Nevertheless, collective bargaining is restrictive of managerial prerogative in some British firms when it covers issues such as manning levels and the right to move men from job to job. The status quo arrangements in parts of engineering have further restricted prerogative by preventing managers changing existing working procedures until new ones have been agreed or until the disputes procedure or a set period of time has elapsed (Elliott, 1978, p. 128). On the whole, however, trade union leaders working through the formal institutions of collective bargaining have been fairly indifferent to job control. Indeed, in the past British and American officials have given up their members' existing controls in certain circumstances rather than trying to increase them. Kuhn (1968) suggested that U.S. unions would sell job control for financial gains, while productivity bargaining in Britain in the mid-1960s was clearly based on the trade-off between workers' customary protective practices, such as overmanning, demarcation lines and control of output, and cash rewards (for example the Fawley agreement reported in Flanders, 1964).

Union democracy

Goal displacement describes the process whereby union members' goals are subordinated to other interests. This has been regarded as an extremely important feature of institutional regulation, because it enables unions to support the economic status quo and to ignore membership goals which appear to threaten the economic order. Michels, as the result of a detailed analysis of the German Social Democratic Party in the early twentieth century, asserted that labour organisations, however democratic their aims, were subject to an 'iron law of oligarchy' (Michels, 1915). Michels's arguments have structured the subsequent debate about trade union democracy, in particular his views that the needs of organisational efficiency conflict with the control by the membership of policy-making and execution, and that the apathy of most members, who choose not to participate in the formal machinery of union government nor to use their power, allows officials to ignore members' interests. Michels' position can be summarised briefly.

Organisation by its very structure creates oligarchy; it does this even more readily in trade unions than in political parties. As they grow in size and permanence, unions become administratively more complex and develop specialised leadership roles. Unions are unable to operate on the basis of 'direct democracy', partly because their size makes this impossible, and partly because the complexity of organisational problems can only be dealt with by people with technical expertise and experience. But once a permanent and bureaucratic organisation has been created, then the leaders who were at first no more than the executive organs of the collectivity may emancipate themselves from the mass and become independent of its control.

Structural factors also tend to concentrate power in the hands of officials. Leaders control the channels of communication and thus the flow of information within the unions, which enables the leaders to manipulate information to their own advantage. Leaders, by virtue of the expertise acquired in office, become indispensable, or at least very difficult to remove even when subject to periodic re-elections. In addition, leaders use all the methods at their disposal to maintain their power, partly for its own sake and also because their standard of living depends on holding office. While members often feel that incumbent officials have some customary or moral right to remain in office.

Once they have this strong position, so Michels claims, union leaders displace membership goals with their own. Thus the revolutionary ideals of socialist political parties and the radicalism of unions disappear and are replaced by bureaucratic conservatism, which serves the leadership's interest in the stability and preservation of their institutions. At the same time, union leaders become fairly prosperous, find that they can satisfy their personal interests within the existing system, and develop an accommodative ideology: a clear split develops between the rank-and-file perceptions of industry and society and those of the leaders. However members rarely resist goal displacement; they tend to be apathetic and uninvolved with issues of union government.

Michels and later sociologists have underestimated one vitally important feature of trade union goal displacement. This is the fact that unions have been weaker than employers for most of their existence, which has greatly influenced how union leaders have pursued more radical objectives. Over time, trade unions have moderated certain of their members' demands lest employers and governments destroy the union movement. Initially, this meant ignoring the radical commitment to the destruction of capitalism which many early American and European unions shared. Latterly, it has meant ignoring their members' control aspirations. However, as the next chapter shows, unions *will* actively pursue control issues when they have the strength.

The sociological interest in union democracy and the representation of members' interests has concentrated mainly on the formal institutions of union government. One approach emphasises participation rates in union meetings and elections. Low rates typically prevail, which has been used as evidence of the small influence that members have on official policy (Goldstein, 1952). A second approach analyses the political processes of union government and internal organisation, because unions may still represent their members despite low participation rates. Toleration of opposition emerges as the vital organisational feature. In *Union Democracy* (1956), Lipset, Trow and Coleman argued that the two-party system of government found uniquely in the International Typographical Union (ITU) promoted democracy by institutionalising opposition and providing for the replacement of incumbent administrations. Subsequent investigations into union organisation suggest that there is no need to go to the extreme of a two-party political system and that unions other than the ITU may be democratic. Martin (1968) asserts that the toleration of opposition factions and the right to campaign against executive policies is sufficient for democracy, and what is needed is some idea of the constraints that compel union leaders to tolerate factions. Edelstein and Warner (1975) have a more restricted conception of a democratic structure, as one where there is competition between equally powerful competitors, close election results, and turnover of officials. This has only a limited usefulness, however, because election results can be interpreted in ways that relate to the competence of officials as well as union democracy, and because most British officials are appointed rather than elected (except at branch and national executive levels).

The pessimism of Michels and later sociologists is exaggerated, as some of these analyses of union politics and organisation suggest. The displacement of members' goals and oligarchic tendencies are *not* inevitable. This is certainly Turner's view in *Trade Union Growth, Structure and Policy* (1962), where he classifies the variety of union administrations on the basis of the relationship between full-time officials, the minority of lay activists (shop stewards and branch officers), and the normally apathetic rank-and-file. He identifies

1. *Exclusive democracies* which typically occur in closed unions based on single occupations, which have few officials (all of whom are ex-rank-and-file members) and high levels of membership participation.
2. *Aristocracies* in old craft unions which were once closed to outsiders but now recruit more widely; one occupational group tends to participate more and have greater influence than other groups (for example, craftsmen in the engineers' union, AUEW).
3. *Popular bossdoms* in large, open or general unions where participation is low for all groups and union leaders emerge as an oligarchy controlling policy.

A number of factors *other* than the formal institutions of government and the structure of the organisation obviously influence the likelihood of union representativeness and membership participation. As Turner's typology suggests, the composition of the membership is very significant. Occupational heterogeneity is associated with low involvement and representativeness. Where unions incorporate a variety of occupational groups with their own individual interests and feelings of solidarity, then the open expression of these interests tends to be suppressed as threatening to organisational unity, and union leaders, faced with conflicting demands, tend to listen only to certain groups. Members of multi-occupational unions are frequently passive in union affairs, except in those matters that directly affect their interests because much of what their unions do appears to have no relevance for them. Other forms of group differentiation have an effect as well: particular groups are typically uninvolved in policy-making and government, notably ancillary workers in otherwise skilled trades, women workers, young workers and immigrants. The size and distribution of the membership is also significant. Unions whose members are dispersed (such as seamen or lorry drivers), or engaged in casual or seasonal work (hotel and catering), are generally marked by low participation rates and lack of communication between officials and members. Dispersion and size are associated with the growth of bureaucracy and the proliferation of organisational levels, both of which impede direct participation and influence.

Conversely, where the membership is geographically concentrated, is based on a single occupation which has a high degree of solidarity and occupational identity, and is small enough to obviate the need for an elaborate bureaucracy, the union is more democratic and officials more in touch with rank-and-file opinion.

The British docks provide an interesting illustration of these contrasts, because two unions operate within the same industry and organise the same type of worker with very different results. The National Amalgamated Dockers' Union (NASDU) is a small union, geographically concentrated mainly in the London and Liverpool docks, and occupationally homogeneous. The Transport and General Workers' Union (TGWU), which has a dockers' section, is an extremely large, general union which organises a multiplicity of different occupations in a variety of industries across the whole country. A recent comparison of the two unions in the London docks found a high degree of membership participation in NASDU, both in routine branch meetings and elections and in the special mass meetings of all London members which were called to discuss important issues, membership control of policy-making and execution, a low degree of bureaucratisation, and a leadership which had no independence of the rank-and-file (S. Hill, 1976b, pp. 127–49). The TGWU, on the other hand, exhibited considerably less rank-and-file participation, a more bureaucratised organisational structure, officials who were largely free of membership control, and less responsiveness to members' aspirations and interest in the formulation and execution of policies.

There is one basic characteristic of trade unions that ought to be central to the analysis of union democracy and responsiveness to members' goals, yet is scarcely considered: the fact that a union cannot coerce its members. The strength of a union derives from the strength of its members, who retain this strength regardless of what their union tells them to do, and unions, therefore, have influence but not power over their rank-and-file (Goldthorpe, 1974). Power in trade unions resides at the bottom rather than at the top, not merely in the formal, constitutional sense of the sovereignty of the people which is then usurped by the executive, but in a way which carries important implications for goal displacement and union democracy.

In the first place, members can effectively *veto* union policies which require them to act or to refrain from action, even when they cannot compel the hierarchy to pursue policies that match their aspirations. This is formally institutionalised in the U.S., where unions commonly require their members to ratify the collective agreements negotiated on their behalf and ratification acts as a check on the hierarchy selling out rank-and-file interests. While not formally institutionalised in many British unions, the *de facto* principle of ratification is assumed in the recognition that members will reject any agreement negotiated on their behalf which does not suit them and will pursue their own interests by means of 'unofficial' industrial action (action that the union does not sanction). Even in those countries where union officials negotiate agreements which are then legally binding on their members without the need to obtain membership ratification, members may ignore both their union officials and the law which supports them and take unilateral action against the agreement. Evidence of this can be found in the large number of unofficial and illegal wildcat strikes in Sweden in the 1970s (Forsebäck, 1976); the growth of spontaneous action in Germany, as in 1969 and again in 1973 when large numbers of metal union members rejected a union-negotiated pay agreement; and the wave of unofficial strikes in Belgium in protest against union-negotiated agreements in the late 1960s (Dubois, 1978). When faced by membership revolts that involve more than a handful of people, unions are powerless to coerce their members. This fact has all too often been ignored by those who assume that unions work like industrial and commercial organisations, with power flowing downwards from the top.

Secondly, since the collective power of labour in any workplace is created by, and 'belongs' to, the labour force itself, not the union, workers may act on their own and deal directly with management. There always exists the possibility that the rank-and-file, while still remaining union members, will create *other* organisations to protect their interests. Workshop industrial relations activity which is outside the control of the union hierarchy has been found in several mature industrial relations systems. The potential for alternative organisation has been realised in its most extensive and systematic form in Britain, which has no structure of legal restrictions designed to prevent unofficial action, for example by making union-negotiated collective agreements legally binding or by restricting the initiation of strike action to the union leadership. The problems of union democracy and the sensitivity of union officials to membership interests are not particularly meaningful, therefore, to the rank-and-file of many British unions: members have been able to pursue their own interests at the workplace and ignore the union hierarchy, choosing to deal directly with their employers. There is a range of issues which remains outside the control of the domestic organisation, notably the trade union representation of workers' interests in the political realm, and here the question of trade union democracy may perhaps assume more significance for members. But in the day-to-day dealings of labour and management which most concern workers, unions have been by-passed if their members have found them inadequate.

In Britain, one paradoxical effect of independent workplace organisation has been to make trade unions *more* responsive to their members. In the 1970s, workplace representatives (shop stewards) were at last formally incorporated into the union hierarchy. At the same time, they were delegated union functions (including local collective bargaining), most of which they had performed in the past unofficially. The union response was prompted partly by fear. Domestic organisation showed how little influence some unions had in the workplace and how unrepresentative they were of their members. This, in the long run, threatened their ability to recruit new members, to retain existing membership levels where there were no closed shops, to maintain the loyalty of the large number of unpaid, lay officials (such as branch officials and some stewards) who constituted the union organisation at the local level and usually collected union dues, and to be recognised by employers for negotiating purposes. But the significance of normative influences, that unions *ought* to be democratic, should not be ignored: despite the actual practice of some unions, democratic values are firmly entrenched in the union movement in Britain and elsewhere (Hyman, 1971, pp. 30–1).

The British experience suggests that the ability to negotiate meaningfully with employers at the workplace is of great significance for goal displacement, because collective bargaining at this level provides the membership with its best chance to control the issues which are being bargained and the conduct of negotiations. The structure of trade union representation and collective bargaining in continental Europe has mainly prevented this sort of decentralisation. Outside the Scandinavian countries an essential element of the industrial relations system in the advanced Western European nations after the war and through to the 1970s was the lack of effective union organisation and bargaining at the workplace itself. The main vehicles of worker representation within firms were the works councils. These councils were mainly created by government during the postwar reconstruction as agencies of social partnership, in which workers and managers would deal in an amicable manner with a variety of workplace issues. They were designed as 'essentially non-union, even anti-union, bodies based on an assumed community of interests between employers and workers, and providing little scope for the pursuit of workers' sectional interests' (Carew, 1978, p. 197). Their role was consultative and informational with few negotiating functions. Works councils inhibited trade unionism at the workplace by coming between workers and unions and taking some of a union's normal representational functions. Union organisation and collective bargaining over wages and conditions were effective at a level beyond individual plants and firms, in regional and national negotiations which took place between unions and the employers organised collectively. The law backed the system in various ways, defining the councils' role and making it difficult for union officials to organise or in some countries even visit their members at work, but at the same time supporting union hierarchies and the national collective bargaining system against challenge from below. For example, the right to initiate strike action might be limited to union officers and union agreements might be binding on members as in the majority of European nations.

Union members have therefore depended heavily on their leaderships in the absence of local organisations which they might control. For most of the postwar period, however, European unions were dominated by officialdom to a greater extent than in Great Britain. Control of the executive functions of administration and the major influence over the representational and legislative agencies such as the conference or general council were in the hands of the permanent hierarchy (Carew, 1978, pp. 196–7). The centralisation of union activities away from the workplace and the oligarchic tendency of union government combined to thwart the adequate representation of members' interests.

The response of European workers in the late 1960s and 1970s to a system of bargaining which ignored their aspirations was shown in various degrees of unregulated shopfloor action and unofficial strikes. These simultaneously challenged the structure of the industrial relations system and the oligarchic behaviour of the unions. In Italy the challenge was most widespread and intense. It also had the most far-reaching consequences which showed just what the rank-and-file acting together might achieve, when workers created their own shopfloor representational system based on workers' committees and shop stewards (*delegati*). Government and management accepted the new movement and endorsed the idea of plant-level collective bargaining directly between managers and workers' representatives, which involved changing the law relating to works councils. Trade unions recognised the implications of autonomous organisation, accepted stewards within the union structure, and decentralised their activities to the shopfloor organisation. The challenge and the consequences were less dramatic elsewhere, but unions in Belgium, France, Germany and Holland strengthened or established workplace organisations linking officials with members and became more sensitive to rank-and-file aspirations. The law regulating the workplace was changed where necessary to permit unions more access to their members and plant organisations to develop. German works councils were even allowed to negotiate on matters affecting the wage structure and working conditions of the individual plant. There was no decentralisation of power within the structure of industrial relations or trade unions to rival what happened in Italy, however. (For detailed accounts of these developments see Carew [1978]; Crouch and Pizzorno [1978].)

Changes in the Regulation of Industrial Conflict

Liberal pluralists writing in the 1950s, or those whose views were shaped during the early postwar period, were probably correct to believe that institutionalisation could successfully regulate conflict in the ways in which they assumed because industrial relations were then at their most stable and well-regulated for many years. The overt manifestation of conflict in strike rates was at a low ebb in most capitalist economies (Shorter and Tilley, 1974, pp. 318–34), collective bargaining between employers and union officials concentrated on issues which were capable of being resolved without endangering the accommodative relationship between the two parties, and agreements seemed to create a framework of rules and procedures to guide workplace relationships. Conversely, for those who decry unionism for the way it displaces members' goals, this period is one in which oligarchic tendencies reached a high level in the U.S. and several European nations (Martin, 1978). Since then, however, certain developments have shown how the institutional framework of conflict regulation no longer ensures industrial peace.

The British 'informal system'

A celebrated inquiry into the state of British industrial relations in the late 1960s came to the conclusion that

> Britain has two systems of industrial relations. The one is the formal system embodied in the official institutions. The other is the informal system created by the actual behaviour of trade unions and employers' associations, of managers, shop stewards and workers.
>
> (*Donovan Report*, 1968, p. 12)

Informal industrial relations activity was largely *autonomous*, because it was outside the control of the official institutions; *fragmented*, because inconsistent rules developed and different concessions were made to different groups at different times; and *informal*, because it was based mainly on unwritten understandings and 'custom and practice'. Custom and practice rules are sometimes the result of a recognisable process of bargaining, but usually emerge as the result of unilateral actions by workers or managers, informal adjustments, ambiguities and mistakes that establish precedents which are difficult to change (W. Brown, 1973). Fox and Flanders (1969) characterised workplace industrial relations as bordering on anarchy: normative consensus and hitherto-agreed frameworks of rules for dealing with industrial conflict had disappeared, and the institutions of conflict regulation no longer had much effect. There was little sign of any popular consensus about the fundamentals of economic organisation, nor even about the rules which were to regulate the conflicts inherent in the employment system.

Donovan noted three specific changes that reflected the underlying collapse of institutional regulation and the increasingly overt expression of conflict. The first was the rising number of strikes in all industries expect mining, and particularly the increase in unofficial (not sanctioned by the union) and unconstitutional (in breach of procedures negotiated in collective bargaining) stoppages which accounted for 95 per cent of strikes at that time. The second was wage drift, the gap between officially negotiated wages and what workers were actually paid, which resulted both from local collective negotiation and from unilateral worker action. The third was labour utilisation: workers were able to restrict managerial prerogative and insist on overmanning, rigid job demarcation, worker control of the rate of production, and who should be transferred from job to job. Workers fought to dispossess managers of their control over work organisation.

Donovan produced a distorted account of national industrial relations, because he extrapolated from the engineering industry, where the informal system was the most highly developed, to other sectors. Even within engineering, there were significant differences amongst firms. Nevertheless, a sociological investigation of the informal system allows us to present a more detailed account of the factors that underlie *all* shopfloor industrial relations.

Labour power The power of labour varies in response to a variety of influences. Labour market strength, the scarcity of supply relative to demand, is one obvious source of power. The political commitment of British and many other European governments to full employment in the period from the end of the Second World War to the mid-1970s resulted in greater labour market strength for nearly all grades of worker. In addition, specific groups had additional scarcity value by virtue of their skills or, and this often goes with skill, by virtue of their ability to restrict supply. Skilled workers organised into craft unions have long been able to regulate the supply of labour and so maximise their strength *vis-à-vis* their employers. Indeed, there is some doubt whether they have remained skilled because of the inherent nature of their work and the tasks they perform, or because of their ability to restrict labour supply and to maintain demarcation lines (Turner, 1962, p. 242).

Government action has also increased labour power in other ways in Europe. The creation of welfare services which reduce the individual's dependence on his or her employment for the provision of the essentials of life interferes with the forces of the labour market: the relationship between excess labour supply (unemployment) and a decline in labour strength is attenuated when unemployment no longer has the same personal consequences that it used to. The establishment by law of individual and collective employee rights, which restrict managers' freedom of action in personnel matters and give employees some sort of property rights in their jobs, strengthens labour in its dealings with management.

The production system can be seen as a separate source of strength. British and American case studies emphasise how labour power derives in part from work organisation (Sayles, 1958, pp. 41–9; Kuhn, 1961, pp. 144–66; Batstone *et al.*, 1977, p. 258), the result of the machinery and the division of labour imposed by management. Whether or not the system allows a major part of production to be halted by a group of workers is particularly important. In complex production systems, work organisation typically places some groups in more powerful positions than others and these are often the groups that prove the most active in the pursuit of their interests. Changes in the organisation of work towards a greater division of labour and greater interdependence between the different components of organisation, largely the result of applying the principles of rationalised shop management, have increased the scale of the disruption that small groups of workers can cause.

Organisation Another variable is the degree of organisation, how far workers take advantage of their potential power and mobilise for action. This in turn involves collective awareness. Empirical evidence suggests a number of features of industrial work which promote organisation and awareness. Work organisation has an effect when it creates discrete social groupings, such as the work groups which are required for many production processes, which foster collective attitudes and behaviour among people who work together and share concrete interests (Sayles, 1958, pp. 70–9; Batstone *et al.*, 1977, pp. 137–53). The occupational structure of a firm is also significant because members of some occupations typically display sentiments of 'occupational community' and share a collective awareness of belonging to a distinct group. Such sentiments are most commonly found in craft occupations which control the socialisation of new recruits by means of apprenticeships. But such feelings of community are by no means confined to craftsmen and are found among less skilled groups, especially in one-industry areas where recruitment is highly localised and where people spend a lifetime in one industry (Goldthorpe *et al.*, 1968b, p. 74).

Payment-by-results provides a major incentive to organise. Group bonuses paid for the output of a whole producing unit obviously foster collective awareness and organisation, since individuals see that their own earnings depend on what other group members do. But individual schemes also promote group solidarity, because collective action by members of a workshop mitigates various adverse consequences of piece-work: restriction of output on a group basis prevents individual earnings rising so high that management is tempted to cut the rate for the job, deceives time-study engineers when they assess jobs, minimises fluctuations in earnings by maintaining a steady level of output and protects weak or infirm workers.

Management Management policy and structure are significant features of workplace industrial relations. Despite the long-term tendency of managerial control systems to curtail worker autonomy, it is clear that individual managers may frequently permit domestic organisation to flourish and impose restrictions on managerial freedom, and that acquiescence or collusion is essential for the emergence of industrial relations behaviour that is outside the scope of the formal institutions of conflict regulation. American and British studies show how widespread are the informal accommodations reached between supervisors and middle managers, on the one hand, and shop stewards or groups of workers on the other. These accommodations range from practices which are bargained over and explicitly agreed to those which workers develop unilaterally and which managers have to tolerate when labour is strong. The resulting custom and practice rules help to protect workers against managerial domination and control systems. Managers themselves rarely regard such webs of rules as legitimate or morally-binding. They accept them as necessary evils, which are to be preferred to naked conflict and which may temporarily help to achieve managerial goals (Batstone *et al.*, 1977, p. 264). Accommodation normally occurs without the knowledge or consent of senior management.

The state of the market for a firm's goods has some influence on managerial policy towards shopfloor power. By and large, British product markets were fairly soft in the period from the Second World War through to the mid-1960s, and manufacturers were able to pass on the costs of inefficient production to the consumer (Phelps-Brown, 1966). There appears to have been little incentive for manufacturers to risk industrial action which would halt both production and profits when they could maintain what they regarded as a satisfactory level of profitability even with weakened managerial control of the shopfloor. A case study of industrial relations in two British firms provides empirical corroboration of this argument and demonstrates that where markets are stable and not very competitive, managerial resistance to shopfloor power may be low (Lupton, 1963, pp. 97–182).

Management is not a unified team, and different groups have a variety of objectives which influence their treatment of the shopfloor. While managers acknowledge the importance of profitability and the need for managerial authority, managers in different hierarchical levels and functional specialisms develop a variety of interests which may conflict in certain circumstances with senior managers' concern with profitability and capital accumulation and with the principles of rational management. The evidence suggests that low- and middle-level managers, when faced by a powerful labour force, may collude with workers for several reasons. As the representatives of management who deal directly with labour, foremen and production managers find themselves in the front line of industrial conflict. Inevitably, they attempt to reduce the stress that results by informal deals which keep the men off their backs: they act counter to principles of economic rationality and modern management for the sake of a peaceful life. This may keep their own superiors off their backs as well, since informal deals which buy peaceful production may give senior managers the impression that everything is running as it should be (Kuhn, 1961, p. 76).

But managers can also have an interest in collusion that arises out of their own work roles, when acceptance of shopfloor organisation enables them to perform some of their own tasks more effectively.

Even in the most completely rationalised production systems, effective production depends on workers putting a certain amount of effort and application into their tasks, which neither incentive payment systems nor discipline can guarantee if collective action perverts piecework and if managerial authority has been rendered partly ineffective by the collective strength of labour. In less rationalised systems, and particularly where there is considerable production variability, managers depend on the co-operation of workers and their using whatever discretion they have in the interests of effective production. Managers directly involved in the production, when faced by a powerful labour force, may make deals with their operatives in order to fulfil their production goals. In these cases, output is bought at the cost of increased wages and deteriorating control systems. The division of labour within management is obviously intended to divide and co-ordinate tasks in a way that promotes the profitability of the company. But it often happens that managers interpret the firm's overall objectives in terms of their sectional, departmental interests. It is therefore common to find production management pursuing its output goals in ways which conflict with the interests of those other departments, such as cost-accounting and personnel or industrial relations, which are concerned with controlling the costs and maintaining the profitability of what is produced, or with the long-run preservation and extension of managerial control.

Thus the internal structure of management is relevant: the tightness of the control exercised by senior managers over those below them is what determines the scope that lower managers have to re-interpret senior managers' goals. The complexity and depth of the hierarchy is important: the greater the range of departmental interests and the more extended the lines of communication, the more difficult senior managers find it to control the division of labour. Modern information-processing technology has eased the communication problem to a considerable extent, so that senior managers now have a better idea of what is going on below them, but this by no means completely solves the problems of internal control. Managers at the top have a clearer view, one that is less distorted by the specialised sub-goals assigned to different departments, of the means by which to maximise capital accumulation. They are more aware of the pressures of the market place and, as individuals, they are better integrated into the capitalist order (see Chapter 4). The economic rationality that guides modern management is usually fairly clear at the top, though it may become blurred nearer the bottom of the hierarchy.

Labour leadership The final factor is labour leadership. Collective awareness and organisation do not emerge spontaneously in the struggle between labour and management. Rather, they have to be encouraged to grow and then be channelled into an effective course of action. This is why shop stewards are so important in British industrial relations. They teach workers the values of unity, collective interest and organised opposition, which are necessary if workers are to become collectively aware and learn to translate their potential strength into action. Stewards provide interpretative frameworks which structure the way that people see the world and create appropriate patterns of behaviour. Although they express the conflict and struggle of shopfloor life, these frameworks frequently depend on external resources, rather than being developed indigenously. As Lenin argued in another context, how best to create a revolutionary class consciousness, effective labour activity depends to a large extent on concepts imported from the outside in order to explain the objective reality of industrial life and to provide practical guides to action. For Lenin it was the revolutionary party and socialist theory which performed this role; for shop stewards it is the external trade union movement and the values of trade unionism. Stewards depend on their unions, not so much for concrete help or intervention, which some of them would indeed reject, but for a philosophy and a set of prescriptions which enable them to lead their constituents (Beynon, 1973, pp. 211–41; Batstone *et al.*, 1978, pp. 217–23). Stewards thus have a crucial leadership role in mobilising and guiding collective action, and trade unionism, which embodies the knowledge learned by previous generations of workers, provides a significant intellectual resource for this task.

Stewards provide leadership in other ways as well. Because they represent their constituents' interests on what is often a full-time basis, stewards build up a good working knowledge of what is possible in any given set of circumstances. They learn whether individual managers are soft or tough, when the company itself is likely to give way or resist, and what sorts of activity can be concealed. They thus have tactical and strategic knowledge which is denied to the ordinary rank-and-file worker and which adds to their effectiveness.

Effective shopfloor activity usually depends on the co-ordination of different groups of workers within a workplace, and here stewards are extremely important. Most large plants have informal networks of shop stewards and organised mechanisms of integration such as steward hierarchies (senior stewards and conveners) and joint shop stewards committees. These co-ordinate the actions of disparate groups of workers, and offset the tendency of individual groups to become isolated from each other and to define their collective interests in purely sectional terms. This is a particularly important role in the conditions of multi-unionism found in parts of British industry, where competing unions are unable to provide a unified organisation (W. Brown *et al.*, 1978). But the role exists wherever large-scale production and extensive division of labour make it difficult for workers on their own to organise effectively. The same articulating and universalising functions are found in what is now the other largely decentralised system of workplace industrial relations in Europe, the Italian *delegati* movement (Zoll, 1978). This too has to cut across the divisions of multi-unionism (in this case unions divide politically rather than occupationally).

The changing pattern of regulation

Where does this leave the regulation of conflict? It is now apparent that several features of the old system of regulation have been ignored by the traditional accounts of institutional and normative regulation, and that industrial conflict may always have been more extensive and more intense than was previously believed to be the case. Historical investigation shows that workplace activity was normal in the engineering industry in Britain from the mid-Victorian period onwards, that labour – management conflict was often bitter and created the first shop steward movement during and after the 1914–18 War (Hinton, 1973, pp. 71–81), and that the 'formal' system in fact flourished only during the second quarter of the twentieth century. This was an era of labour weakness as the result of economic recession, when workers in their individual factories had insufficient strength to oppose management successfully and national collective bargaining via trade union institutions provided greater collective power than could be mobilised in one place of work. During these two-and-a-half decades, workplace activity itself did not entirely disappear, rather it became less visible to outside commentators. The traditional indicators of workplace activity, strike rates and wage drift, would obviously be influenced by the weakness of labour, but informal worker organisation in opposition to management never entirely disappeared.

The years of orderly industrial relations in Britain may be explained as much by the *power disparity* between management and labour as by the normative consensus which the regulatory institutions were supposed to have created. Changes in the relative power of labour in the post-war era revealed that workers were unwilling to tolerate the terms on which conflict in the past had been regulated: when they had the strength, they overturned the traditional patterns of conflict institutionalisation. It became clear to several observers in the mid-1970s that the apparently agreed frameworks of rules which used to guide conflict resolution and the apparent consensus on the basic details of the organisation of industry were based largely on worker acquiescence in the face of superior managerial power, rather than on any institutionalisation and legitimisation of norms and customary procedures (Fox, 1974; Goldthorpe, 1974; S. Hill, 1974).

The failure of traditional regulatory institutions has not led to complete anarchy, because there are new forms of regulation. These, however, provide only a precarious state of peace. The custom and practice rules of the shopfloor, which grow out of bargaining and unilateral action, help to regulate relationships. Shop stewards replace trade unions as the institutional representatives of workers' shopfloor interests, and the shop steward system develops into a complex and permanent domestic organisation. Stewards assume the trade union function of managing discontent, mediating between labour and management and channelling conflict into tolerable forms. The discussion of the stewards' leadership role emphasised how stewards raised workers' consciousness and taught them to use their collective strength. But it is also true that the adoption of a trade unionist perspective and strategy places limits on the ways in which conflict is expressed and reconciles people to improving conditions from within the system rather than overthrowing it.

This new regulation is of course quite unstable. The webs of rules have little binding force, because there is no real consensus about the legitimacy of rules which represent the ability of one party to impose its will on another. Consequently when it is advantageous to do so, or when the power balance shifts, both sides ignore the rules which they have endorsed, or at least tolerated. There is thus a real struggle at the 'frontier of control', in which both labour and management try to extend their control at the cost of the other's. Consensus about the legitimacy of existing forms of industrial organisation is also missing. Workers rarely formulate any coherent view of alternative forms of organisation, but their commitment to existing industrial and economic institutions is one of pragmatic acceptance rather than of real endorsement (Mann, 1973b, p. 68). This parallels the absence of an agreed framework of regulative rules. The two together help explain why industrial peace is precarious, why power is important, and why there is so little social integration or cohesion in the economy.

Nor can shop stewards restrain industrial action in the way that unions once did. Stewards are more responsive to rank-and-file opinion than union officials because they depend entirely on their constituents for their position and have no organisational independence of the rank-and-file. Therefore, they more faithfully mirror the antagonism inherent in employment. Union democracy has been a 'problem' because officials, in their own interests, have entered into accommodative relationships with employers and have been less effective in pursuing rank-and-file interests, and this goal displacement is precisely why unions in the past have played an important role in the regulation of conflict and the preservation of peace. Shop stewards do have a regulative function, but it can rarely be exercised against the wishes of the rank-and-file and does not provide the sort of stability associated with traditional regulative institutions.

Shopfloor activity is centrally concerned with job control. This, of course, reflects workers' innate interest in such issues. But it also reflects the fact that economism and control are far more closely linked than sociologists have been willing to concede. The employment relationship is concerned with the balance between the financial rewards received and the time or effort expended, as Chapter 2 made clear. The British informal system shows that workers can alter the balance between reward and effort in their favour when they establish some control over work processes: their concern for their pay leads them logically to an interest in control.

Comparative evidence shows that Britain is not alone in having new forms of conflict which escape the traditional regulatory institutions. American commentators have for many years noted the significance of informal, 'fractional' bargaining in which powerful work groups, often led by stewards or activists, renege on agreements negotiated by their unions, ignore formal procedures and take direct industrial action which may culminate in unofficial, unconstitutional and illegal 'wildcat' strikes (Sayles, 1958; Chamberlain, 1961; Kuhn, 1961). These groups are in effect independent units over which neither the union nor management has much authority. More recently, following the wave of industrial unrest in the late 1960s and early 1970s, the rise of more intense conflicts and the increasing inadequacy of traditional regulatory mechanisms to cope with these have become apparent in many European societies. It has been noted that Italian industrial relations are now developing along a somewhat similar path to that followed in Britain, with the rise of a powerful and semi-autonomous shopfloor organisation and intensified conflict, though this is not the most significant case since Italy has never been a society which fits the classic institutionalisation of conflict thesis. More interesting is the growth of shopfloor action in Sweden, where there has been a significant increase in the number of unofficial strikes since the late 1960s (Forsebäck, 1976, pp. 68–69), a symptom of a decay in customary regulation. Unofficial activity and strikes have also posed problems for management and unions in Belgium and Holland (Molitor, 1978; Akkermans and Grootings, 1978). Since 'wildcat' strikes are illegal in Belgium, Holland, the U.S. and Sweden and many therefore go unrecorded, the real extent of unofficial action in these societies is difficult to establish. But the fact remains that even such apparently tightly controlled systems as these display unregulated shopfloor activity.

Rationalised control This is an appropriate point to look once again at rationalisation and managerial control. It is obvious that considerable differences exist between the circumstances of the second and third decades of this century, when the collective strength of labour in unions and at the workplace was not great and consequently scientific management could be introduced against the opposition of the shopfloor labour force, and those of the present day. Shopfloor activity in many firms in Britain now reduces the benefit which accrues to management from rationalisation. Even in continental European nations, where managerial prerogatives in the area of production organisation have been accepted for far longer than in Britain, shopfloor workers have begun to resist rationalisation and to demand that new working methods should be the subject of negotiation between men and management, with the aim of reducing the ill effects of these innovations. German and Italian evidence suggests that rationalisation which intensified worker effort and reduced worker autonomy grew rapidly in the mid-1960s, stimulated by worsening economic conditions which reduced business profitability, and that this was responsible for much of the industrial unrest in the closing years of that decade (Zoll, 1978; Müller-Jentsch and Sperling, 1978). Workers experienced rationalisation as exploitative, and reacted with demands for more control over the organisation of work. In Germany, political pressure from the labour movement ultimately led the government in the early 1970s to modify the law governing works councils to give worker representatives some rights to determine jointly with managers the consequences of further rationalisation for work intensity (Müller-Jentsch and Sperling, 1978). In Italy, there was industrial pressure to increase employee influence on the organisation of work and to develop participatory democracy within firms. The employees involved in this struggle included the traditional, blue-collar working class and the so-called 'new working class' of white-collar workers and technicians in technologically advanced industries. The industrial unrest of 1968–72 produced substantial gains for Italian labour, which institutionalised the power of worker representatives as checks on the exercise of managerial prerogative (Low-Beer, 1978, pp. 24–42; Zoll, 1978).

Trade Unionism and the Unity of Labour

An important and recurring issue in the discussion of trade unionism is whether unions promote the unity of the working class or foster division. Marx and Engels in their early writings regarded unionism as the collective opposition of labour to economic exploitation and as an important stage in the growth of revolutionary action which would be class-wide, based on an appraisal of class interest and embody class consciousness. Though in later years they realised that trade unionism in Britain had not yet in practice produced the results which they had originally anticipated (Hyman, 1971, pp. 4–11). Subsequent Marxists, following Lenin, have argued against the revolutionary potential of unionism on two grounds. One argument, that trade unionism promotes a non-revolutionary appraisal of the economic system and a 'reformist' consciousness which allows capitalism to 'buy off' discontent, was mentioned earlier. The other holds that unionism promotes sectionalism within the working class, because it follows the contours of the industrial structure. This structure creates a labour force that is divided into different firms and workplaces, and into different occupations. Unionism may to some extent overcome geographical diversity by organising on a national scale, but it has the greatest of difficulty in overcoming occupational stratification and frequently organises along occupational lines. Consequently, unionism comes to express, and indeed to perpetuate, the sectionalism of occupational interests rather than the universality of class interests (Lenin, 1961). In particular, the internal stratification of the working class by level of skill is reflected in trade union organisation. Trade unionism *per se* cannot overcome the stratification and sectionalism which results from the industrial structure. Lenin believed that the task of developing a common class programme, which would show how insignificant are sectional differences in comparison with the interests that all workers share by virtue of their common class position and relation to the means of production, would fall on a universalising, social democratic ideology and the socialist political parties which embrace this.

Modern social scientists have divided along similar lines. It was a common-place in British industrial sociology in the 1950s and 1960s that union membership was a form of class action and indicated some level of class awareness and solidarity (Bain *et al.*, 1973, p. 23), while industrial relations specialists argued on the contrary that workers were 'job' rather than 'class' conscious (Flanders, 1970, pp. 38–47). Unionism clearly embodies a sense of collective awareness and solidarity and is a primitive form of class action. These sentiments may in turn develop into a more coherent sense of class awareness and solidarity. However, there is little to suggest that these class attitudes are the main impetus to unionise or that, when unionised, workers' awareness of class solidarity is dramatically raised. In the first instance, as Flanders has claimed, workers are mainly concerned with the immediate improvements in their work situations which they expect to be the result of collective organisation. Their interests are centred on the job. Given the division of labour in modern industry and the plurality of sectional interests, suggests Flanders, the interests of one job may well conflict with those of another. As a result, job consciousness may segment labour, leading to disputes over demarcation (which union's members are to do a particular job) and jurisdiction (which union a particular group of workers should join), and to arguments about pay relativities between different groups, despite the rhetoric of union solidarity.

The trade union experience in America and Britain supports the argument about sectionalism. Industrial development in both countries created large craft sectors, while labour market conditions (the scarcity of craftsmen relative to an abundance of less skilled labour) ensured that craftsmen enjoyed favourable pay and working conditions. Craft unions emerged and flourished long before the general unions of less skilled workers and protected the craftsman's privileged position and status against both management and unskilled labour. A perennial theme in the labour history of both countries has been the division of interests between craftsmen and the less skilled, manifest in the relations between individuals and groups on the shopfloor and in the relations between trade unions acting as the institutional embodiments of job and occupational interests.

Unionism does not cause stratification, which is the consequence of industrial structure, but it certainly used to amplify sectionalism by creating organisations based on occupational differences. Changes in the pattern of American and British trade unionism mean that the structure of the trade union movement now no longer positively promotes division in the way it once did. Craft unionism has now declined in importance in the U.S., partly as the result of legislation favouring single union representation for all workers in a firm or industry and partly because rationalised production methods have destroyed so many of the old skilled occupations. The trend over the last twenty years in the U.K. towards very large, multi-occupational, open unions, as smaller and occupationally-based unions merge with the giants, has also reduced the amplification of occupational differences to a limited extent. Nevertheless, rivalry between the skilled and the unskilled, between different groups of skilled workers, and even within the ranks of the unskilled, constitutes a major factor in the conduct of industrial relations at the workplace and within or between unions (see, for example, Sayles, 1958, on the U.S. and Turner *et al.*, 1967, on the U.K.).

A more positive attempt to overcome sectionalism can now be found in certain British factories, where factory-wide committees and steward hierarchies have developed into fairly effective institutions (W. Brown, *et al.*, 1978). The drive to overcome sectionalism depends on workplace initiatives rather than official trade union leadership. It reflects no change in political ideology and makes no attempt to create a class movement. It is a pragmatic response to the growing size of manufacturing plants and the occupational complexity associated with this, which attempts to increase unity in order to increase labour's bargaining power. In multi-plant companies, stewards often set up co-ordinating committees which attempt to unify action in all plants. These new departures have not entirely overcome sectionalism and unity is still highly precarious. Should they in future prove more successful, there would then be good evidence that rank-and-file unionism can create organisations which transcend the old forms of sectionalism. In these circumstances, the rhetoric of trade union solidarity would no longer ring with its customary hollowness.

Trade unionism outside America and Britain has had a less divisive record, notably in continental Europe. France and Sweden show how different patterns of industrial development and structure have helped to create different union movements. The rapid industrialisation of the Swedish economy towards the end of the nineteenth century did not create the sort of craft sector found in America or Britain. Differences in industrial structure may explain why craft unionism never became entrenched in Sweden and facilitated an undivided manual union movement (Korpi, 1977). French industry was marked by occupational and skill differentiation, but labour shortages after the mid-nineteenth century raised significantly the material rewards of unskilled workers and reduced differentials with craftsmen. Craftsmen were unable to maintain their élite status against the pressures of the market, thus sectional differences became less important (Sellier, 1973). In both cases, economic factors created a relatively less differentiated labour force, which facilitated the trade union organisation of manual workers regardless of occupation, in contrast to American and British experience (though in France the trade union movement *is* divided along political lines, a major division being between communist and socialist unions).

Unionism in France, Germany and Sweden shows the effect of a second influence, which also helps to account for the way in which occupational sectionalism has been resisted in all three countries: the historical legacy of a universalistic philosophy, which in this case was socialism. Whereas trade unionism in America and Britain has always been largely pragmatic, non-ideological and concerned with the bread-and-butter issues of improving pay and conditions, and whereas strong unions existed long before the growth of political parties representing working-class interests, continental unionism has typically been heavily influenced by socialist theory and intimately linked with, indeed sometimes created by, socialist political parties. Early German unions were organised along craft lines, but they were so closely connected to the Social Democratic Party, and their members were so committed against capitalism, that the craft unions were first opened to less skilled workers and then amalgamated to form industrial unions in the late nineteenth and early twentieth centuries, and sectionalism within the industrial sphere was subordinated in the interests of unity in the political arena (Lösche, 1973). In Sweden, socialist political parties were actually founded after the first stable trade unions, but then provided the links between different unions before federations of unions were organised (Scase, 1977, p. 27). The manual trade union movement has from its earliest days been intimately associated with the Social Democratic political party and has shared this party's socialist ideology, which laid emphasis on the necessity for political action to transform capitalism in addition to the purely industrial action of trade unionism, and on the importance of class unity in the fight against capitalism. The largest union federation in France, the CGT, was created by revolutionary socialists in 1895 and ever since has been committed to a programme of class unity and struggle. It follows an orthodox Leninist line on the need for labour unity and the subordination of trade unionism to the practical and ideological leadership of the political party, since the 1920s the French Communist Party (Dubois *et al.*, 1978).

These three examples support Lenin's contention that unions

need a universalistic ideology if they are to create a united labour movement, and that this ideology is normally created and sustained within a socialist political party rather than growing naturally within unionism itself. The ideological orientations of the three movements are now very different, despite their common origins in Marxism in the last decade of the nineteenth and the early decades of this century. The Swedish manual federation (LO) and Social Democratic Party have chosen to collaborate with capitalism, which has involved working to increase capitalism's economic efficiency and the return on capital, while at the same time reforming it by means of union activity in industry and the Social Democratic Party in politics. Nevertheless, the trade union and political wings of the labour movement maintain a clear commitment to the radical reconstruction of capitalism, and there are signs that this may now be translated into more concrete action as the limits of the collaborative reform of capitalism are reached (see Chapter 8). The German union movement and Social Democratic Party have both shed their traditional socialism over the last quarter of a century and no longer pay even lip-service to fundamental social and economic reconstruction, at the same time that they have increasingly divorced themselves from each other (Lösche, 1973). Of the three, only the French movement has entirely maintained its original ideological purity. The historical legacy of a universalising ideology imported from outside the movement remains important, however, because once a union organisation based on non-sectional principles had been established and firmly institutionalised into the structure of industrial relations, it could then persist regardless of any subsequent change in the original ideology. In Sweden and France, the universalistic ideology still has a considerable practical force. The Swedish LO pursues a policy of wage equalisation, which is designed gradually to remove pay differentials attached to occupational or skill differences within the manual labour force and between manual and non-manual workers (Scase, 1977, p. 29). French unions have recently adopted a similar policy designed to reduce disparities (Dubois *et al.*, 1978).

8 Trade union effectiveness

How successful are trade unions? This question is not raised very often, though it is one which should be posed in any evaluation of trade unionism. The answer can be divided into several parts, since success and effectiveness can be discussed in relation to various union functions which cover the advancement of members' interests and the contribution that unionism makes to institutional regulation.

Economism

The effect of trade unions and collective bargaining on the wages and living standards of union members is one obviously important issue. This has been the main area of union activity, as part of the strategy of giving primacy to workers' economic interests. The effectiveness of trade unions in collective bargaining has been evaluated in several ways: the structure and level of wages, which includes differentials between unionised and non-unionised labour and the effect of unions on the growth in money wages or wage inflation; the share of wages in national income over time; trends in real disposable incomes and living standards. Economists who have dealt with these issues believe that the extent to which unionism delivers the goods, in particular how far union members are better off than they would be without a union, cannot be determined accurately. It is even debated whether unions provide any wage benefits at all. The evidence suggests positive though unquantifiable financial gains for union members.

Investigation of the *structure* of pay shows that union members and others covered by agreements have wage differentials over those outside. In America, research comparing the remuneration of union members and others, or wages and salaries in unionised and non-unionised industries, has found that the average union differential is between 20 and 25 per cent, with a range of 10 to 50 per cent according to the ethnic, skill and sexual composition of the employees in question (G.E. Johnson, 1975). In Britain, workers covered by collective agreements negotiated by unions (and these workers include non-unionists) have a wage differential of 25 to 35 per cent (Metcalf, 1977). The issue is whether unions and collective bargaining cause higher wages, since other factors may be at work. High wages, unionism and bargaining may all be determined in part or in whole by some other factor, so unionism and bargaining may be wrongly credited for raising wages when these depend on some extraneous variable.

Labour quality is one such variable. Firms that are highly unionised or covered by good agreements may be the ones in which managers have chosen to operate high wage policies, in order to attract high quality labour and keep turnover rates low, perhaps because the production process requires specific training or worker commitment and application. Unions for their part like recruiting in these firms, because a stable labour force means that once a person has been recruited he remains a union member, which is particularly important in the U.S. where organisation by firm and less by trade means that workers who leave a firm often leave the union as well. British unions also prefer stable workforces and find it more difficult to organise industries with many small firms and high labour turnover. The firms that pursue high wage policies are often large in size, which means that there is a large number of potential members in one place and the cost of organising each member is comparatively low. Unions also find negotiating rewarding when companies in any case want to pay well. Employees, in turn, have a strong incentive to unionise for *non*-wage reasons: as pay is good they are unlikely to want to move elsewhere, so they have a strong interest in negotiating improvements in their non-wage conditions of employment (G.E. Johnson, 1975). Controlling for labour quality reduces the union differential. G.E. Johnson (1975) estimates that the differential is negligible in America. Metcalf (1977) thinks that it may be as high as 20 per cent in Britain. The evidence is scanty and not very convincing in either case, and these estimates contain a large element of guesswork.

In Great Britain certain types of collective bargain are worth more than others. National agreements provide no real advantage over wages outside agreements, and the real benefits go to people with supplementary agreements on top of a national one or with local agreements only (Metcalf, 1977). Union membership and collective bargaining as such do not significantly determine wage differentials. Other factors have to be considered. The association of relative gains with domestic bargaining suggests two avenues of enquiry. On the labour side, differentials may be associated with the strength of the shopfloor and shop steward bargaining. Labour strength is the product of a variety of factors, including effective collective organisation, that were noted in the last chapter. Simply being unionised is perhaps unimportant for relative wages, but being powerful at the workplace and having the union organisation (stewards and full-time officials) to channel that strength may be more significant. On the employers' side, one might reasonably assume that any policy of recruiting high quality labour and the profitability of a firm and its ability to pay, which are the explanations favoured by many economists, would show through in decentralised bargaining where the differences between firms are not submerged as they are in national bargaining.

Unionisation is associated with wage inflation and levels of pay that are higher than would otherwise be likely to occur. American evidence shows in the first place that wages in poorly unionised industries are largely determined by company profit rates, whereas in strongly unionised industries wages are much less influenced by profits (and presumably the ability of the firm to pay), and secondly that the pressure of surplus labour reduces wages in the poorly organised sector but not in the other (G.E. Johnson, 1975). In other words, wage levels in the union sector are higher than economic analysis suggests they would be in the absence of unions. This reinforces the case for believing that collective organisation has some effect on relative wage levels and the structure of wages. How far bargaining inflates the *general* level of pay depends on how far the wages outside the unionised sector, or in Britain the area covered by local agreements, are influenced by those within. Economists disagree on this issue, because the mechanism that transmits wage inflation from one sector to another is not specified and there is anyway a shortage of good empirical evidence here as elsewhere (G.E. Johnson, 1975). Moreover, it is clear that if there is a simple or fairly direct relationship between unionisation and wage inflation, then more unionisation should lead to more inflation. In fact the per annum increase in unionism is small and does not appear to explain the actual amounts of inflation. Against this line of reasoning, it must be said that politicians who are concerned with the practical problems of economic management believe that general wage levels are greatly influenced by union pressure, which is why incomes policies designed to restrain union wage-bargaining have been popular on both sides of the Atlantic.

Unions have aimed to win a larger *share* of the product for their members, to redistribute surplus away from its appropriation as profit and into higher wages. In the 1950s and 1960s, rising living standards in Britain appear to have been the result of a growing national income, which meant more for all, rather than any great change in proportionate shares. This indicated that unions had little effect (Flanders, 1970, pp. 213–40). However the effectiveness of labour pressure on the distribution of the product has increased since the mid-1960s. British and American evidence shows that the share of profits in company net output has fallen while that of wages has risen slightly (Glyn and Sutcliffe, 1972; Nordhaus, 1974). Rowthorn (1976) indicates that, over the last decade, the share of post-tax profits has declined throughout the advanced capitalist world. The immediate causes of this decline are rising state expenditure, the rising price of primary products such as oil and other commodities from the non-industrialised world, and the existence of a strong working-class movement which protected people's real wages. Popular pressure for better social services and benefits is one of several pressures working for higher state expenditures which have absorbed a growing proportion of national income, yet popular pressure has also prevented the cost of such expenditures and of higher primary product prices from being passed to labour as reduced living standards. Because workers have refused to shoulder the burden of higher taxes and prices and have often negotiated wage increases that largely maintain real wages, much of the burden has fallen onto company profits. The exact contribution of unionism to these developments cannot be disentangled from the role of mass political parties, though unions have probably played a part.

Discussion at this aggregate level, however, may be too much of an amalgam of different factors to tell us much, particularly as different industries have widely different wage shares according to the amount of capital invested: in a labour-intensive industry the share of wages is naturally higher than in a capital-intensive one. Phelps-Brown (1966) suggests that the division of the product between wages and profits in each industry is more informative, and in a survey of the evidence suggests that the main effect of unionism and collective bargaining is to prevent this share *falling* as it would have done without these institutions. The wages' share has followed a level trend this century through periods when a progressively growing capital investment should have increased the share due to capital (Phelps-Brown, 1966). If the recent data on aggregate national income are correct, then the wages' share of the product actually increased between the mid-1960s and the mid-1970s.

Fox (1975) claims that to maintain even a constant share while at the same time reducing the working week and the amount of physical effort expended does say a lot for unionism. Against this is a line of reasoning that devalues the contribution of unionism. This suggests that because these developments have been generalised and are not confined to unionised employment, they represent the workings of the market for labour: employers have to offer these conditions in order to attract the sort of labour they require. This sort of contradiction is typical of the controversy that bedevils the analysis of the economic effects of union bargaining: advocates of strong trade unionism attribute improved pay and conditions to the union influence, while opponents argue that any improvements are a result of other factors. The evidence is usually inadequate to resolve the argument satisfactorily. Economists tend to favour a market forces explanation, and it has been suggested that in the past many economists were either hostile to unionism or misunderstood its nature and effects (Fox, 1975; Mathias, 1978). However, the present discussion indicates that bargaining has some real effect on remuneration, even though this is not at present quantifiable and may be small.

The effect of unions on *real wages* is highly variable, as it depends not only on the strength of labour in its dealings with management but also on the economic policy of government. One conventional explanation of increases in real wages, which applies particularly in America, is that union wage pressure leads firms to raise productivity by sacking workers, introducing more efficient machinery and increasing worker effectiveness by means of new control systems. Wages may go up, but the wage cost per physical unit of output remains constant. In America, where under a quarter of the working population was unionised in 1980, any wage increase in the unionised sector normally results in a decline of employment there (Lewis, 1963), so that workers must transfer to the lower-paid, non-unionised sector, where they compete for jobs and to some extent keep wages down. Productivity gains increase the real wages of those left in the primary area of the economy, while the displacement of labour helps to depress real wages in the secondary. This latter phenomenon has prompted economists to conclude that

> most, if not all, of the gains of union labour are made at the expense of non-unionised workers, and not at the expense of earnings on capital.
>
> (H. Johnson and Mieszkowski, quoted in G.E. Johnson, 1975)

In Britain, productivity gains have not followed wage increases in the same proportion for many years, because labour strength is sufficient to resist the full plans for redundancies, new controls and the new working methods associated with new equipment. The greater spread of trade unionism and the measures of employment protection legislation mean, in addition, that there is not the same gap between unionised and non-unionised sectors nor the same degree of labour mobility between them. Employers are therefore faced with the choice of absorbing wage rises either by reducing profits, thus increasing real wages by increasing the wage share of the product, or by raising prices. The latter course of action has been the one most commonly pursued. It was helped by the relative weakness of competition from overseas in the first quarter century of the postwar period (British firms tended to pay similar wage increases and thus to stay in the same competitive position relative to each other), and by government policy which permitted monetary demand to match rising unit costs and removed the risk of bankruptcy (Phelps-Brown, 1966). Assuming that wage increases are spread widely and not confined to a few groups, the long-run effect is for increased money wages to provide little or no increase in real wages because price rises cancel out wage rises. In the short term, which is often the main concern of those involved in collective bargaining, real wages rise for a while before they are eroded. However, should only a few groups increase their money wages, then a more lasting real wage rise is possible to the extent that inflation is borne by others, usually by the poorly organised and those outside the labour market (the sick, unemployed and retired populations). In this case, unions succeed in negotiating wage premia at the cost of the rest of the population rather than at the expense of capital. With the development of international competition which forced price rises to be restrained, labour-force pressure in the 1960s put the squeeze on corporate profits and wages did indeed rise partly at the cost of capital. The decision of government to permit continued monetary expansion and to rescue any major company that failed, meant that even the risk of bankruptcy provided little constraint on the shopfloor in the decade after 1965.

Government economic policy, which is beyond the reach of trade unions acting through collective bargaining and the pressure of the shopfloor, is clearly an important influence on the outcome of collective bargaining. Indeed, recent British experience suggests that the satisfaction of workers' economic aspirations may be less a consequence of collective bargaining and traditional forms of industrial action which involve dealings between the two sides of industry than of political decisions made by governments. Governmental decisions such as those about manipulating demand so as to encourage economic growth, expanding the money supply, or taking into public ownership or subsidising major firms influence the stance that managers take in collective bargaining and the level of wages that they will concede. But, government also intervenes more directly in the fixing of living standards – by means of incomes policies which set limits on the pay rises that can be negotiated in collective bargaining and by taxation policy which determines the amount of take-home pay. Three years out of every four in the period from 1965 to 1980 saw government pressure on collective bargaining, though the serverity and effectiveness of the various incomes policies varied considerably. An analysis of real disposable incomes between 1960 and 1974 – that is to say how much money a worker received in his or her pay packet after tax and social security deductions and what it was actually worth in terms of purchasing power – showed how variations in workers' living standards were greatly influenced by changes in the amount which government deducted from pay packets (Turner and Wilkinson, 1975). The authors of this study concluded that,

> an ultimate return to free sectional collective bargaining is an illusory sacred cow. Each year's change in workers' living standards now depends not on nominal wages and prices, but on the government's tax decisions.
>
> (p. 136)

Government has become more important for the satisfaction of workers' economic interests in another way. Political rather than economic processes now determine how a significant part of the product is to be distributed, particularly in those nations which have a tradition of social democratic governments which are committed to promoting popular interests. Wage negotiations lose some of their previous importance for living standards and the distribution of surplus, when government transfers decisions about the distribution of the product between wages and capital from the economic to the political realm. In Scandinavia and Great Britain, for example, an increasing proportion of the national product is channelled to and distributed by the state, and public spending is an important allocative mechanism. What in Britain is called the 'social wage', the range of goods and services which government provides either at artificially low prices or at no direct cost to the consumer, which people would otherwise have to purchase in the market place out of their wages, makes an important contribution to living standards in advanced social democracies. Public ownership of a large part of the economy, as in Britain, is another means by which distribution is moved from the economic to the political realm, because in this case in the final analysis it is politicians rather than managers who make decisions about investment, return on capital, and the share of wages in the product.

Whether the outcome of decisions is in fact any different is a separate issue, one which depends on whether the state really promotes popular interests or covertly supports the interests of business (see Chapter 11). What matters here is that customary forms of trade union activity such as collective bargaining and strikes may become less effective in satisfying economic interests, if living standards are indeed more heavily influenced by political decisions than collective action in the economic realm. British unions have reacted to the new role of government and increasingly participate in politics in order to influence government.

Economism has dimensions *other* than bargaining over wages with employers or governments. The defence of economic interests leads to union influence in the labour market, for example by restricting labour supply in order to increase both pay and job security. Unionised labour may restrict managers' prerogative to decide how many employees a firm will employ, by resisting redundancies and imposing restrictive practices which increase manning requirements. This sort of union influence over the volume of employment seems to be greater in Britain than in most other advanced capitalist economies. In this way unions maintain job security, an important economic goal. Unions may also influence the quality of the labour a firm employs. By insisting that skilled craftsmen do de-skilled tasks, as happens for example in the British newspaper printing industry, unions artificially raise the required skill levels and thus the levels of pay and job security. This aspect of trade union economism provides further evidence of trade union effectiveness, though it remains largely unquantified.

Control

With regard to workers' control aspirations, the conventional argument, that unions are less concerned with control issues than with economism and are less effective in this area when they do choose to pursue control, has been presented with some qualification in this discussion. Broad generalisations about control, however, may conceal any variations that exist between systems of industrial relations and give no hint of certain prospective developments that may modify the traditional relationship between unionism and control.

On the subject of variations between systems, Herding has suggested that union strategies *vis-à-vis* management in the U.S. and West Germany differ in the extent to which they represent members' control interests (1972, pp. 37–42). U.S. unions pay less attention to these issues, because they adopt a 'countervailing power' policy which does not allow them to become involved in the formulation of managerial policy. Whereas German unions have legal rights of joint determination on some issues, as the result of co-determination legislation which gives unions some influence over the formulation of company policy, and members' aspirations are satisfied more fully in this system.

Neither the facts nor the interpretation of these which Herding puts forward bear close scrutiny. The claim that the German system of industrial relations reflects trade union concern with control and embeds unions in the decision-making process in such a way that they can severely curtail managerial prerogative is mistaken and exaggerated. German works councils have been designed to exclude unions from workshop issues and to confine union functions to centralised pay bargaining. Councils represent all workers, regardless of whether or not they are union members, have a legal obligation to strive for industrial peace and pursue the interests of the company as well as those of the labour force, cannot call strike action, and act as the other part of the dual system of worker representation in which unions are confined to wage issues and mainly operate outside the plant. Unions do organise their members in order to ensure that councils are controlled by trade unionists, but councillors are in no sense union representatives since their obligations are to the employee collectivity and the company (Müller-Jentsch and Sperling, 1978). Nor are the powers of works councils very great. Prior to 1972, councils were in effect consultative organs which made few inroads on managerial prerogative as in most European nations. Legal changes introduced in late 1971 in response to pressure from organised labour gave councils more power to determine wage schemes, various benefits not covered by union-level collective bargaining, working hours and certain items relating to recruitment and dismissal; these issues are now subject to co-determination between managers and councils (Müller-Jentsch and Sperling, 1978). However, encroachment on managerial prerogative in the area of control systems is limited to the right of co-determination only when alterations in the workplace increase the workloads of employees.

The other level of the co-determination system is the supervisory board, which makes the broad policy decisions for a company as a whole. This does not concern itself with the detailed administration of the company, which is in the hands of a board of management appointed by the supervisory board, nor with wage negotiations which are dealt with by national and regional negotiations between unions and employers' associations. German trade unions have placed great weight on this level of employee representation. During the 1970s they campaigned for an increase in representation, from one-third to one-half of the places on the supervisory boards in private industry. (Private firms in the iron and steel industry already had a system that gave employees five out of eleven votes.) In 1976, legislation provided near-parity representation for employees, with the casting vote of chairman assigned to shareholder interests. The employee side also includes a representative of management, who can normally be expected to vote with the shareholders. Co-determination allows employee representatives some influence over broad policy issues but not over managerial decisions that most concern workers' daily lives and to which control aspirations are oriented. Even at this level, employee influence is significant only on a few issues such as closure and redundancy where shopfloor support is easily mobilised (Marsden, 1978, p. 19). In practice, the union slate always does well in elections to the board even though in theory representation is not organised by the union but remains open to any employee. Herding's claims must be qualified. German unions have little effective jurisdiction within the workplace and display little interest in job control. Works councils can consider only a narrow range of control issues and must always promote the company's welfare. Unions are more concerned with broader company policy, and have a limited effectiveness at this level.

Nor is Herding correct to conclude that U.S. unions have of their own volition chosen to act only in response to managerial initiatives and to leave managerial prerogatives untouched. One reason why unions act as 'countervailing powers' in America is that they are fairly weak organisations, without the strength to push for anything more than this limited influence over management. There is a significant difference between union power in Britain and West Germany, on the one hand, and the United States on the other. Union power in the two European nations is in part the product of the efforts of trade unions themselves over the years, the success of which can be seen in their moderately high membership densities. It also results from favourable environmental conditions, notably the cumulative effects of political decisions regarding the management of the economy and social policy. American unions have enjoyed less favourable conditions than their European counterparts over the last thirty years, and in particular they have not benefited from the sort of political management which strengthens labour's hand in collective bargaining.

During the Second World War, when economic conditions, notably severe labour shortages and soft markets for firms' products, provided workers with a greater degree of collective power than they have enjoyed subsequently, U.S. trade unions did push for and win substantial concessions at the cost of managerial prerogative. Leaders of U.S. 'business' unions, who are notoriously concerned with economic rewards such as cash and fringe benefits, proved that they were able and willing to pursue an aggressive control strategy when the conditions were right (Herding, 1972, p. 220). But once the economic environment changed, then the unions no longer had the strength to resist a new managerial offensive which rolled back the earlier gains (1972, pp. 221–2). The failure of American unions in the control area in recent years reflects the weakness of trade unionism as much as a lack of concern. Moreover, this American experience shows how ineffective collective bargaining is if labour does not already have considerable collective strength, a strength which in turn depends partly on conditions beyond the control of workers and unions. Those commentators (for example Clegg, 1976) who assign collective bargaining an independent role in the regulation of conflict ignore the fact that this institution is dependent on certain antecedent conditions and is the product rather than the source of labour strength.

The experience of German and American trade unionism since the war reinforces an observation made in Chapter 7, that there is nothing inherent in unionism that stops it becoming more effective on non-economic issues. What matters are the *conditions* under which trade unions operate, and in certain circumstances control issues which disrupt established patterns of accommodation will be pursued. Developments within the European trade union movement suggest that in future trade unions are more likely to be concerned with a range of control issues, because some of the conditions which used to govern union action are now changing. The most significant changes are increased labour strength that allows unions to take a more aggressive line without endangering their own survival; the growth of pressure from below and unofficial action that makes it more difficult for union bureaucracies to ignore their members' voices and increases the likelihood of union democracy; the appreciation on the part of trade unions that collective bargaining is of limited usefulness even for the realisation of traditional union objectives and needs to be supplemented by more effective forms of action.

Increased labour strength in industry since the Second World War has resulted not just from the actions of unions but also from the changed politico-economic environment of the period. Governments have provided workers and their unions with a degree of strength in their dealings with management that they would not have achieved by their own efforts within the industrial arena. Western European nations have witnessed several decades of political intervention in the economy which has reduced the disadvantages under which labour operates in collective bargaining. Political commitment to full employment, successfully maintained by manipulation of the economy until the recession of the mid-1970s, the creation of welfare services which reduce the individual's dependence on his or her income for supplying the essentials of life, and the establishment by law of individual and collective employee rights which restrict the freedom of management in personnel matters, have together increased the power of labour when dealing with managers.

The new labour strength is translated into union action on job control if the hierarchy is responsive to members or if it finds that more control is necessary in order to pursue its traditional economistic objectives. American evidence indicates that those unions which are more democratically organised, where the hierarchy cannot easily displace member goals, are more militant in pursuing control issues (Herding, 1972, pp. 53–5). In Britain the integration of stewards into the union structure has made official unionism somewhat more responsive to job control issues.

At the more aggregate level, most European trade union movements have pursued policies that acknowledge the importance of greater job control, but only in Scandinavia (particularly in Sweden) has this concern been transformed into concrete action. In Sweden, the original impetus toward humanised work in the late 1960s came from management which sought to raise productivity and reduce absenteeism without encroaching on managerial prerogative, rather than from the unions. The Swedish LO was content merely to endorse this managerial activity until the early 1970s, when a new generation of leaders who were more responsive to the growing aspirations of the membership led the union movement into confrontation with management on the control issue (Brannen and Caswill, 1978). The LO strategy now is to work to make industry democratic by the destruction of managerial prerogative and the introduction of the direct participation of employees in all the levels of managerial decision-making (Strom, 1976; Janérus, 1978). Union pressure on government has resulted in a major encroachment on managerial prerogative in the job control area: legislation in 1977 has established the right of unions to negotiate before managers can introduce major changes in operations, working conditions, and conditions of employment as well as co-determination rights over the management and distribution of work; in the event of any disagreement, the union interpretation is to prevail until the dispute is resolved. At the same time, legislation for a minority of worker directors has introduced some employee influence into top-level decision-making, though the main purpose of this provision has been to supplement other measures aimed at greater democracy. Unions see it as a means of gathering more information useful in collective bargaining and checking on management.

Union strategies regarding allocative control

The most decisive break with the accommodative tradition of trade unionism in Europe, however, has occurred over a *different* type of control issue. Rather than fighting with all their energy in the arena of job control, union movements have developed a much greater interest in the possibility of controlling high level company policies unrelated to the routine administration of control systems. There is a distinction to be made between control issues at the 'operational' and 'allocative' levels (Pahl and Winkler, 1974). The first concerns work operations and workers' immediate interests in autonomy and creativity, which reflect the second and third levels of appropriation noted in Chapter 1; while the other concerns control over the allocation of a company's resources and the use to which capital is put, the first level of appropriation. The majority of Western European trade union federations are now concerned to transfer to employees and their representatives a significant share of the control over capital which owners and managers presently enjoy.

The German approach to this issue has been to create insitutions of 'industrial democracy', which provide for employee representation on the supervisory board and a say in major strategic decisions. This notion of democracy, that the supreme policy-making body in a firm should include a substantial degree of employee representation, has proved to be particularly influential with national governments and international civil servants, with the result that several European nations now have employee representation on company boards and the EEC actively encourages industrial democracy. Union movements, however, differ in the amount of support that they give to the German method. Several federations, notably the Swedish and Danish manual worker federations and both the communist and non-communist movements in France and Italy, see little role for board representation apart from its function in providing information about company policy. Industrial democracy creates two problems for trade unions. In the first place, it is felt that the effect may be to integrate workers and unions more fully into the capitalist order, and for this reason union movements which maintain an anti-capitalist ideology are unwilling to go along with plans that give them or their members a substantial representation on company boards (Sorge, 1976). Secondly, the German experience shows how industrial democracy may create a conflict of roles even for those unions which are well-adjusted to capitalism:

> A trade union movement in a capitalist milieu cannot perform both the functions of the entrepreneur and those of the union. For in attempting to do so, it internalises the conflict between capital and labour...
>
> (Kirkwood and Mewes, 1976, p. 304).

Unionists on supervisory boards may find themselves siding with capital rather than labour and opposing rather than representing workers' interests. This is why in Britain several important unions oppose the TUC's policy directed towards placing trade union representatives on boards of directors: they claim that unions cannot bridge the capital – labour divide and still perform their true functions. Nevertheless, unions still have aspirations for allocative control and those which cannot accept the German solution need some alternative. Once again the Scandinavian movements have taken the lead. The Swedish manual union confederation (LO) has gone beyond the participation of employees in control to develop a programme which envisages the gradual transfer over a number of years of company equity into the hands of 'wage-earner funds' managed by employee representatives, thus socialising capital (Korpi, 1978, pp. 327–30).

The shift towards allocative control, whether by means of co-determination and industrial democracy or by means of the socialisation of capital, is sufficiently recent that one cannot be sure how aggressively and successfully unions will fight for their plans. Nevertheless, this development does show the error of the orthodox view of trade unionism, which stretches from Lenin, through Kerr *et al.*, to Giddens and Mann, that unions will not attempt any major reconstruction of the economic order.

Trade unions appear to have taken up allocative control for a variety of reasons. Unions respond to their members' aspirations for more control over their working lives and environments, which they interpret as control of high level decision-making. At the same time, changes in the industrial environment within which unions are operating give unions an interest in allocative control as a means of pursuing their traditional economistic objectives and as a means of meeting their own institutional survival needs. The long-term, structural change within capitalist economies toward 'late' or 'monopoly' capitalism highlights the weakness of traditional forms of trade union activity. In particular, unions have found it increasingly difficult to perform even the traditional, limited function of protecting their members' economic interests, as long as they insist on using collective bargaining as the means of influencing employers, despite the increased power of labour in recent years, and as long as they make a *de facto* distinction between economic and control issues. The features of 'monopoly' capitalism that are relevant here are the increased size of firms, the spread of multi-plant and international operations, and the rise of conglomerates spanning different industries, which result from the historical tendency in this century toward the concentration of capital. Unions now need to influence decisions on issues of allocative control which, as part of managerial prerogative, have always been excluded from collective bargaining. They need, in particular, far more influence over investment and locational decisions, given the potential mobility of capital within large corporations, if they are to protect their members' living standards and job security and their own membership rolls. For example, there is little point in a union negotiating on pay and conditions if the company has locational plans which involve the closure of the plant concerned, or investment plans which deprive it of new funds, so that it becomes uncompetitive and unable to pay decent wages or to provide secure employment. Despite the relative success of collective bargaining in providing satisfactory outcomes on traditional issues such as pay and conditions because of the increased labour market and shopfloor strength of workers, unions have experienced great difficulty in obliging management to negotiate on issues of allocative control.

The experiences of the recession of the mid-1970s demonstrated the vulnerability of past gains to the union movement and questioned the ability of unionism to protect employees' interests in an economy dominated by giant corporations, this being the case most notably in Britain. Here, a series of factory closures followed by the transfer of capital and equipment within multi-plant corporations produced a spontaneous and defensive union response in the form of factory occupations and take-overs (TUC, 1979, pp. 8–9). In effect, unions claimed the right to veto corporate strategy on issues such as the movement of capital when this strategy adversely affected their members' financial and employment interests. This experience, among others, was influential in changing the orientation of the British TUC, which had for long extolled the virtues of traditional forms of collective bargaining and the potency of unionism as a countervailing power to that of management, towards a concern with new forms of control over a new range of issues. After a discussion of collective bargaining and the benefits which accrue, a TUC policy statement adds:

> However, it is clear that this leaves a wide range of fundamental managerial decisions affecting workpeople that are beyond the control – and very largely beyond the influence – of workpeople and their trade unions. Major decisions on investment, location, closure, take-over and mergers and product specialisation of the organisation are generally taken at levels where collective bargaining does not take place and indeed are subject matter not readily covered by collective bargaining. New forms of control are needed.
>
> (1979, p. 33).

There has thus been a happy convergence at the allocative level between the interest of members in control and the traditional concern of trade unions. It is no coincidence that allocative control should become a live issue in Europe once unionism no longer had to depend solely on the power which union members wield on the labour market and the shopfloor, a power which has normally proved insufficient to support effective union action on any but a narrow range of issues. European trade union plans for 'industrial democracy' depend for their implementation on government legislation which obliges business to share the control or ownership of capital with employees. This may well, of course, be a reason that radical proposals for economic reconstruction have not yet been implemented, because most governments as yet appear unwilling to make a decisive shift in the balance of power in industry. Nevertheless, recent trade union strategy shows how the unions themselves have appreciated the limits of their traditional activities and how they have chosen to pursue new aims. This new strategy indicates that unions can indeed conceive of major changes in the economic system and how to achieve them.

Developments in the late-1960s and the 1970s clearly eroded what was left of the distinction between the 'political' and the 'economic' in industry. The issue 'who rules' is now a live one. Workers on the shopfloor resist managerial control of the workplace. Their means of resistance range from the British and Italian strategy of direct action, in which workers' own shopfloor organisations try to push forward the frontier of control, to the Swedish use of legal regulation, in which unions use their political influence on government to legislate away managerial prerogative. The rights of capital and senior management are also contested in the boardroom, as labour works to win a share in allocative control, perhaps even to dispossess the existing powerholders. Outside industry, the linkage between the political and economic realms becomes more visible when unions attempt to use government to give them industrial rights which they cannot gain by their own efforts in collective bargaining. Access to political power is an important resource in the struggle for control, for trade unionists and employers alike.

Institutionalisation

One essential role of trade unions in capitalism has been to reduce the threat that working-class discontent poses to profitable accumulation. By acting to contain conflict, trade unions perform important and specific personnel functions for management. Unions which negotiate collective agreements provide managers with stable, predictable and disciplined employee relations, provided that the unions stick by their bargains. Managers are concerned with key issues of employee relations during negotiations, but once a contract has been signed they can in effect ignore the issues for the duration of the agreement: the written contract sets the framework of the relations that are to prevail and trade unions ensure that their members abide by these.

Changes in the structure of industry in late capitalism have made this positive trade union contribution to solving industry's personnel problems more rather than less necessary, and employers more rather than less receptive to unionism. The growing indispensability of unionism is more pronounced in the large-scale and capital-intensive sector of the economy than it would appear to be among smaller and less heavily-capitalised firms. Galbraith (1967) and Shonfield (1965) have observed of late capitalism, that increases in the scale of production and advances in technology which vastly increase the amounts of capital invested in manufacturing processes, coinciding with the rise of more integrated and competitive markets, create novel demands on management. Managers can no longer simply respond to changes in the commercial environment in the traditional manner, but must anticipate and, if possible, mould this environment. It is the uncertainty and unpredictability of change, rather than change itself, that have become major problems. Managers therefore seek to routinise, predict and plan all parts of the environment, including the labour relations area which is a major source of uncertainty. This is why, as noted above, such firms pursue 'enlightened' employment policies and why the stability, predictability and discipline that unionism can provide grow in importance. Large firms are also more bureaucratised and for this reason again are more receptive to unionism. Managers and officials alike want the same thing, a coherent, planned and impersonal personnel structure, and the managers rely on unions selling such a structure to their members (Herding, 1972, pp. 8–28).

Trade unionism performs its role as a bulwark of capitalism with varying degrees of success. The discussion of the British informal system demonstrated that institutionalisation via collective bargaining in Britain has failed to create the sort of deeply-rooted and shared values which reduce industrial conflict to fairly superficial disputes between interest groups, as some versions of the institutionalisation thesis would believe. Workers do not participate in an industrial normative consensus as the result of institutional regulation and the webs of rules created in bargaining, and do not legitimate the existing economic order and system of production. Once official unionism loses its grip on member activity, then the precariousness of institutionalisation and the lack of commitment to the normative order are manifest in chaotic industrial relations. It was fashionable in the late 1960s to argue that, because unions had once successfully institutionalised conflict by creating a shared normative framework, this moral order would return if the authority of trade unions over their members were restored (Fox and Flanders, 1969). This analysis rested on a false premise, that unions and bargaining had ever entirely reconciled workers to capitalist industrialism, when worker acceptance of this system was in fact based largely on powerlessness and pragmatism, and when informal resistance to management was always present below the formal surface of regulation. There is no reason to believe that the partial integration of the domestic organisation into the union structure which has taken place recently is likely to be accompanied by any notable increase in the moral density of industry.

In a less extreme form, the institutionalisation of conflict thesis suggests merely that unions and collective bargaining channel conflict into forms that industry finds *tolerable*, and does not concern itself with issues of shared normative frameworks. The evidence is that industry now cannot rely even on this support with complete certainty. The rise of strong and independent shopfloor activity in several mature systems of industrial relations reduces the potency of trade unionism as a force for stable and predictable industrial relations. This can be seen in its most extreme form in Britain and in lesser degrees elsewhere in Europe and in America. The effect of the growth of shopfloor action and unregulated conflict on official unionism is perhaps even more significant than the activity itself. For reasons mentioned before, one of which is the responsiveness of unionism to the challenge from below, unions now demand a price for their continued support of industry which managers are not willing to pay: the channelling of discontent into demands for control of job and allocative issues means that reformism and the institutionalisation of conflict now take forms that industry does *not* find tolerable. The particular form of conflict regulation that liberal pluralists observed in the two postwar decades, and which many thought would continue unchecked in the future, depended on a set of conditions which no longer prevail.

A common trade union criticism of industrial democracy is that it binds workers and their representative bodies to the existing order without any real shift in the balance of power in industry. Moreover, because unions straddle the capital – labour divide, they lose effectiveness as representatives of labour. Both these arguments have force at present, because the schemes of industrial democracy that governments are willing to implement fall short of what unions want and provide only minority representation which does not allow labour to control its fate. It seems likely, however, that the *parity* representation and control to which British and German union confederations aspire would indeed have a major effect were such a scheme ever to be implemented. The division between the two sides might not disappear, but joint control of the power centre would mark a real shift in the balance of power within the firm. Certainly, industrial interests in both countries have bitterly opposed parity or near-parity representation because of fear of the possible consequences of sharing allocative control in this way.

The way unions use their power in systems of shared control is crucial. The German experience of industrial democracy based on minority representation does not suggest that firms have been committed to policies that greatly differ from what would have occurred without representation (Kirkwood and Mewes, 1976). However, this discussion has indicated that when unions are more critical of the status quo or more responsive to their members, and if they have equal strength on the board, they would be more likely to use boardroom power for alternative ends. The pitfalls of the industrial democracy route to control, although they are not inescapable, do nevertheless exist. The radical proposals of the Swedish unions, which include the scheme to transfer industrial equity to wage earners, are especially significant in this context. They show that some unions formulate alternatives that transcend the limits of existing strategies, without incurring the difficulties of co-determination.

9 The structure of social stratification

At this point the focus of attention shifts to issues of social stratification. There is a close link between the sociology of social class and the sociology of industry. Both are concerned with the analysis of economic phenomena and both focus on the same issues: the nature of economic interests, the character of the social relations in the realm of production, the consequences of position in the division of labour for the life experiences of individuals and groups. Economic criteria are central to class analysis, and it is in their economic lives that people most directly experience the reality of class. The subject matters of class analysis and industrial sociology are therefore similar in important respects. The connection has often been ignored, in industrial sociology during the ascendancy of the human relations movement which divorced the study of employment and industrial life from their wider implications, and in class analysis when stratification studies concentrated on status rather than economic factors. But the traditional linkage has been reaffirmed over the past decade, as the consequence of a revived interest in class theory.

In this chapter modern developments in the sociological theory of class are first considered. These divide into two schools: the sociological or Weberian, and the Marxist. It is suggested that the two provide a more unified description of the structure of stratification than is normally acknowledged. Using the concepts from the theoretical section, the substance of class structure is discussed in the remainder of the chapter. This extends the scope of the previous chapters in several ways. The discussion confirms that the major divisions within industry have consequences for stratification outside and that relations across the industrial divisions may be treated analytically as class relations. The discussion also complements the earlier emphasis on work and the labour process with an extended treatment of features of the labour market. It provides in addition a comprehensive account of the structure of the labour force in advanced industrial societies. Chapter 9 concentrates on the objective features of class. The relevance of subjective class attitudes for the character of industrial life are considered in Chapter 10.

Class Theory

The sociological approach

Classes are economically-defined categories, and sociologists regard position in the division of labour as the crucial class determinant. The major class divide was for many years thought to be that running between manual and non-manual occupations. This appeared to correspond to major differences of condition. Non-manual workers had better pay and security, less coercive work relations, jobs with more autonomy, and better lives outside work. In addition, non-manual work was associated with distinctive class attitudes and behaviour. This division no longer seems to be very useful, because the distinctiveness of the manual–non-manual line has become blurred. Routine non-manual work and the consciousness of routine non-manual workers are often similar to what are found in the manual working class. At the same time, significant differences can be found *within* the ranks of the non-manual population.

Modern sociology does away with the crude manual–non-manual division as the means of placing people in different classes. A more discriminating set of criteria is used, which divides the economic basis of class into the two analytical categories of *market* and *work* situations. In Lockwood's original formulation (1958), the two had equal importance. The market situation was the set of material rewards which different groups possessed, such as the amount and security of financial remuneration, and the chances of promotion. The work situation referred primarily to the set of social relationships in which people were involved at work, by virtue of their positions in the division of labour. These criteria allowed Lockwood to distinguish the class location of clerks from that of manual workers during the early part of this century: clerks had a better economic position and privileged working conditions, which associated them with authority and placed them under fewer coercive controls. However, by mid-century these market and work advantages had begun to decline, and the position of clerical workers had begun to converge with that of manual workers.

Subsequently, Giddens has placed more weight on market capacity as the major criterion of class as an economic category (1973, Chapter 6). However, since classes defined on the basis of market power are analytical abstractions, sociologists need some idea of how these are transformed into classes as identifiable social groupings. This process of transformation is called *structuration*. Work situation is one factor which turns economic classes into 'social' classes. This now includes the nature of work tasks and production technology, as well as the structure of social relations and managerial control systems. The class hierarchy is one where market rewards increase at each level, and where working conditions become progressively more pleasant as well. Higher classes have less coercive social and technical controls at work, greater job interest, variety and autonomy, more opportunity to exercise discretion, and the opportunity to command others, in addition to better pay, security and promotion opportunities. These are the criteria used, for example, in allocating occupations to different classes in the major British survey of social mobility conducted at Nuffield College (Goldthorpe and Llewellyn, 1977a). The overlap between this approach to class theory and the concerns of industrial sociology is obvious. The analysis of markets, work, and the social relations of production, which is a central concern of this book, is also central to the sociology of class.

In *The Affluent Worker*, Lockwood and his colleagues added *life-style* factors to supplement market and work criteria (Goldthorpe *et al.*, 1968a and b; 1969). The structure of the economy produces differences outside work as well as in the world of production. For example, there is a tendency towards the physical segregation of social classes outside work into different residential communities. One of the ways in which different economic classes become identifiable 'social' classes, suggests Giddens, is by virtue of different 'consumption' patterns outside work and different patterns of social relationships. Sometimes a concern for the life-style aspects of structuration has distracted attention from the proper consideration of market and work criteria. The *Affluent Worker* research, for example, claimed that market and work factors were important, but has rightly been criticised for its excessive interest in non-work life at the cost of a proper investigation of the work situation (Mackenzie, 1974). The modern approach is usually labelled 'neo-Weberian', because it uses a multi-factor model and because of the weight it places on life chances in the market.

The neo-Weberian criteria in principle allow for a multiplicity of classes based on different levels of market rewards, different types of work situations, and different combinations of the two. This poses problems of interpretation. When are market and work situations sufficiently different to mark a class division? In practice, the criteria have been used for a fairly modest extension of the two-class model to form a three-class one. The Nuffield team, indeed, have identified seven separate classes, but they have aggregated these into three basic clusters for most analytical purposes (Goldthorpe and

Llewellyn, 1977a). They split the old non-manual category into two major clusters and slightly blur the manual–non-manual line. The new intermediate class cluster is composed of routine white-collar occupations, self-employed artisans, the supervisors of manual workers, and technicians whose work may be partly manual.

Certain combinations of market and work factors fit rather uneasily into the conventional neo-Weberian model. It is noteworthy that neo-Weberians normally use their criteria to subdivide the non-manual class, leaving largely intact the old division between manual and non-manual, despite the greater discrimination of the new criteria. They justify keeping the traditional divisions on the grounds that there are still major discontinuities between the work and market situations of manual and routine non-manual workers. As the rest of this chapter shows, this interpretation of the facts is not clear cut. Clerical and other routine white-collar occupations may in certain instances be placed on a par with manual work, when the neo-Weberian criteria of market and work situations are applied. It may be noted here, in anticipation of some of the later arguments, that many of the more obvious cases of convergence between manual and low-level, non-manual occupations are ignored, because the white-collar jobs concerned are done by women. Women are thought somehow not to count in class analysis. For example, the Nuffield team studied economically active *males*, while Giddens placed feminised occupations in under-classes which were peripheral to the main class divisions, rather than in the working-class location which market and work criteria indicated (1973, p. 288).

There are also significant differences within the upper class. These raise the issue of what range of different market and work situations is allowable for different occupations to be classified together in the same class. The Nuffield team defined what they called the 'service' class as including higher professionals, senior administrators in government and industry (including company directors), managers of large companies, and proprietors. (I shall retain the customary usage 'upper' class.) Of the employed male population 10–15 per cent are in this class. If the subaltern or cadet positions of these occupations are included, that is, lower professionals, less senior officials and managers, then the size of the upper class is further increased. However, they also found that there is an inner, élite group within the upper class which has greater market power and substantially higher financial rewards, and the social power, moreover, to close access to outsiders (Goldthorpe and Llewellyn, 1977a). The same differentiation of a small and particularly advantaged élite appears in other categorisations of market factors (Giddens, 1973, pp. 169–70). It is highly likely that members of this élite also have more favourable work situations. Company directors, for example, seem to have more power, autonomy and variety than the managers below them. Here we enter territory that is poorly charted in sociology, because the scholarly literature dealing with firms and occupations does not provide evidence of work situations above the level of middle management or its equivalent in other administrative occupations and the professions. Nevertheless, casual observation suggests significant differences between directors and senior managers, and particularly between the managing directors or chairmen of companies and others.

Weber regarded both capital and marketable skills as providing advantage to those who possessed them. This insight informs the concern with market capacity. Skill is now emphasised, and is used to cover both the market resources of trained manual workers in skilled occupations and those of managerial and professional workers who have succeeded in the educational system. Interestingly, Weber was more concerned with the effect of capital on class structure than secondary accounts of his work have credited until recently. He suggested that property owners constituted a separate class. He maintained that property created self-perpetuating privilege, that it was the basis of social power and provided the capability to manipulate markets, and that it gave its holders control over the management of industry (1964, pp. 425–6). Unlike Marx, however, Weber identified at least four classes, as the result of adding the skill criterion (the working class; the traditional lower middle class of economically independent small businessmen and shopkeepers; the intelligentsia and administrative class; the privileged, propertied class). The modern approach in principle deals with the mechanisms (skill and capital) which lie behind class placement, but in practice its users place less weight on property than other resources and less weight than Weber himself placed. The power and privilege stemming from property are largely ignored by those who focus on the rewards stemming from the division of labour. It is simply assumed that the interests of those with property are similar to those in the higher reaches of the division of labour (Parkin, 1978, p. 613); that people who own capital or effectively possess the powers of economic ownership, for example owner-entrepreneurs or board-level managers, share the same class interest as lesser managers who are both relatively propertyless and excluded from ownership powers.

In Weber's accounts the relational aspects of class were not confined to the internal structuration of classes, but applied equally to relations *between* classes. He saw conflict between classes as common, being most evident between combatants whose interests were immediately opposed. Thus workers would mainly organise against managers, rather than against the owners who controlled industry and drew the profits (1964, pp. 425–8). In his broader discussion of capitalist industrialism, Weber saw this as a class society whose central class relations derived from relationships in the labour market, including the class relations between capital and wage labour (Giddens, 1973, pp. 44–51). This contains an important insight which has rarely been taken up in the sociology of industrial organisation. Analytically, the divisions between workers and managers and between labour and capital may be seen as class divisions and the social relations involved in production as class relations. The Weberian perspective which has so influenced modern sociology provides the means of viewing the major divisions of interest in industry in class terms. Though the neo-Weberian emphasis on structuration correctly reminds us that classes and class relations defined analytically do not always have a concrete reality and that real social class groups and social class relations exist only in certain circumstances.

Parkin (1974) has revived the older concern with class relations which was common to Marx and Weber and which is otherwise neglected in modern orthodox sociology. His particular scheme adapts Weber's treatment of economic competition as a means of analysing class relations. The central focus of class activity, Parkin suggests, is the distribution of scarce resources. Class relations are characterised by mutual competition for scarce resources, which provoke one of two general strategies for staking claims to these resources. The first is exclusion: those who have access to scarce resources attempt to exclude others, and to pass on privileges to their own kind. The second is solidarism, which is the collective mobilisation of the dis-privileged aimed at collective advancement. These strategies are not limited to dichotomous class structures but apply to multi-class systems equally, since the intermediate classes may simultaneously practise strategies of exclusion against those below and solidarism against those above.

The Marxist approach

Marxism also regards class as an economic category, but analyses it in relation to capital rather than the division of labour. Marxist class analysis lost popularity among sociologists, when it appeared that the separation of capital ownership from the administration and control of industry made propertylessness such a broad category, embracing all levels of employee, that it no longer distinguished between groups with widely different economic positions; for example, between senior managers and shopfloor workers. More recently, however, there has been a revival of interest in Marxism and various suggestions have been made, reformulating the classical theory of class. These attempt to solve the problem posed by occupations which, *prima facie*, do not belong in the capitalist class nor in the proletariat as traditionally conceived. This problem *must* be solved, if the dichotomous, twofold class model based on the conflict between capital and labour is to be preserved.

All Marxists agree that manual workers who are directly concerned with the manufacture of physical goods on behalf of capital are members of the working class. But they disagree about other propertyless wage earners. Poulantzas (1975) makes three distinctions to be used to locate classes. The first is the difference between productive labour which creates surplus value, which is to be found in material production that adds to the stock of capital, and unproductive labour. The latter includes the labour performed in service industries and government which, because it does not directly create surplus value, cannot be classified as proletarian even if it is performed by manual workers. The other two distinctions are between mental and manual labour, and between supervisory and non-supervisory positions. Only the performance of manual, non-supervisory, productive labour qualifies a person for inclusion in the working class. Unproductive manual workers, clerical workers, foremen, low-level technicians and government employees are all categorised as members of a new petty bourgeoisie. Other modern Marxists have condemned this reformulation, not least because it reduces the proletariat to tiny proportions – one in five of the population in America according to Wright (1976). The distinctions between productive and unproductive, and mental and manual labour, have been rejected as valid criteria of class placement (Wright, 1976).

A number of modern Marxists have proposed schemes which are based on a distinction between those who perform the functions of capital and exercise the powers of ownership (in this way defining the capitalist class regardless of whether they actually own capital or not) and those who perform only the function of labour and are thus in the working class (Carchedi, 1975; Crompton, 1976; Wright, 1976). These schemes are not identical and there is not the same consensus within neo-Marxism that exists within orthodox sociology. The simplest and most elegant analysis is Wright's (1976). This revives the distinction between ownership and non-ownership, which is now conceptualised as the division between those who exercise the various powers of ownership, whether or not they are the ultimate legal owners, and those who do not. The capitalist class comprises those who have ownership powers. Ownership can be divided into three aspects. These correspond to the three modes of appropriation discussed in Chapter 1, which create the opposition between the material interests of capital and labour and place owners and workers into a relationship which is objectively one of conflict. The three aspects are control over investment and resource allocation; control over the physical apparatus of production, the material means of production; and control over labour power. The capitalist class controls the overall investment process, and has ultimate control of the physical apparatus and of labour power. The proletariat is excluded from all three aspects. Capital and labour stand in an antagonistic relationship, and the social relations between the classes that represent these interests are laden with conflict.

This way of dichotomising the class structure allows Wright to establish the two basic classes and to allocate concrete jobs to the two analytical categories of capital and labour. The top corporate executive – principally the board of directors – peoples the capitalist class. Low-level manual and non-manual employees comprise the proletariat. In between, one finds *contradictory* locations. These reflect differing strengths of control over each of the three ownership functions. Senior managers who are not on the board of directors have firm control over the physical apparatus of production and over the labour power of others, but only partial control or influence over resource and investment decisions. Middle managers have partial control over the apparatus and labour, but very little over investment and resource allocation. Technical experts – professional and technical employees – have a little control over apparatus and labour, but none over resources. Foremen have some control over labour but nothing else. Thus the contradictory nature of any particular intermediate location is a variable quality: some are near the boundary of the working class and others near the boundary of the capitalist class. The most contradictory locations are those of middle managers and technical experts, who have one foot in the bourgeoisie and the other in the proletariat, according to this line of analysis.

The division between the functions of capital and labour suggested by Carchedi (1975) and developed by Crompton (1976) in relation to routine white-collar workers is more complicated than the exercise of ownership powers. It incorporates a series of distinctions between labour functions, which are those that would exist in any complex production system and therefore are not specific to capitalism, and capitalist functions. Certain groups unambiguously belong in the capitalist class as the agents of capital: they have *real* control over the material means of production, labour and the acquisition of surplus value, even if they are not the ultimate legal owners. Boards of directors and senior management fall into this category. Others are clearly part of the working class, because they perform only the labour function and have no involvement in the capitalist one. In between are groups whose jobs involve *both* capital and labour functions, whose class position is therefore ambiguous. Foremen, for instance, act to supervise labour. This is a task which forms part of the capitalist function, since it is only necessary in order to extract a surplus and would disappear in a non-exploitative economic system. Foremen also perform technical and co-ordinating roles which are not specific to capitalism and are needed in any complex production process, and belong to the labour function. Many routine white-collar workers carry out capitalist functions associated with the extraction of surpluses as well as technical and co-ordinating duties, and share an ambiguous class position on this basis. Certain jobs create ambiguous class locations for a different but related reason, because they exist only in the capitalist mode of production. Because activities such as banking, insurance and accountancy are concerned with the management of capital and are thought to exist only in capitalism, white-collar workers in such industries perform the functions of capital, even when they are subjected to the same sorts of work organisation and manner of expropriation as manual workers in other industries (Crompton, 1976).

There are some obvious points of similarity between modern sociological and Marxist theories. Both deal with class in economic terms, as noted above. Both give work a central place in class analysis: the nature of the labour process and the quality of the social relations of production are significant aspects of class structure in both approaches. Both have an interest in inter-class relations and conflicts. The two approaches, however, are clearly informed by different theories and to some extent are addressed to different issues. Marxism claims to have identified a central principle that explains the development of capitalism both as an economic and as a class system, namely the incessant drive to accumulate as capital the value created by labour. The differentiation between capital and labour is the source of class differentiation, the determinant of class relations, and the impetus to class action. Classes are believed to exist 'as real social forces', as social actors with a political potential and the capacity to change society (Wright, 1976). Weber claimed it was rationalisation, which also implied bureaucratisation, which was the organising and developmental principle of modern society. The concepts he used to analyse class, however, were not tied to a particular view of economic processes or development, and modern sociologists employ them largely as descriptive instruments. This allows them to view class as an analytical abstraction with little concrete presence in the real world, and as a collection of individuals who happen each to have similar economic positions but who share nothing else that welds them into an identifiable group. However, the interest in structuration does reflect a sociological concern with the issue of how classes may change from analytical categorisations of economic position into tangible collectivities with social identities, and perhaps act as classes and have social consciousness.

The rest of this chapter discusses structuration and the next deals with consciousness. The neo-Weberian criteria of market and work situations are used here because they allow more precise description, particularly in the case of occupations in intermediate or contradictory locations. Disagreement within the neo-Weberian approach about such occupations centres on the interpretation of the facts of market and work situations, and on the place of women within the class structure. The orthodox sociological criteria do not build confusion and contradiction into the theoretical apparatus, which is what the modern versions of Marxism do in order to adapt a two-class model to the modern occupational structure. One of the things to emerge in the following pages is that neo-Weberian and neo-Marxist concepts may provide broadly similar *descriptions* of the objective placement of groups and class structuration, despite their different theoretical premises and despite the often-encountered assertion that they are incompatible forms of analysis. There is a series of Marxist-like effects that flow from Weberian analysis. The reason is that orthodox sociological criteria dealing with the division of labour pick up the consequences of an industrial system which, with respect to market and work situations, is much as modern Marxists describe.

The following pages show that the manual section of the British working class is homogeneous and well structured; that the full working class in addition includes a substantial proportion of the low-level, white-collar labour force; that there is a small, well-structured élite that can be distinguished from other classes; that there is a fair measure of agreement, using the orthodox and some of the neo-Marxist criteria, as to which groups occupy intermediate or contradictory locations. The unity of the working class, including routine white-collar workers, is hardly surprising: the degradation of work argument which was endorsed in earlier chapters obviously suggests a growing homogenisation of the lower strata, and the neo-Weberian criteria chart these consequences. The separation of a small élite class is suggested by Weber's own identification of a socially powerful propertied class as well as by the strict application of the neo-Weberian criteria. These interpretations are not the ones usually found in conventional sociology, but they are suggested by the evidence. An account of the class system oriented around the issue of structuration confirms the importance of class analysis for the sociology of industry, reinforcing and extending the findings of earlier chapters. It shows that major social divisions within industry are also class divisions. It provides a description of the employment market that is the essential complement of earlier analyses of work and the labour process.

Social Mobility

Social mobility is one starting point for an investigation of structuration, because this provides a good measure of the amount of rigidity in the class system and the stability and homogeneity of class membership. Data collected in the late 1940s by a team of sociologists at LSE (Glass, ed., 1954) showed that mobility rates were low in Britain and the class system was rigid. The conclusions derived from these data dominated sociological thinking for nearly a quarter of a century, until the results of the Nuffield investigation were published in the late 1970s. These have substantially changed the picture of the postwar era. They show that modern rates and patterns of mobility differ considerably from those found in the LSE research (Goldthorpe and Llewellyn, 1977a and b; Goldthorpe, Payne and Llewellyn, 1978). There are three major findings relevant to structuration. First, absolute mobility rates since the war are much higher than were previously believed. Secondly, mobility has often been long range, into the upper class from the working class (and from all levels of the working class in equal proportions). Previously it was assumed that mobility was short range, between immediately adjacent strata, and that, within the working class, only the top stratum of skilled men had much mobility. Thirdly, the membership of the upper and intermediate classes has been far more fluid than sociologists have realised.

The major explanation of this change in class structure is the 'occupational transition' which all advanced industrial societies have experienced: the postwar growth in Britain of jobs for which higher formal qualifications are asked leads to an expansion of 'middle-class' occupations of professional, technical, managerial and white-collar varieties, and to a contraction of manual occupations (Goldthorpe, Payne and Llewellyn, 1978). Differential fertility is also part of the explanation, because the relatively low level of fertility in the élite, at a time when upper echelon jobs have been expanding, creates space for recruits from lower classes. The Nuffield team makes an interesting distinction between 'absolute' and 'relative' mobility data. Because the occupational transition is so important in creating high mobility rates and the appearance of a system which is fluid and open at the top, they present the data after 'allowing' for these structural influences. These relative data show that, but for the occupational transition, the system would in fact have been stable, have lacked openness, and counter-balanced mobility openings in one channel by the closure of another (Goldthorpe, Payne and Llewellyn, 1978).

The implications of the Nuffield research for class structuration are simply stated. The rapid expansion of the number of people in higher and intermediate classes, the heterogeneity of the social backgrounds of recruits to these classes, and the fluidity of class membership in the upper reaches of the hierarchy (the result of a sizeable number of people moving in and out of different class locations during their lifetimes), do not provide particularly favourable conditions for upper-class structuration. It is clear, however, that existing upper-class members have succeeded in passing on a privileged position to their offspring, and that the fluidity of the upper class is due to expansion bringing in new recruits rather than to people dropping out of the class on a large scale. The Nuffield research also identifies an inner élite which is smaller than the upper class as a whole, is considerably more advantaged, and which is largely closed to outsiders: this inner élite *is* highly structured. The use of neo-Weberian criteria in fact creates an upper class which is larger than Marxist sociologists would allow, and it is this inner group which appears to correspond more with the Marxist notion of a capitalist upper class (Goldthorpe and Llewellyn, 1977a). Conversely, the stability of the manual working class is high, in the sense that any movement is outward to other classes and very few new recruits join, which leaves a dwindling, but stable and homogeneous class. This is a situation where common experiences and life chances are reproduced over the generations, which provides a foundation for structuring into an identifiable grouping.

The Working Class

Despite the evidence for increased structuration within the working class as traditionally defined, that is, the manual working class, there is little sociological consensus about its homogeneity and unity. Two issues stand out. The first is whether the working class is becoming more or less homogeneous: in particular, whether the differences that exist within the working class are sufficiently great and sufficiently permanent to segregate different groups into different strata. The second is whether or not various non-manual groups should be included in the working class.

The earlier discussions of managerial control systems and production technologies showed how the work situation of the manual working class has become more homogeneous in this century. This has implications for class analysis because, as the Marxist perspective suggests, the convergence of work situations should have produced a less differentiated working class. When one looks at what has happened to the internal divisions which once stratified the manual working class into discrete and rigid strata, then a greater unity of objective condition is indeed apparent, a unity that is confirmed by the application of neo-Weberian criteria. However, new sources of potential differentiation have emerged at the same time.

Labour aristocracy

There have traditionally been enormous differences in market and work rewards surrounding differences in skill. In the most extreme case, apprentice-trained craftsmen at the summit of the skill hierarchy formed an 'aristocracy' of labour in Britain and America in the nineteenth and early twentieth centuries. Historians and sociologists have often identified this as a stratum which prevented homogeneity of class experience and stood in the way of united class action. Engels and Lenin suggested that stratification by skill and the emergence of the labour aristocracy inhibited working-class radicalism, because the aristocracy enjoyed a privileged position within capitalism. Indeed, if one applies either the modern sociological or Marxist criteria of class location, then the class positions of craft and non-craft workers in early capitalism were different. The market situation of labour aristocrats provided higher pay, greater security of income and some chance of advancement by means either of self-employment or promotion within a firm (Hobsbawm, 1964). In comparison with less-skilled labour which tended to be casually employed by the hour or the day, the aristocrats' job security and secure earnings were perhaps their most significant market advantages. The aristocrats also enjoyed better work situations. Chapter 2 showed how British and American craftsmen had considerable autonomy from employer control and considerable intrinsic work interest, which separated their work experience from that of other manual workers. They also performed, in the jargon of modern Marxism, various functions of capital, that is the range of managerial activities noted in Chapter 2, which in some cases amounted to the 'co-exploitation' of unskilled workers. Outside work, there is clear evidence that the labour aristocracy lived in social isolation and residential segregation from other workers, had a distinct life-style based on superior market rewards, and participated in a self-contained community with its own distinct culture (Crossick, 1976; Gray, 1976).

It is difficult now to identify any equivalent labour aristocracy in British industry, because internal stratification on the basis of skill has become much less important as a division within the working class. Historically, labour markets were segregated in such a way that fully-qualified craftsmen and unskilled labourers were scarcely ever in competition for jobs. Craftsmen and labourers inhabited different worlds. Craftsmen were formally trained, usually by means of apprenticeships, and they had job rights which were guaranteed partly by their skill, which was a scarce resource in the market, and partly by their own craft unions, which used trade union power to supplement and preserve market advantages. Official bodies still classify workers into unskilled, semi-skilled and skilled, and about 60 per cent of the modern manual labour force in Britain is classified as skilled (by the Office of Population Census and Surveys). But this classification is really most misleading, because its definition of skill embraces most of the jobs that popular usage treats as semi-skilled (for example, all driving jobs), and because very few workers within this category even remotely resemble the old-style, fully-trained and formally-qualified tradesman. In an investigation carried out in 1971, the OPCS found that two-thirds of all the workers who were classified as skilled for census purposes had no qualifications of any kind, including apprenticeships (OPCS, 1973, p. 243). Even the minority of skilled workers who possess formal qualifications have usually undergone a far less substantial training process than the popular image of tradesmen might suggest. A tiny proportion of those British apprentices who participate in City and Guilds training courses successfully complete these courses; nevertheless an apprentice can still receive craftsman status by merely serving his time. In many industries, unskilled labour is promoted into craftsmen positions and craft unions agree to recognise a certain number of these 'dilutees' each year. In engineering, where the skill levels required by the job are thought on average to be fairly high, apprenticed craftsmen are more common but still account for only just over a half of all tradesmen (D. Robinson, ed., 1970, pp. 58–60).

This shows that the amount of market segregation which exists today is not as great as might be expected. There are obviously industrial and occupational variations, and the decline of segregation and rigid stratification is unlikely to have been an even process. There may still be a few pockets of formally-trained craftsmen, whose levels of skill and market capacity approach those of the traditional labour aristocrats. This is likely to be true of those areas of industry where the rationalisation of managerial controls and the application of information-processing technologies have not yet made much headway. Such men seem likely to occupy segregated labour markets, though it is difficult to say much about them in the absence of hard information. But it is clear that skilled workers of this sort are a very small minority indeed. Most workers now classified as skilled have at some point in their lives competed with non-skilled workers in some labour market, while their present market capacity as skilled men is not greatly different from that of the non-skilled. The market rewards of skilled and non-skilled labour have converged, as pay differentials have been eroded in most advanced capitalist economies (OECD, 1965). This convergence is powerful evidence of growing homogenisation.

Blackburn and Mann's research into one local British labour market (the city of Peterborough) took those jobs performed by male manual workers which employers did not regard as requiring apprentice training. These included many jobs officially classified as 'skilled' and covered about four-fifths of the manual labour force (1979, p. 41). Their evidence shows how homogeneous the market and work situations of manual workers indeed are, and they claim that the application of neo-Weberian criteria produces a Marxist-like picture of manual work (1979, p. 296). They found that there was very little difference between supposedly skilled and unskilled work. Of those interviewed 81 per cent used less skill in their jobs than they would have done if they drove to work, and 85 per cent of the sample could have done 95 per cent of all the jobs in this local labour market (Blackburn and Mann, 1979, p. 280). There was a unified labour market which did not segregate the mass of workers into groups with different market capacities. Of course, the jobs themselves were not homogeneous and could be graded hierarchically into those which were better paid and somewhat more interesting, and those which were neither (financial rewards and job content tended to be linked and to vary together). Workers were selected for these jobs on the basis of their seniority within the firm and the extent to which they impressed management with their co-operativeness (the two are of course linked since unco-operative workers do not last as long in a firm as those with the right attitudes). Managers in Blackburn and Mann's firms did not recruit for higher posts on the open or 'external' labour market, because the qualities for which they searched could not be assessed there. As Chapter 3 suggested, in circumstances where jobs are within the capability of most people, and where the only real difference between jobs is the amount of damage that the failure of a worker to act responsibly may cause, then employers are often more concerned with employees' attitudes rather than their marketable skills.

The de-skilling of work and the rationalisation of managerial control systems lead to the convergence of work situations. The autonomy and intrinsic job content of skilled work is rarely now what it used to be. Skilled men no longer perform those managerial or 'capitalist' functions which marked them off from other manual workers, now that occupational principles of administration have been eroded. The full extent of the change in the traditional crafts has been obscured by the success of some craft unions in restricting access to certain types of work, regardless of the level of skills which the work actually requires. For example, compositors who have been apprentice-trained retain the right to set copy in the British newspaper industry, even on modern computerised type-setting equipment which requires little more skill than the ability to type. Elsewhere, unions have been unable to resist the consequences of rationalisation and de-skilling, and have co-operated in making labour more homogeneous. Unions in British shipyards in the 1960s agreed to a plan of rationalisation which destroyed the old stratification within the labour force, opened old craft jobs to outsiders, and thus created a more unified and more proletarian labour force (R. Brown, *et al.*, 1972).

It is a paradox, given the apparently greater strength of the rationalising principle in American industry, that the only real evidence of the continuation of the labour aristocracy comes from the U.S.A. Mackenzie's research (1973) into the conditions of craftsmen in Rhode Island (on the northern Atlantic seaboard where the system of delegated management described in Chapter 2 flourished in the nineteenth century) shows how craftsmen there still enjoy superior market and work rewards, and still constitute an identifiable social community which has its own separate existence. There is no equivalent evidence for Britain, and it seems unlikely, moreover, that such clear evidence of an aristocracy would be found elsewhere in America, particularly away from the traditional industries of the northern Atlantic seaboard.

Under-classes

While the traditional axis of working-class stratification along the line of skill has declined in significance, other forms have assumed some importance. Two criteria which are often cited as new principles of stratification in advanced capitalist societies are *ethnicity* and *gender*. Differentiation along these lines has caused problems for the analysis of stratification, because sociologists have for long assumed that the purposive rationality of capitalism and the homogenising tendencies of industrialism have destroyed ascriptive and 'status group' criteria as important principles of action or as significant axes of differentiation (Parkin, 1978, pp. 621–30). It was taken for granted that such characteristics of pre-industrial society had been replaced by economic categories such as class. Giddens suggests that although the bases of class and status group formation differ, there is an additional impetus to class structuration when class and status group criteria coincide, because status is transformed into a *market* capacity (1973, p. 112). Ethnicity and gender are held to be the foundations of an 'under-class', in the sense that they serve as 'disqualifying' market capacities which place ethnic minorities and women into the lowest-paid, most unpleasant and least secure occupations, or even disqualify them from employment altogether (Giddens, 1973, p. 112).

The analysis of class stratification along under-class lines is often associated with notions about the segmented nature of labour markets which follows the workings of a 'dual' economy. The association has been particularly common in American labour market literature (for example, Doeringer and Piore, 1971). The dual model suggests that the economy is divided into primary and secondary sectors. The first sector is based on large and profitable firms, which include monopolies, and capital-intensive and technologically advanced firms. The second sector includes smaller, less advanced or capital-intensive firms, which operate within highly competitive markets. The labour market is divided along the same lines. The primary labour market has the following characteristics: jobs are highly paid and fairly secure; unions are strong and regulate the conditions of employment effectively; there are internal labour markets which provide manual employees with some chance of promotion through a manual job hierarchy or 'career structure' of limited range. In the secondary market, jobs are insecure and poorly paid, unions are uninterested in organising or face practical difficulties in recruiting in numerous small workshops with constantly changing workforces, and firms provide no career structures. Economic concentration creates primary sector firms which are large and monopolistic and control their product markets. Their production needs are consequently stable and predictable, and what such firms value is a reliable labour force which has low rates of turnover and absenteeism and which works with steady effectiveness. Capital-intensive production processes reinforce this requirement for a reliable labour force. It is suggested that, in the American dual economy, white males predominate in the primary sector while women and coloured workers are relegated to the second. There are difficulties in generalising this economic model outside the U.S., and it may not even be a very close fit in America. But the division of employment into different sectors, which contrasts those firms and labour markets which provide high pay, good security and an internal career structure to those that do not, is a distinction which has a general validity.

The view that the working class has been stratified by ethnicity and gender to such an extent that they now form separate under-classes, and the related contention that labour markets are split into two separate segments, involve two distinct propositions which can be assessed empirically. The first is the contention that there are inequalities of condition within the working class which follow the lines of ethnicity and gender. To demonstrate that this is so would be to show that the working class is internally *differentiated*. Stratification, however, implies something more than the inequality shown, for example, in the average differences between the wages or working conditions of blacks and whites, women and men: it also implies *segregation*.

Ethnicity Blackburn and Mann (1979) have evaluated the existing evidence of stratification along ethnic lines in Britain, and in addition have provided their own evidence from one local labour market. Part of the following discussion draws on their analysis. The investigation of the hypothesised market stratification which informs under-class and dual labour market theories can be couched in terms of three criteria of segregation: wage levels, occupations, and legal rights in the labour market. American and British wage data do show clear differentiation, but these inequalities are not as great as those between men and women, nor enough to indicate definitely a segregated labour force (Blackburn and Mann, 1979, p. 25). Moreover, the differential between blacks and whites has been closing in America over the last three decades (Szymanski, 1975). In Britain and most European nations, the wage differential between immigrants and natives occurs mainly because immigrant job levels are on average lower than those of native workers: workers who do the same jobs have the same wages. This raises two questions. What access do immigrants have to normal labour market freedoms? How segregated are occupations?

Almost all continental European capitalist economies employ substantial numbers of immigrant workers who have the status of semi-free or 'bonded' labourers, a status which is reminiscent more of feudal than of capitalist societies. They form a 'reserve army' of labour, which can be hired or fired (and returned to their countries of origin) according to economic fluctuations and the demand for unskilled labour (Baudouin, Collin, Guillerm, 1978). These immigrants do not possess full labour market rights. They cannot normally change their employer without permission from the immigration authorities in continental European nations. They are denied residence once they lose their jobs in several countries and in Switzerland they can only live and work for a certain period of time before they have to return home. Although this legally-imposed dualism is not the sort which the dual economy thesis describes, it undoubtedly serves to segregate the labour force into free and semi-free categories which have the force of law. Ethnic minorities in America and Britain normally have citizenship rights and therefore employment rights equal to those of the white working class, but even these nations do not give the full range of market freedoms to all groups immediately upon arrival.

Occupational segregation varies in Western Europe according to the proportion of the labour force that is immigrant or of separate ethnic status. Castles and Kosack have shown that the proportion is highest in Switzerland, where about a third of the manual labour force in the late 1960s and early 1970s, at the end of the postwar boom, were foreign workers (1973, p. 61). Moreover, this large volume of immigrants was in turn concentrated into certain industries in the 'secondary' sector of the economy, and into the worst jobs in these industries, and segregation along dual labour market lines was obviously the norm. But elsewhere there is little evidence of concentration and segregation on the Swiss scale, and immigrants have even begun to work in parts of the 'primary' economy, when they take well-paid (but unpleasant or boring) jobs in the automobile and electronics industries for example. Immigrants are overwhelmingly unskilled workers and, even where they are not segregated into different economic sectors, they remain occupationally differentiated by their low skill levels and the lack of any opportunities to become more qualified or to advance through internal labour markets (Baudouin, Collin, Guillerm, 1978).

Ethnic minorities form a much smaller proportion of the labour force in Britain than in continental Europe – no more than one-twentieth of the workers in any industry, and no more than one-quarter of any specific occupation (Blackburn and Mann, 1979, p. 25). National figures such as these may not reveal local variations, and 'micro-level' knowledge of local labour markets is required to supplement the 'macro-level' evidence from the national scene. The evidence shows that on a few occasions race may lead to a form of segregation in which white and coloured workers do not compete for the same type of work (Mayhew and Rosewell, 1978). Segregation is not widespread and even where it occurs it is not complete. For example, while there may be some segregation at the extremes of the job hierarchy, there is considerable overlap in the middle. 'Secondary' workers rarely have jobs which offer high rewards on all dimensions (pay, intrinsic content, working environment), and 'primary' workers rarely have jobs that are generally bad. But in between there is similarity. Blackburn and Mann found that most of Peterborough's immigrants (two-thirds) shared jobs with native-born British workers, they had the same pay and conditions of employment, and were integrated into the native job structure (1979, pp. 254–6). They were employed in both primary and secondary firms. However, these immigrants were mainly in lower level jobs, and were more likely to stay there because they did not have the same chance of promotion to better jobs. The remaining third of the immigrant population had segregated, low-level jobs. Even when ethnic minorities work for 'secondary' firms, those firms have good jobs which are on a par with bad jobs in the 'primary' sector. There are also jobs which offer unbalanced rewards, such as very high pay to offset unpleasant jobs and poor working conditions (for example, in foundries and automobile assembly), and it is not unusual to find ethnic workers in such jobs. Additionally, piece-work payment schemes often allow less-skilled and ethnic labour to offset the wage disparity between lower and higher level jobs, albeit at the cost of extra effort. This suggests that the ethnic labour force is not homogeneous, does not experience one typical market and work situation, is only in part segregated from the rest of the working class, and does not form a well-defined under-class in terms of the economic criteria of class location.

Ethnicity does work against working-class homogeneity and structuration, not so much because of differentiation along class criteria as because of the segregation which results *outside* the world of market and work situations. Segregated residential communities, segregation in the educational system, prejudice and discrimination against ethnic minorities on the part of the established native working class, and ethnic cultures which differ from the indigenous working-class culture, are all well-known forms of segregation. In other words, stratification occurs in the social rather than the economic sphere, as the result of life-style differences. Ethnicity does not lead to an under-class, but it does inhibit the structuration of the working class.

Gender Unlike ethnic minorities, whose plight has provoked a body of sociological research which tries to understand and explain their situation, women have been discriminated against equally in the world of employment and labour markets and in the conceptual universe of sociology. Sociological class theories normally concentrate on economically active males and ignore female employees altogether. In a few cases, the class location of women has been conidered, but Giddens' conclusions, that women are 'peripheral' to the class system and their location is mainly determined by ascriptive and non-economic criteria (1973, p. 288), are fairly widely accepted. Giddens in fact appears to consign women to two under-classes, one attached to the non-manual middle class and the other to the manual working class (1973, pp. 219, 288). Therefore, the task is not simply to examine the extent of the differentiation and stratification of women workers on the established criteria of market and work situations, but also to consider the adequacy of the sociological conceptualisation of women's place in the class system.

Class theory makes a variety of assumptions which lead to women and the occupational composition of the female labour force being ignored in the analysis of class structure. The basic unit of analysis is assumed to be the family, because this is the mechanism which transmits class position through the generations. It is further assumed that the head of the household is male, that his economic position determines the class location of other family members, and thus a woman's class is determined by her husband's or father's (when women live in households with husbands or fathers as heads). These assumptions may be questioned.

Garnsey (1978) points out that the usual consequence of taking the family as the unit of analysis and the man's job as the determinant of family position is a belief that the determinants of class structure are to be found in the occupational composition of the male labour force alone, rather than the whole labour force including women. This is an entirely illegitimate confusion of levels of analysis: the class position of families and the shape of the class structure are different things. Because sociologists attach little importance to the economic position of women for the class placement of families, it does not follow that one area of the occupational structure should be regarded as unimportant for the class system. Nearly 40 per cent of all the employed people in Britain are women (CSO, 1979, p. 84), and this large female labour force is mainly concentrated in a narrow range of occupations. However sociologists concerned with industry and class show little interest in women's work. This is unpardonable. To ignore working women is to understand only part of the industrial and class system. Individuals rather than families must be the basic units of class analysis. Moreover, the existence of single adults, families with female heads of households, and families where the male head is unemployed (and where the wife may in fact be employed) means that the emphasis on families and male heads cannot be maintained even by those who regard women as peripheral to class. In Britain in 1971, nearly thirteen million women could be classified on the basis of their husbands' jobs, but about five and a half million could not be classified in this way because they were single, widowed or divorced (Garnsey, 1978). In America, the proportion of households which did not have male heads in the early 1970s has been estimated at nearly 40 per cent (Acker, 1973).

There is extensive labour market segregation, as measured by wage levels and occupational patterns. Barron and Norris (1976) have analysed sex differences in wages in Britain, and find that the area of overlap between the hourly rates of men and women is less than one-third of the total combined distribution. This indicates a greater degree of segregation than is found between the different ethnic populations. Pay differentials between men and women exist at all levels of the occupational hierarchy, but are greatest at the bottom (Westergaard and Resler, 1975, p. 97). Women are heavily concentrated in clerical and sales occupations in the non-manual area, and in unskilled factory and service (for example, cleaning) occupations in the manual (though some women are of course found at all levels of the occupational hierarchy, including the most senior). In routine white-collar occupations, women's pay is below that of men in skilled manual work.

This aspect of labour market segregation has vitally important implications for how sociologists view the class structure. If feminised occupations are ignored, then the traditional class division at this point of the occupational hierarchy can still be defended to some extent. Male non-manual jobs are mainly better paid than manual ones, though this is not the case when men work in low-grade, white-collar occupations. Once women are treated equally with men in class theory, then the old distinction becomes completely untenable. The feminisation of routine non-manual work, which was a feature of the expansion of white-collar jobs that began before the Second World War in America and Britain, was accompanied by proletarianisation. This is apparent if one takes work situation criteria in addition to market rewards. The work situations of female sales staff have never been much better than those found in manual occupations. But, in the past, office work was superior. However, the progressive degradation of office work, which was portrayed in Chapter 2 and elsewhere, has made significant inroads into the traditional differences between the work of manual and low-level, non-manual employees. On neither of the economic criteria adopted by the neo-Weberians can manual and low-level, non-manual jobs be separated. There remain slight differences of material condition, such as the somewhat shorter hours worked by routine non-manual workers, their access to a few fringe benefits, and the absence of petty restrictions such as clocking-on (Wedderburn and Craig, 1974). But these differences are insignificant in comparison with the similarity on the main criteria. Thus, conventional sociology and the Marxist class theories of Braverman and Wright can be shown to produce the *same* conclusions in this instance.

Garnsey (1978) suggests that women can be accommodated within class analysis without recourse to new concepts such as under-class that depend on ascription, and that discrimination results from the operation of economic rather than status criteria. She argues, in effect, that the quality of female labour is lower than that of male, because of women's position in the household. The unequal division of labour in the household means that women are responsible for childcare and domestic duties, in addition to childbearing. As the result, women are not suited for paid employment in the 'primary' sector of the economy, because employers there look for people who will give them long-term, uninterrupted employment, will work full-time, and in some cases will be geographically mobile, all of which effectively disqualifies most women (Barron and Norris, 1976). Women are therefore employed in the 'secondary' sector where wages, job security and job content are all inferior. Female office workers are of course employed in 'primary' companies. But they usually have the worst jobs in these firms, because they are low quality labour when judged by the standards of the 'primary' labour market. It is, therefore, the lower market value of female labour which results from the household division of labour that leads women into inferior jobs, rather than the prejudice and convention of male employers and co-workers.

This re-integration of women into orthodox class analysis has two major virtues. It is an elegant and parsimonious conceptualisation, because it simplifies class theory by the removal of excrescences such as 'under-class'. It focuses on the market mechanism which determines occupational placement and class location, rather than the social attributes of women or the prejudices of men. Two issues remain, however, which suggest that ascription and status considerations should not be underestimated as significant influences on female employment.

It is not clear *how* widespread are job hierarchies and internal career structures in British industry, nor that Blackburn and Mann's findings are typical of other British labour markets. Firms with 'primary' characteristics, which are large, profitable, capital-intensive and operate in oligopolistic markets, are not necessarily 'primary' employers. Automobile manufacturers, for example, provide high pay but little job security and no job hierarchy of rising pay and more enjoyable work – in other words no career structure of increasing responsibility. Their employment policies are traditional, based on the cash nexus and the commodification of labour (Beynon, 1973). Firms which do have job hierarchies and provide careers may have several 'ports of entry' which offer upwards movement to those without long and uninterrupted service. A comparative analysis of three local labour markets for skilled workers shows that this is often the case, and applies both to firms in the 'primary' sector and to those outside (Mackay *et al.*, 1971). The existence of large areas of well-paid and male-dominated employment which do *not* require the labour qualities contained in Garnsey's hypothesis, and from which women are nevertheless excluded, suggests either that there are more non-ascriptive market disabilities than have yet been identified, or that non-economic criteria are at work.

Secondly, what can be explained as a weak market capacity at the level of class theory is clearly at another level ascription. This can be phrased in another way. The economy receives female labour that is not of the same quality as male labour, and purely economic criteria may determine its occupational placement. But the difference in quality is itself the result of conventional, ascriptive practices in the home, which deprive women of the attributes which are valued in the best jobs. In addition, the ascriptive practices in the educational system, which reflect the belief that certain manual and intellectual qualities are appropriate for boys rather than girls, and the prejudice displayed in unions and professions which control access to their trades prevent women from enhancing their market capability by acquiring the sorts of skills that do have a market value irrespective of the length and continuity of periods of employment.

Employment patterns are of course mutually reinforcing. Women are concentrated in jobs that have high rates of labour turnover, in firms that operate in highly competitive product markets and are also labour-intensive, which leads managers to minimise all costs including wages while maximising output, and in firms which are often small in size. The characteristics of the economic sector in which so many women are employed militate against women organising effectively to improve their market power by means of collective action. It is popularly believed that women are by nature (or social conditioning) less likely to unionise than men. But, in reality, proportionately fewer women than men are unionised because of the kind of jobs that women do. Chapter 7 shows how unionism flourishes most in large firms which are bureaucratically organised, have stable labour forces, high wage and enlightened personnel policies. These tend to be the characteristics of primary rather than secondary firms. The different economic environments of men's and women's work account for much of the difference in unionisation. The traditional reluctance of male unionists to organise women, rather than any reluctance of women to join unions, may explain the rest. Indeed, the proportion of women workers who are union members has risen sharply in Great Britain in recent years, from approximately 29 per cent in 1964 to approximately 37 per cent in 1974(Price and Bain, 1976). This compares with nearly 57 per cent of the male labour force which was unionised in 1974. The rapid rise in female unionisation suggests that many women do not lack interest in the use of collective strength for market improvement. But the relative weakness of trade unionism in the sorts of firms in which many women work, means that low wages, poor conditions and high turnover persist, and in turn make organisation more difficult.

It is therefore true that women are more obviously segregated within the working class than are ethnic groups and, on the face of things, they are more likely to constitute an under-class. However, the relative contributions of conventional class criteria and status factors to women's disadvantage are not easy to assess. Economic segregation cannot entirely be explained away as the consequence of ascription rather than rational economic calculation, though the balance may fall towards ascription. The consequences of this segregation and internal class stratification for structuration are also ambiguous. There is the paradox that ethnicity does not stratify the working class along market and work lines, but creates isolated communities when life-style criteria are used; whereas women are stratified within the working class economically, but are more integrated outside the sphere of production – in other words men and women live together even if they do not work together.

New and old working classes

There were several attempts in the sociology of the 1960s to divide the working class into 'old' and 'new' sections. The different classifications bore little overt similarity to each other, but they shared a deeper and concealed unity in the common belief that capitalism develops in a way which continually segments the labour force. The incessant transformation of the forces of production which is intrinsic in capitalism divides labour in two ways, by bringing new groups into the labour force and by the continual modification of existing industrial and occupational structures. These general processes of change can be outlined, before considering two of the more influential accounts of the new working class.

Industrialism in the past expanded by bringing new groups into its labour force: agricultural workers, women, immigrants. Industrial growth has often depended on readily available supplies of labour, preferably of cheap, docile and unskilled workers, to work in labour-intensive industries where productive techniques make few demands on anyone's skill. The continuous expansion of the economy creates a division between the labour force which is already established and those brought into industrial production (or latterly into services) for the first time. There is, as a result, a further division between the working classes of old industrial economies with slow rates of growth and others which are more recent or are still expanding vigorously. In Europe, this difference can be seen most clearly in the comparison between the British working class, on the one hand, and those of France and Italy on the other.

The British working class has, by international standards, been quite stable and homogeneous for many years. The shift from employment on the land to employment in industry, and from rural to urban residence, was largely complete half a century ago.

Unskilled immigrant labour has not been imported on the scale of other European nations in the postwar period. Moreover, that substantial part of the immigrant labour force which is Irish does not segment the British labour force along under-class lines, nor in the manner of the southern Europeans and north Africans working in northern European societies. The rising proportion of working women marks a substantial addition to the employed population. Women have *always* been part of the labour force: what is new is only the number who now work.

In contrast, even twenty-five years ago, France and Italy had large agricultural populations. Subsequently, there has been a dramatic shift from 'pre-capitalist' employment into employment in the capitalist economy, from self-employment as a peasant farmer or unpaid labourer for some other member of the family into employment in manufacturing and service industries. This initially involved extensive internal migration in both societies, the displacement of manpower from rural to urban areas and from agriculture to established industrial regions. At a later stage, industry itself was decentralised, and manufacturing plants were moved into traditional agricultural regions in southern Italy and western France (Bauduoin, Collin, Guillerm, 1978). These transformations have now created a segmented class composed of old-established urban and industrial families, migrants who have since the war moved from pre-industrial society to the modern sector, and pre-industrial workers transposed directly into industry without any change of locale. The inflow into France of more than a million foreign workers in less than fifteen years, between 1956 and 1968, in order to meet the labour shortages which internal migration and industrial decentralisation could not overcome, has been a further major source of division (Bauduoin, Collin, Guillerm, 1978). The size of the underemployed agricultural population in Italy has been so great that there has been no need to import labour. It is only in the growth of female employment that the British working class resembles those of France or Italy.

The transformation of the forces of production also threatens to divide the working class by changing the industrial and occupational structures. It is widely believed that the increasing complexity of industry and occupations leads to greater differentiation of the employed population (see the views reported in Hyman, 1978b; Low-Beer, 1978, pp. 7–22). This line of argument can be summarised as follows. The pre-war tendency towards more mechanised and simpler work in conventional manufacturing industry had promoted the expansion of semi-skilled at the cost of skilled labour, which homogenised the manual element of the working class. But the expansion of clerical and other routine white-collar jobs in the pre-war years introduced a *new* principle of differentiation, between manual and non-manual work. The postwar era has seen further divisions, as the result of new automated technologies, the growth of whole new science-based industries, the rise of the service sector of the economy, and the decline of traditional industries (textiles, coalmining, steel, shipbuilding, railways). The manual labour force itself is now thought to be divided into three strata: the new, technically-trained (though not apprentice-trained) stratum working on advanced technologies and in the new industries; semi-skilled labour working in conventional mass-production industries with a high degree of rationalisation; and those who work in declining, traditionally-managed industries. The continued expansion of non-manual employment has been maintained, in the form of the recent growth of technical and professional occupations. This growth, indeed, has blurred the distinction between manual and non-manual tasks, when the tasks of process workers and technicians are compared. Some of these new technical and professional occupations in the advanced sectors of the economy can even be included as part of the working class.

Several points of a general nature can be raised which suggest that class homogeneity is not much altered by the transformations of the capitalist economy. First, occupational heterogeneity and change have always been typical of capitalism but, with the exception of the labour aristocracy, have not fundamentally stratified the working class. Secondly, occupational differentiation is only important for class position if it is accompanied by differences in market and work conditions, or in the relationship to capital. There is no evidence that manual work is being divided along such lines. There *is* evidence that manual and routine non-manual work have converged in feminised occupations, and it will shortly be suggested that a similar convergence may be found in some male clerical work as well. Thirdly, the test of whether or not new segments have been added to the working class is the application of the conventional class criteria, whether neo-Weberian or neo-Marxist, rather than the industrial location of the occupations.

Goldthorpe *et al.*, in the *Affluent Worker* research (1968a and b; 1969), were concerned with the consequences for the British working class of the growth of mass-production manufacturing, which replaced traditional industries belonging to an earlier economic era. They maintained that postwar economic growth in Great Britain had produced industrial and occupational diversification, the breakdown of an old pattern of single-industry towns or areas of towns, and the geographical mobility of the working class as labour moved from old to new industrial areas. Workers in traditional industries – and their evidence is drawn from the coalmining, shipbuilding, deep-sea fishing and docking industries in the 1950s – had distinct work situations and life-styles which separated them from other sections of the working class. The major contrast was between these traditional workers and the 'affluent' workers to be found in the more modern sector of the economy, notably in certain mass-production industries. Traditional workers had unrationalised work situations which provided interesting tasks, freedom from managerial and technical constraints, and teamwork. The important life-style elements concerned the structure of family and community life. Traditional workers lived in occupational communities of workmates who were also neighbours and friends, in single-class areas which were geographically and socially isolated from the mainstream of society, in stable and long-established communities. Family life was gregarious and looked outwards to extended kin. The more modern, 'affluent' workers of Luton, in contrast, had chosen to leave their old areas in order to work in high-paying and mainly unskilled jobs in the engineering industry, including motor assembly. In exchange for affluence, they endured highly rationalised work and 'privatised' life-styles. Workers with these life-styles displayed no communal sociability: their occupational and kinship networks scarcely existed, their leisure time was centred on the immediate family and was inward-looking, and they lived in neighbourhoods that could in no way be described as 'communities'.

This typology exaggerates the lack of homogeneity among the British working class and can be challenged in two ways. The implicit model of a stable industrial society which has been dislocated by economic growth and changes to the industrial structure does not fit the facts of British economic history nor does the historical movement from traditionalism to modernity ('affluence') have much validity, as Lockwood (1975) now acknowledges. The working class has always experienced geographical and occupational flux as the result of the transformations of the forces of production, and today's traditional industries and communities are yesterday's centres of industrial and social expansion (Davis and Cousins, 1975). Modern Luton can itself be seen as an industrial centre that is now becoming traditional: it relies on a largely stagnant section of the British engineering industry with an old-fashioned technology, and no longer provides an expanding labour market which supports inward migration.

Secondly, the typology underestimates the extent to which certain secular trends have occurred in the work situations and life-styles of *all* British workers. It appears that the changes affecting 'affluent' workers are more typical of the wider working class than Goldthorpe *et al.* have credited. 'Traditionalism' is not an adequate description of any section of the modern working class. The effect of new productive techniques and greater managerial intervention in the labour process has subjected 'traditional' industries such as shipbuilding and the docks to the same rationalising tendency found elsewhere (R. Brown, *et al.*, 1972; S. Hill, 1976b). Organised labour has slowed the pace of rationalisation, but the direction of change is clear. Detailed investigation of the docks in eastern London, an area and an industry which are both renowned for their traditionalism, has shown that dockers are scarcely distinguishable from Luton engineering workers in terms of the life-style factors which were mentioned above (S. Hill, 1976b, pp. 163–78). Dockers are geographically mobile, they no longer form tightly-knit occupational communities, and they no longer mix with extended kin. Instead, they are home- and family-centred and merge socially with the wider working class in the areas where they live. This wider working class includes 'affluent' workers from the Ford assembly plant at Dagenham and 'new working class' process workers from the oil refineries and paper mills along the Thames estuary. Another investigation, that of the working class in the Liverpool area, has also failed to find evidence of a distinctively traditional working class (K. Roberts *et al.*, 1977).

The other major attempt to differentiate traditional and modern sectors was formulated in France in the 1960s (Mallet, 1963 [1975]; Gorz, 1964 [1967]; Touraine, 1969 [1971]). This was the division between people employed in advanced, high technology industries who made up the 'new working class', and the rest of the working class. Proponents of the new working class thesis claimed that advanced capitalism had introduced structural changes into the labour force. It was suggested that high technology required better-educated workers, provided more interesting and involving work, organised production along communal, teamwork principles, and integrated workers into their firms. These arguments about high technology are indistinguishable from Blauner's view of automated processes in the American oil industry. Unlike Blauner, however, these theorists maintained that such structural changes promoted greater industrial militancy, because they made more apparent various 'contradictions' of capitalism.

One fundamental contradiction, which the new working class is supposed to experience acutely, is that between the communal production of goods and the private appropriation of profits. As highly-educated technicians, the new workers fully understand the workings of production processes in ways which ordinary workers do not, and moreover, they have real control over these processes. Teamwork brings home to them the communal basis of production. Moreover, knowledge of the hidden secrets of the productive forces, control over the process of production, and the communal character of production have enabled the new working class to penetrate the contradiction which is hidden from other workers. 'Precisely because it is placed in the centre of the most complex mechanisms of organisational capitalism, the new working class is brought to realise more quickly than the other sectors the contradictions inherent in the system' (Mallet, 1963 [1975], p. 29). The consequence for structuration is that the work situation of the new working class separates it from the rest of the labour force. Another contradiction which underlies these theories is that between the responsibility, skill and education of new workers, and their lack of institutionalised power. They have power over production, high social status, and a strong bargaining position, but as individuals and collectively they are unable to exert much influence on company policy. Mallet and Gorz find no significance in the division between manual and non-manual work, though Touraine is concerned with non-manual technical and lower professional groups. In Mallet's account, which is the more extreme, the new class comprises ordinary blue-collar workers and highly trained professionals, including graduate engineers. Gallie's investigation (1978) of two French oil refineries suggests that many blue-collar, new working class employees are little more than semi-skilled labourers.

The arguments about consciousness and action will be dealt with later. What is at issue here is whether these various accounts correctly identify a new principle of stratification within the working class. The answer must be that they do not. The earlier discussions of Blauner and Braverman clearly demonstrated that manual employees working on high technology have no more control and no greater understanding of the production process than other workers. Indeed, they compare unfavourably with traditional craftsmen. Secondly, there is a huge variety of work situations within the ranks of qualified technicians. Low-Beer (1978) notes in his investigation of the new working class in Italy how some technicians are engaged in routine tasks which are repetitive and make few demands on their skills or education, while others are involved in innovative tasks. Gorz, in a revision of his earlier position (1976), suggests that it is the job of some technicians to remove the intellectual content from manual workers' tasks and to take this over for themselves, thus allowing manual jobs to be de-skilled and performed by semi-skilled labour. In such cases, technicians themselves enjoy stimulating work at the cost of the working class. In neo-Weberian terms, these technicians are separated from the working class by virtue of their superior work rewards. Neo-Marxism arrives at the *same* substantive conclusion, for different reasons: these technicians are differentiated because they perform certain functions of capital. Conversely, some technicians have not benefited from the division between manual and mental labour (Gorz, 1976). Indeed, some technicians have been de-skilled to a point where their work begins to resemble manual labour in terms of control and mental stimulus. This is the case with draughtsmen in many large drawing offices. This parallels the closing of wage differentials between certain technicians and skilled manual workers (B.C. Roberts *et al.*, 1973). There may thus be some warrant for the inclusion of various low-grade technical staff in the working class, though this case is not clearly established on either neo-Weberian or neo-Marxist criteria. But there is no warrant at all for the sweeping generalisations of the new working class theorists. Finally, Mallet and the others have introduced a new criterion of class placement which appears to have no obvious validity or usefulness, when they assume that class can be defined by the *industrial location* in which people are employed. The conventional criteria are still more appropriate.

Intermediate and Upper Classes

The evidence above indicates that the old divisions within the manual part of the working class are less important, that homogeneity is greater, and that structuration is higher, than previously believed. New divisions, however, threaten some of this unity. Above the working class, division is endemic in the British class structure. Neither the upper nor the intermediate classes, following the modern bifurcation of the old sociological category of the 'middle class', appear anything like as well structured. This reflects, in part, the activities of sociologists, who have been more concerned with manual workers than the rest of the employed population and have a less extensive knowledge of the non-manual world, particularly its upper echelons. However, the fragmentation of the new intermediate and upper classes appears in fact to be real, and is not just an illusion created by the relative shortage of evidence.

The Fragmentary Class Structure (K. Roberts *et al.*, 1977) suggests that upper and intermediate classes have become less homogeneous since the Second World War. Popular contemporary accounts of the English middle class just after the war painted the picture of high market rewards, based on a mixture of earned income and some personal wealth, and work situations which allowed a great deal of independence and control. Comfortable prosperity and independence, when they went together with high levels of formal education, produced the characteristic middle-class involvement in 'high' culture (Lewis and Maude, 1949; Bonham, 1954). In these accounts, the typical middle-class occupations were in the traditional professions or in business, often as the owners of small- or medium-sized firms. Such accounts may have been idealised, and doubtless there were people in routine office employment with pretensions to middle-class status. But they do point to the basic unity of material conditions and culture within the class in that era. Big industrialists, large landowners, and the leading figures in financial capitalism belonged to a separate upper class.

Sociology defines the modern upper class to include the old upper and middle classes within the same classification. The resulting amalgam, however, is fragmented. This is partly the consequence of combining two previously distinct classes, and partly because the old middle class is no longer as homogeneous as it once was. Taking the old upper class first, this still remains separate from other strata and does form a well-structured group. The commercial, industrial and financial élites remain fairly distinct from rank-and-file management in British industry (Stanworth and Giddens, 1974; 1975). Recruitment patterns show this. Directors of large companies, particularly non-executive directors, are drawn disproportionately from the old upper class. Executive directorships, notably those filled by internal promotion within the company from senior management, are somewhat more open to recruits from other social backgrounds. The growing importance of formal qualifications in management suggests that company directors may increasingly be drawn from more varied social backgrounds. But the differential class access to higher education ensures that a substantial proportion of directors, chosen on achievement rather than ascriptive criteria, do continue to be drawn from the old upper class. Investigations into large firms in the 1950s found that just under a half of directors had fathers who had also been directors, and nearly two-thirds had been to private schools (Copeman 1955, pp. 92–120; Clements, 1958, pp. 173f). A study of bank directors over the period from 1939 to 1970 found that about half came from élite backgrounds, despite a clear trend towards higher educational qualifications among these directors (Boyd, 1973). Company chairman are still overwhelmingly drawn from traditional sources (Stanworth and Giddens, 1974).

Recruitment to élite positions creates a stratum that is still self-perpetuating and partly closed to outsiders. It is also well integrated. Multiple directorships serve to integrate the various segments of the traditional upper class, integrating industrial, commercial and financial sectors and linking different company boards within the various sectors. Friendship and family networks, and common life-styles, unify this stratum. A common educational background of private schools and Oxbridge reinforces the development of common values and culture. New recruits appear to absorb the common culture, whatever their social origins (Rex, 1974). The landed segment of the old upper class is also integrated. Wealth created in business is frequently invested in agricultural and sporting land, and landed families often have business interests which link them with corporate and financial worlds (Newby *et al.*, 1978). It has been suggested that members of the old upper class have a feeling of community, even a class awareness, as the result of these integrative processes (Scott, 1979, p. 126).

The old middle class also survives in a compressed form. Small-scale businessmen, self-employed professionals and employees who have risen to the top the hard way, have not disappeared, but no longer dominate their class (K. Roberts *et al.*, 1977, pp. 104–22). The proportion of people who own their own businesses may have declined, but there is still an entrepreneurial middle class throughout Britain. K. Roberts *et al.* found that a significant minority, about 16 per cent, of their sample of non-manual workers in the Liverpool area was entrepreneurial middle class. These self-employed respondents enjoyed high market rewards and extremely comfortable styles of life (1977, p. 112). In his study of Swansea, Bell (1968) distinguished a local bourgeoisie, made up of locally-born tradesmen and professionals who ran family businesses and professional practices. They were distinct from the 'spiralists', who worked for large organisations and moved around the country as they progressed in their careers. The 'locals' were the town's 'burghers', who dominated local life and constituted a fairly cohesive and integrated middle-class group within the town.

A major influence on the structure of the old middle class has been the growth of the large-scale, corporate sector of the British economy since the war. This has created a new segment of 'organisation men' in addition to the local bourgeoisies. It was a popular theme in the sociology of the 1950s that large organisations created new and distinct work environments, and were associated with distinctive styles of life outside work. C.W. Mills, in *White Collar* (1953), and W.H. Whyte, in *The Organisation Man* (1956), suggested that the rise of salaried managers at the cost of the independent middle class created a new breed of executives who had sold themselves to their corporations. Large firms demanded total commitment and expected their executives to be willing to move from town to town, and even between continents, as they were shifted from one post to another. The more successful the executive, the more moves he was likely to make, as he spiralled upwards within the firm. Organisation men therefore can make roots in no community, find it hard to maintain contacts with kin other than those members of the immediate nuclear family who live in the same house, and frequently have many acquaintances but no real friends. The total dedication to work which an ambitious executive needs if he is to advance leaves little time or energy to become involved in 'high' culture. The working environments of large firms tend to be highly bureaucratised, and the literature of the 1950s suggests that executives adapt their personalities to fit their environments. Thus, the organisation man thesis suggests that there is a complete contrast of work experience and life-style between the old and new business strata.

Modern research into British business management shows that the organisation man thesis has a lot of relevance. In a study conducted by Pahl and Pahl (1971), most managers had changed jobs once every five years, or more frequently. Only about a half lived within even one hundred miles of their parents. Few had any close friends, because they were never in one place long enough to make roots, and the outside social life of the family was constantly disrupted. K. Roberts *et al.* (1977) document a similar set of demands that large organisations make on their managerial employees. The corporate executives in their research changed jobs more frequently, moved between areas more often, and had different patterns of social life outside work than those who worked for small firms (1977, pp. 121–2). Bell found that a belief in continuous career advancement was a key expectation, and that the great value placed on individual achievement was a cornerstone of the middle-class value system (1968, pp. 13–20).

A fourth part of the sociological upper class is the segment once known as the 'intelligentsia'. As the term applied in the immediate postwar era, it included occupations such as writing, broadcasting, publishing, university teaching and some levels of school-teaching, which were 'intellectual' and constituted the liberal professions. The rapid growth of employment in education, communications and welfare has led to a huge expansion of these and similar liberal–professional occupations. They typically provide high levels of autonomy at work, even when this takes place within large organisations, because employers accept the claim that good performance is possible only when controls are few. This autonomy is greater than is found in the corporate managerial segment, except at the top of the executive level. Market rewards are adequate rather than generous by upper-class standards. Life-style differences also mark off these occupations from others in the same class (K. Roberts *et al.*, 1977, pp. 153–4). The level of educational attainment is higher than for the rest of the upper class, career patterns of long service in one job are common, and there are very high rates of geographical and social mobility which are linked with participation in higher education. People in 'intellectual' occupations participate more fully than anyone else in community life, political parties and religious organisations (p. 154). They also subscribe to an intellectual and principled form of radicalism, what Parkin labels 'middle-class radicalism' (1968). This remains outside the institutions of organised radicalism, such as the trade union movement and the Labour party for example, and typically finds expression in protest movements; for example in CND in the 1960s (Parkin, 1968).

The intermediate level of the class hierarchy in Britain is even more fragmented. This can be judged by the variety of different types of occupation which the Nuffield team lists, including foremen and self-employed artisans, who have reached the summit of a traditional working-class career, people in low-level, white-collar jobs who will stay in these all their lives, whose class position has become increasingly proletarian over the years, and others at the start of careers that will provide them with long-range mobility into the upper class before they reach middle age. The Nuffield research shows that the intermediate level is in a state of perpetual flux and has the most disorderly patterns of mobility (Goldthorpe and Llewellyn, 1977b). This middle mass contains the highest rates of inwards and outwards mobility. It includes short-range mobility, as people move between hierarchically adjacent occupations, and long-range, as people move through the intermediate level into the upper class.

Fragmentation is not just a question of the different types of occupation found at the intermediate class level. Fragmentation occurs even within single occupations, when these include wide ranges of condition that vary from the proletarian to those that are not conceivably proletarian. The occupation of technician fits this category. Laboratory staff earn about the same as semi-skilled workers, but draughtsmen earn considerably more even than skilled manual workers (Wedderburn and Craig, 1974). A study of 1100 technicians in the late 1960s (B.C. Roberts *et al.*, 1973) found that all suffered restricted promotion opportunities because of the new practice of recruiting technical managers from graduates and professionally qualified people. But the experience of de-skilling varied. Some performed routine tasks which made no demands on their skills, while others had a high cognitive-planning element in their work. In some cases new technology rationalised work, while in others it created more challenging jobs. The nature of technical work clearly varies, between what is structured and can be rationalised, for example draughtsmanship, and what is less structured and more difficult to rationalise, for example experimental work in laboratories (Low-Beer, 1978, p. 213). There are also differences between jobs in the extent to which they are involved in the functions of capital, particularly in the de-skilling or control of other workers' labour (Gorz, 1976). Proletarianised work and market situations do not necessarily coincide, as is demonstrated by draughtsmen whose work is proletarianised but highly paid and laboratory staff where the reverse applies. It is difficult to make useful generalisations about the variety of conditions within the technician category.

It is also difficult to generalise about the class position of *male* clerks. On the one hand, certain indicators suggest that there is little difference between the situations of clerical and manual work. Earnings surveys show that male junior clerks earn less than semi-skilled manual workers, that intermediate clerical grades are on a par with semi-skilled work, and that many senior male clerical posts are paid less than most skilled manual occupations (Wedderburn and Craig, 1974; *Diamond Report*, 1979, pp. 92–3). Some minor relics of clerks' old middle-class status can be found in their terms and conditions of employment, but these are insufficient to separate them from manual workers. More clerks than manual workers can have time off with pay for domestic reasons, can arrive a few minutes late for work, and have company pension schemes (Wedderburn and Craig, 1974). Apart from these differences, rationalisation and de-skilling by means of job re-design, increased division of labour, and office automation have made manual and routine white-collar work more alike. Shopfloor working conditions have further encroached upon white-collar work, with the growth of large 'pools' of clerks in open-plan offices and more formal controls over working practices.

On the other hand, it is clear that many male clerks have a very different market situation in one crucial respect: career prospects or life chances. For the majority of men who start work in clerical occupations, being a clerk is only a transitional stage before promotion into more senior non-manual jobs. An investigation of the career patterns of British clerks in the early 1970s shows that men starting their working lives as clerks, or becoming clerks at an early age, can realistically expect promotion (Stewart, Prandy and Blackburn, 1980). The bulk of promotion occurs while men are in their twenties. Thus the market situation of male clerks, in this crucial respect, separates them from women. An implication of these findings is the paradox that the feminisation of clerical work *enhances* the market capacity and mobility prospects of men. At a moment when promotion opportunities for clerks as a whole are restricted, the female element disqualifies the majority of clerks from being considered for career advancement, thus improving the life chances of the minority of men (in 1971 only 27 per cent were men).

Clerical work is not at all homogeneous and when one follows the neo-Weberian criteria, the occupation of clerk does not define a *single* class location. Most other neo-Weberians, however, do not reach this conclusion, as this chapter has demonstrated. Some male clerks do share the same proletarian situation as women. These are long-established clerks who have failed to gain promotion and middle-aged, late entrants who have no chance of promotion. Late entrants include manual workers who move into clerical work when their manual work proves too arduous, and for whom clerical work may represent a loss of financial rewards rather than an improvement of material condition. Indeed, there is considerable movement, in both directions, as clerks take up manual work for its greater financial rewards and manual workers (including ex-clerks) move into clerical work because it is less arduous. Women clerks, unpromoted clerks and late entrants have very different class situations from the young high-flyers.

Both Braverman's labour process approach and Wright's ownership functions approach contradict the conventional sociological treatment of clerks in Britain. Much of the difference can be explained by their correct appreciation of the centrality of women in the class system. A strict application of the conventional criteria that does not discriminate on the grounds of gender would agree with much of the neo-Marxist description, though it would distinguish between types of clerk. The other variety of capitalist functions approach makes no claim for the class unity of clerks, but suggests that they divide into the proletariat or capitalist class according to their role in the extraction of surplus and the management of capital (Crompton, 1976).

It used to be assumed that white-collar workers were similar to the rest of the 'middle' class in their life-styles. The fragmentation of the old middle class suggests that this may no longer be a tenable assumption. There is not a great deal of information about the life-styles of the intermediate class. However, two case studies of single occupations suggest that there may be no distinctive, intermediate class life-style. A study of foremen shows many similarities between intermediate and working-class life (S. Hill, 1976b). Consumption patterns, leisure activities, family and community life were the same for foremen and the men they supervised. There were two areas where foremen and men differed, however. The foremen mixed more with other white-collar employees in their social lives than did the men, and a small proportion had friends who were all in non-manual jobs. They also appeared to support to some extent the 'middle-class' emphasis on individual achievement. There was some variation between those who scarcely differed from the men and those who did. The criteria of market and work situations excluded them from the working class, and they were allocated some of the functions of capital, notably in their formal control of the labour process. Yet their life-styles were ambiguous when evaluated for class content and differed from the working-class pattern in only a limited way.

As part of the *Affluent Worker* research, Goldthorpe *et al.* (1969) compared the life-styles of a sample of men clerks with those of affluent manual workers. (The clerks were employed by the same companies as the manual workers.) They found some small differences in friendship patterns. Clerks were more likely to go beyond the circle of kin, workmates and neighbours to make friends, to entertain those friends at home more often, and had more friends shared jointly between husband and wife. Clerks belonged more often to formal associations, to clubs, societies and political parties. The evidence shows that none of these differences was large. Family life was home-centred and privatised in both cases. There were no differences in the aspirations which people held. Many clerks lived in working-class areas. But clerical workers did differ in how they tried to realise their aspirations: they planned their lives more systematically in order to realise long-term objectives and involved their wives more in this planning, for example in family budgeting. This was not so among manual workers nor was such a strategy possible, because their employers provided far less job security for manual employees than for clerical workers.

This investigation revealed a particular stereotype of the middle-class life-style, derived from research into managerial and professional occupations. The model suggested that middle-class social life was gregarious, that most friends were the joint friends of husbands and wives, that there was a lot of home entertaining, and that making friends was a conscious decision rather than something people just drifted into as the result of close proximity (with kin, neighbours and workmates, for example). The middle class were thought to be 'joiners', who participated heavily in formal associations. Family life was based on the nuclear family. The husband–wife relationship was close and involved a lot of joint activities. Middle-class aspirations were based on a set of beliefs, that careers were progressive, that an orderly improvement in the quality of life followed career progression, that the future could be planned for, that there was a hierarchy of social prestige, and that individual achievement was the crucial measure of a person's worth. This model differed in all respects from the 'traditional worker' model of working-class life. Except in the analysis of family life, it also differed from the model of the new working class contained in the 'affluent worker' concept.

Since there are in fact few life-style differences between 'traditional' and 'affluent' workers, the evidence of Goldthorpe *et al.* indicates that clerks do have quite a lot in common with the generality of manual workers. However, like foremen, these clerks differ from the manual working class in two particular respects: the tendency to make non-manual friends and certain 'middle-class' orientations. Because *The Affluent Worker* does not stratify by age or promotion prospects, it is impossible to distinguish between clerks destined to remain in routine clerical work and those who are just passing through. Consequently, it is also impossible to ascertain whether the different objective circumstances of the various types of male clerk are reflected in different life-styles.

One may conclude that the intermediate class is unstructured. High rates of mobility prevent class stability, heterogeneous jobs inhibit common class experience, and life-styles are not distinctive. The intermediate class may have an analytical existence in sociology but it does not form a tangible collectivity with a distinctive social identity in the real world. Large sections of this class in any event properly belong in the working class if the principles of classification are followed strictly.

10 Classes and consciousness

The major approaches to class analysis treat the division between managers and lower level employees as an important class boundary. In Marxism it denotes the division between capital and labour. In orthodox sociology it marks a significant point of change in market and work situations and in life-styles. Both approaches regard relationships across this class boundary as having a conflict potential. Marxism contends that the potential for class conflict follows simply from the exploitative relationship between capital and labour. Some neo-Weberians see it differently, in terms of the ubiquitous competition for scarce resources manifest in the clash between workers' and managers' utilities, and the consequential strategies of exclusion and solidarism which embody conflicting class interests. Weber himself also emphasised the significance of the expropriation and subordination which lay behind the conflict between managers and workers, as was shown in Chapter 1. It is clear that, in either approach, industrial relations may be visualised as class relations and the regulation of industrial conflict as the institutionalisation of class conflict.

Class has subjective as well as objective features, in that people have views about their own position, the class to which they belong, and the relationships amongst classes. Modern sociology is concerned with the way that people perceive class, because it believes that these views provide a link between the objective features of the class system and social behaviour. The issues on which industrial sociologists concentrate arise out of the conflict potential that the class system contains. These are how people view the class system; how far members of a class are aware of the interests that they share with each other; how aware low-level employees are of the conflict of interest between the working and upper classes; what alternative forms of social and economic organisation are visualised; and what action people will take to realise these. An implicit assumption in much recent discussion is that, if the working class understood how the class system is constituted, then it might act to change the pattern of inequality, and this action would inevitably take the form of political action.

The Working Class

Sociological explanations of consciousness

The male manual working class in Britain since the Second World War has in fact shown little interest in bringing about radical change by political means. This apparent passivity has been the object of considerable sociological analysis. There are two types of explanation why it has not been more radical and active. The first claims that the working class is not homogeneous and that this affects subjective class perceptions. The second argues that the working class has been 'incorporated', that it has been indoctrinated by a dominant ideology which distorts the subjective awareness of class.

Homogeneity The argument about the lack of homogeneity moves from structural factors to consciousness. If labour is divided into segments with different life experiences, then there will not be sufficient unity of condition to promote the sorts of consciousness and action which might otherwise be expected. At one time it was the labour aristocracy which prevented a united class consciousness and class action, for it felt that it shared little in common with the rest of the working class. Nineteenth-century divisions clearly no longer segment labour. But the idea that fragmented consciousness follows structural divisions was given a new lease of life in the mid-1960s by the *Affluent Worker* research. Lockwood (1966) identified traditional proletarianism and affluence, two structural categories that have already been discussed, and a third category of the traditional deferential worker. Deference was associated with work that brought workers into persistent, face-to-face contact with paternalistic employers and with local communities in which there were frequent contacts between lower strata and the upper class. Agricultural workers and domestic servants were seen as the classic examples of the deferential working class.

The typical forms of consciousness believed to be associated with each of these categories can be summarised briefly. Traditional workers were supposed to have strong feelings of collective solidarity. Their work culture was based on comradeship and shared experience, and manifested itself in a close attachment to work groups. These groups formed the building blocks of wider community and class loyalties outside work. Collectivist values were heightened by the isolated and inward-looking nature of traditional communities. Collectivism was both solidaristic and oppositional: workers believed in the unity of the working class and the unity of the industrial and political wings of the labour movement, rejected middle-class individualism, and had a class-conscious social imagery. This image divided industry and society into two antagonistic classes, 'us' versus 'them', and the relationship between them reflected the greater power of the upper class at work and outside. This was therefore a 'power' model of society. The proletarian image that Lockwood described is one where people visualise class both as an objective social position and in relational terms, involving relations with other class members and between classes.

'Affluent' workers were presented as economic men, who regarded work simply as a means to earn money and did not invest it with a group or communal meaning. They were indifferent towards co-workers and individualistic in their outlook on many issues. This individualism led to the typical privatised, family-centred social life. Collectivist values still informed their social perspectives, however, because they realised that as individuals they were powerless to protect their interests. These collectivist tendencies had strongly instrumental overtones: trade unions were highly valued, but for the material benefits they would bring rather than as the result of some deeper collective or class loyalty. Their social imagery contained a 'money' model of society, which saw differences in spending capacity as the basis of stratification and was unconcerned with the relations between classes (though it did not deny that there were classes).

Deferential workers deferred socially and politically to people whom they recognised as their superiors. They voted Conservative because they believed that government should be in the hands of the country's 'natural' rulers. They had a vision of society as a status hierarchy rather than as a structure of class or money inequalities. This was the 'prestige' model of society.

The other modern structural segmentation theory, that of the so-called new working class, also has implications for consciousness. These are discussed below.

Incorporation and dual consciousness This approach minimises the importance of segmentation. Indeed, it assumes that working-class culture is uniformly distributed. Working-class perspectives, however, are thought to be shaped by social values from outside the working class. Dominant social values are hegemonic: they are all-embracing, set limits to people's social perceptions, even determine how people see themselves and society. At one time sociologists were little concerned with the origins of dominant values. Functionalists took it for granted that all societies needed shared values in order to cohere, and that this need explained why values existed. The popularisation of the Marxist view, that dominant values represent the ideological hegemony of a dominant class, challenged this perspective (Anderson, 1964). The newer view asserted that the working class may at times appear to have an independent consciousness, but in reality this is subordinated to and enclosed by the dominant culture. Action is shaped by what the dominant class can safely allow, which is trade union economism in industry and reformism in politics. This line of argument has given rise, in turn, to the notion of dual consciousness which is influential in contemporary industrial sociology.

Parkin (1972) distinguishes the dominant, subordinate and radical value systems in society. The dominant originates among those with power and advantage, and is embodied in the institutional order (for example, in the state, in education, even in the labour movement's own institutions). This value system legitimises inequality, and its institutional expression means that it permeates the consciousness of subordinate groups. While people accept dominant values, they add to them their own subordinate ones, which modify but do not destroy the system. Subordinate values are those of traditional working-class communities, such as an 'us' versus 'them' image of class and industrial relations and a belief in the distinctiveness of the working class. These are held to be 'accommodative' values which somehow reconcile people to their position in the class system. Trade union economism, for example, buttresses dominant values and the status quo says Parkin, since collective bargaining implies acceptance of the present economic and social order: 'Organised labour directs its main efforts towards winning a greater share of resources for its members – not by challenging existing frameworks of rules but by working within this framework' (1972, p. 91). Parkin believes that radical values are only found in socialist political parties. But as the British Labour Party has become less radical with time, it can no longer be a source of radical, oppositional views.

Mann (1970; 1973b) has a slightly different approach. Workers accept dominant values, he suggests, partly because they have been indoctrinated into these and partly because of a realistic, undistorted appraisal of the facts. For example, workers may accept the dominant value that stresses the need for industrial co-operation if workers' own interests are to be protected, because they see this to be factually correct within the existing economic system. Standing against the full acceptance of dominant values, however, is a commitment to 'deviant' values. Hence the dualism in working-class consciousness. Mann then suggests, however, that in reality workers may have few values of any description, and that they may accept the existing order on an unthinking, pragmatic basis. Mann thus has three accounts of why there is not a more active opposition: indoctrination; undistorted appraisals of self-interest; pragmatic apathy.

All incorporation accounts assert the confused nature of consciousness that arises out of dualism. Workers simultaneously endorse and reject different parts of the dominant value system. Sociologists within this tradition conclude that the dominant ideology disguises the true nature of the class system, inhibits a generalised sense of collective identity in the working class, and prevents a coherent critique of existing principles of stratification.

An evaluation

We can now assess the evidence for the claims that working class consciousness lacks homogeneity or displays an incorporated quality. Not surprisingly, the following pages show that both explanations of working-class quiescence are considerably exaggerated. Moreover, because of their concern for political action they ignore the great significance of working-class action in the economy.

Homogeneity Just as Chapter 9 demonstrated that the structural fragmentation of the working class is low, so the evidence of working-class consciousness demonstrates considerable unity. Inspired by Lockwood's typology, a number of investigations into working-class perspectives were carried out in the late 1960s and early 1970s. K. Roberts *et al.* (1977) found that the proletarian image of society, which embraced a power and conflict model of society, was dominant among the manual respondents to a survey in Liverpool. The basic difference was simply between the more and the less class-aware workers, that is, a variation in the intensity and consistency of proletarian consciousness which is a difference of degree rather than kind (1977, p. 55). The only separate image was an imprecise, 'bourgeois' model held by about a quarter of manual workers, who saw themselves in the middle class (1977, p. 50). Moorhouse (1976) has come to a similar conclusion after re-examining existing research: he notes the prevalence of a dichotomous, power-based social image throughout the working class. He suggests that there is really one working-class image that is articulated in a variety of terms and often imprecisely, rather than a variety of different images that are fairly precisely formulated. Workers are aware of their common identity and do understand the privileged and powerful position of the upper class. Moorhouse claims that the distinction between money and power models of stratification is an empty one, because the language of money is simply how people express power differences: a common finding is that people divide society into the rich and the poor, but this perspective should not be dismissed as 'simplistic' or 'populist' as some sociologists contend, because it constitutes the money representation of a dichotomous model. Wealth creates power so far as workers are concerned. In turn, power is expressed in the relationships between members of different classes.

These claims for the unity of consciousness are supported by two detailed case studies of supposedly deferential and traditional occupations. Newby found that only a small proportion of a sample of farmworkers adhered to a reasonably consistent deferential image of society (1977, p. 44). Most farmworkers were quiescent, which reflected their dependence on farmers for work and housing and had nothing to do with their social perspectives. Most were consistently and unambiguously proletarian. A large minority had less consistent, more ambiguous perspectives, though many of these farmworkers subscribed to some elements of the oppositional view. The investigation of London dockers found that in most respects their industrial attitudes and social perspectives resembled those of the Luton 'affluent' workers, even though Lockwood's classification placed them at opposite extremes of the working class (S. Hill, 1976b). Collective and oppositional values were typical of both groups. Dockers and 'affluent' workers clearly perceived the opposition of interests and the latent social conflict in industry, and both reported that the actual social relations between men and management remained peaceful while their instrumental demands were satisfied. Like the rest of the working class, dockers and 'affluent' workers advanced their interests by means of economic trade union strategies. Collectivism was an important industrial value for both groups, and involved a conception of trade union action for the defence of collective interests, though it did not extend to a conception of the united industrial and political labour movement in either case. Dockers vested this collectivism with a greater moral content than 'affluent' workers. There were also some differences of emphasis in social perspectives, since dockers gave somewhat more 'left-wing' answers to questions about power, social justice and inequality. However, their social imagery and models of social stratification were fairly similar to those of the Luton sample, supporting the view that money models are normal in the working class. This lends weight to the claim that the major difference within the working class is simply the strength with which workers subscribe to the proletarian image.

The evidence of the docks shows that industrial and socio-political imagery is related, but not in the direct way commonly assumed. Dockers appraised class relationships in society and politics as being manifestly antagonistic, but this appraisal went together with a peaceful view of the existing state of industrial relations in the docks. There was no question of dockers' views about overt conflict in society and industry going together. (It was noted in Chapter 2 that the docks were administered on delegated control principles and dockers had autonomy at work, which partly explains dockers' perceptions of management–labour relations.) But dockers were aware of the latent conflict, which suggests that, where it deals with opposition in industry, the proletarian image of society is concerned with the *structural* clash of interests. There need be no immediate link between how people experience actual social relations in industry at a particular time and their ongoing awareness of the structural conflict between opposed interests. Variations in workers' class consciousness or the strength with which they hold the proletarian social image are unlikely to predict with accuracy variations in industrial militancy, for instance the incidence of strikes. The proletarian image may contain a radical appraisal of society and politics without overt social conflict in industrial relations necessarily following.

The effect of including low-level, non-manual employees in the working class, as Chapter 9 showed they must be, is difficult to assess. There is no information about how women non-manual workers perceive class, yet they fill the bulk of routine occupations at this level. Most research into the perspectives of men does not clearly distinguish between those who share the proletarian situation and those who do not. Nevertheless, there are indications that the perspectives of some men in routine non-manual occupations may be converging on those of the manual working class. Clerks in the *Affluent Worker* research were almost as likely as manual workers to subscribe to certain elements of the oppositional ideology, believing that there was one law for the rich and another for the poor, and that big business had too much power in society (Goldthorpe *et al.*, 1968b, p. 26). There was evidence of some 'normative convergence' of clerks and manual workers (1969, p. 163), partly as the result of converging life-styles and partly just because of converging perspectives. However, a far smaller proportion of clerks than manual workers voted Labour and oppositional perspectives were not translated into voting behaviour in the same way. In *The Fragmentary Class Structure*, K. Roberts, *et al.* reported that proletarianised male white-collar workers at the base of the non-manual hierarchy, in routine jobs and with similar pay and status to manual workers, endorsed the oppositional and proletarian class perspective that was the norm for manual workers (1977, p. 139). This research highlights the importance of exactly locating different class positions among non-manual workers, and suggests that those who share the proletarian condition tend towards the proletarian social imagery.

Variations in working-class perspectives, between the more and the less proletarian, can partly be explained by the networks of social relationships within which people are enmeshed. The proletarian condition, consisting of low market rewards and a particular type of work situation, disposes workers towards a proletarian view of their place in society and a set of oppositional values. Within this overall tendency, different social settings may strengthen or weaken the predisposition. The extent to which people have friends and relatives in the manual working class and absorb working-class culture is important. Those with a more proletarian outlook tend to be more enmeshed in manual working-class society. Conversely, those with a weaker proletarian awareness or with a bourgeois perspective tend toward social relationships with non-manual workers (Goldthorpe *et al.*, 1968b; S. Hill, 1976b; K. Roberts *et al.*, 1977). So far as political radicalism is concerned, comparative international research shows that variations are associated to some extent with political socialisation: parents' political views and exposure to the ideology of radical political parties are both significant influences on political attitudes (Lash, 1980).

Incorporation If working-class perspectives are fairly homogeneous, how far is this unity the consequence of incorporation? To answer this question, it is first necessary to specify the dominant ideology or value system into which people are indoctrinated. This is no easy task, because the incorporation thesis does not spell out the content of the values in a coherent manner, nor in the real world are they self-evident. Following the account in Abercrombie, Hill and Turner, *The Dominant Ideology Thesis* (1980, Chapter 5), there would appear to be four significant elements: the ideology of accumulation and property; the managerial ideology; the ideology of state neutrality and welfare; bourgeois culture as ideology.

Sociologists commonly regard the rights of property as one of the 'core assumptions' of the capitalist order (Westergaard and Resler, 1975, p. 17). But the evidence does not unreservedly support this view. The principle of accumulation and some property rights are clearly part of dominant values: the gearing of economic activity to profit-making and the reproduction of capital, and the right to own property privately, are both central elements. But other property rights have a less certain place: the right to transfer property by means of inheritance and the right of owners alone to decide how to use or dispose of their property are not so well established in the dominant value system. This emerges if one considers the actions of those institutions that the incorporationists cite as representing upper-class interests, for example the state 'which is the political embodiment of the values and interests of the dominant class' (Parkin, 1972, p. 27). Taxation restricts inheritance, and other legislation has given non-owners the power to prevent owners using their property as they see fit (for example, tenants have rights against landlords and employees against employers). Nevertheless, many individuals within the upper class still subscribe to the traditional property values (Newby *et al.*, 1978).

The managerial ideology explains class stratification as income inequality (rather than as inequality of property and wealth) which is determined by the laws of supply and demand in the market-place or by the functional importance of various occupations. The importance of individual achievement is emphasised, in order to justify inequality as being inevitable and income differentials as fair and just. As is well known, this conceals a reality where privilege is often inherited and where the powerful to a great extent determine the qualities that are to be rewarded (Parkin, 1972, p. 27). This is a managerial ideology because it justifies the economic and social position of the relatively propertyless, managerial stratum in modern industry rather than the rights of property. It also justifies power and privilege within the firm by reference to managers' meritorious success and professionalism (see Chapter 2).

Values of state neutrality and welfare play an important part in the political culture of pluralist societies like Britain. The state is presented as neutral, even-handedly balancing the interests of a plurality of competing institutions and groups. If it has any bias, this is to mobilise resources for welfare purposes in order to alleviate the worst effects of inequality on the poor. At the same time, the state has an economic role, which is to maintain economic growth and business profitability. This is portrayed as a neutral activity which is in everyone's interest. The possibility that the state is not pluralist but 'capitalist', because its economic role means that it promotes the interests of those who own or control capital (see Chapter 11), is not raised.

The last element is bourgeois culture. The working class is thought to absorb this, in particular the value of individualism which colours all aspects of the dominant social value system. In addition, the cultural traits of empiricism, which inhibit philosophical thinking about the true nature of society, and deference to authority are present in the working class (Anderson, 1964).

The dominant value system is frequently inconsistent. The welfare policy of raising the poor above their market or functional worth conflicts with the managerialist perspective that wages ought to be determined by market principles or functional importance. State neutrality conflicts with the belief that the state should also promote the interests of capital accumulation. The rights of property lie uneasily with the managerial ideology of meritorious achievement, especially when property buys advantage for children and grandchildren. Nor do all dominant groups support all the dominant ideology, because there is a wide range of material interests within the upper class which leads different groups to respond differently to the various elements (Abercrombie, Hill and Turner, 1980, Chapter 5).

The British manual working class is *not* as well socialised into this dominant ideology as existing accounts suggest. Major parts of the ideology of property and accumulation are rejected. When people assert their tenant rights against landlords, they encroach on property rights in a way that is sanctioned by law. When they assert the legitimacy of squatting in empty houses, or the right to occupy factories which threaten to make workers redundant, they deny property rights in a more radical manner. Squats and factory occupations became a feature of working-class protest in the 1970s and they are often endorsed within the working class as legitimate actions (Moorhouse and Chamberlain, 1974). In some circumstances, for instance the right to own a second home, even the right to own property is rejected. Profit as the criterion of economic activity is frequently denied in favour of non-economic criteria, which is to reject the principle of accumulation itself (Moorhouse and Chamberlain, 1974). On the labour side, wage-bargaining embodies ideas about what is a just wage which depend on social rather than economic criteria and find no relevance in arguments about ability to pay, profitability, and the market principles of supply and demand. Appeals to need or customary differentials simply ignore the accumulation principle.

The managerial ideology is less challenged in one respect.

Workers tend to accept the *structure* of incomes as fair and endorse the meritorious justification of this in terms of individual achievement (Hyman and Brough, 1975, pp. 199–207). However, the actual *levels* of earnings, the cash values of the differentials between occupations, may be decisively rejected (Abercrombie, Hill and Turner, 1980, Chapter 5). Workers accept that they should be paid less than company directors, but also believe that existing differentials are too broad and cannot be justified. There is thus little effective normative consensus or feeling that existing pay arrangements are natural or legitimate. Indeed the opposite holds, because workers believe that they have a right to higher wages and the fruits of affluence enjoyed by others, and use their trade union strength to push for these. For these reasons, Goldthorpe (1978) suggests that when price inflation results from wage pressures, this is an indicator that dominant values and consensus have failed. Where the managerial ideology deals with power and privilege within industry rather than the occupational structure of wages, then it is challenged. Workers reject the implications of the firm as an organic community with a harmony of interests and the justification of managerial power, as Chapter 2 showed. At the same time, there is a rejection of authority and no consensus of values in British industrial relations, as Chapter 7 demonstrated. In other words, it is in the *economic* and not the political sphere that the incorporation thesis breaks down with the most concrete results: excessive wage demands and chaotic industrial relations are proof that dominant values and regulatory institutions cannot maintain the normative consensus which is required to contain conflicting interests. The disruption of the economy rather than political *incivisme* is the consequence of the failure of normative regulation to preserve class harmony.

There is little to suggest a generalised acceptance of the picture of a pluralistic liberal democracy. Opinion surveys show that most manual workers believe that big business has too much power in society and over government, that there is one law for the rich and another for the poor, that the upper class is hostile to working-class interests, that government is not disinterested between interest groups, that ordinary people have little influence over government (Abercrombie, Hill and Turner, 1980, Chapter 5). Even the master symbols of the political system, the House of Lords and the Monarchy, receive only lukewarm support (McKenzie and Silver, 1968, pp. 145–52). Nor is there evidence that working-class culture, with its oppositional and collective values, has been much permeated by bourgeois culture.

The amount by which the British working class deviates from the dominant value system is greater than the major dual consciousness accounts have suggested. It is greater than the equivalent disparity between working-class and dominant values that exists in the U.S. (Huber and Form, 1973, pp. 100–16). These deviant values are also more radical and less vague in their conception of alternatives than present dual consciousness accounts credit. This is suggested by the critical appraisal of property rights and the principle of accumulation, and the acceptance of alternative criteria on which to base economic activity. Socialist ideologies have become less significant in the mainstream of the labour movement since the war, but the historical legacy of an earlier radicalism remains within contemporary working-class consciousness in the elevation of need over profit and property. This component of the radical value system has not disappeared just because the Labour Party is committed to the dominant value system (Moorhouse, 1976).

Conventional accounts are nearer the mark when they note the lack of coherence within working-class consciousness. The rejection of the dominant ideology is not complete and some elements are indeed endorsed. It has been suggested that these may have negative rather than positive effects, that although they do not incorporate people or bring about social cohesion they perhaps inhibit and confuse the formulation of coherent alternatives. The partial acceptance of meritorious, achievement values has been cited in this context (Offe, 1976). This suggestion is difficult to prove or disprove. What is clear is that people manage to accommodate a variety of perceptions which often appear inconsistent to sociologists. Any lack of coherence is of course hardly surprising, when coherent, well-formed and clearly-articulated philosophies are rare in *all* social classes, including the upper.

Accounts of the social stability of class societies that depend on normative integration, which include modern theories of incorporation and traditional sociological assumptions about shared values and common cultures, exaggerate the importance of values. They regard social harmony between classes as essential for stability, and interpret working-class acquiescence in the status quo as endorsement of the values underlying class relations. Yet, as some sociologists recognise, the stability and integration of a society may be unrelated to shared values, even to social harmony. Lockwood (1964) has suggested that attention should be focused on *system integration*. This term captures the sense in which a complex division of labour establishes interdependencies which must be realised, indeed usually are realised. System integration may rest on the self-interest of workers and on various forms of external constraint.

Self-interest leads workers to perform their roles, because this role-performance maintains a system on which they depend, which is why for instance they co-operate with management in the production of goods. Workers depend on capitalism for their livelihoods. It would only be in labour's interests to transform the economic and social system if there were a real chance that the alternative would reduce domination at work and in society, if the material benefits that have already accrued within the capitalist framework were not jeopardised in the change, and if the individual freedoms associated with bourgeois individualism were also maintained. The experience of state socialism, the most widely-spread alternative, suggests that none of these conditions is easy to fulfil. Postwar capitalism in advanced societies has undoubtedly increased the stock of wealth and raised everyone's living standards, whatever conflicts of interest it may create over the way wealth is distributed and the manner in which surplus is extracted. A significant effect of the increased affluence and mass consumption has been to reduce the intensity of these conflicts though not to conceal them. Capitalism has typically tolerated a wide range of individual freedoms which may benefit workers as well as others. Provided that workers in practice do their jobs, system integration is not destroyed by the rejection of dominant values or non-violent social conflict in industry. Pragmatic acceptance, rather than normative consensus or endorsement, is what matters for system integration. In addition, the overwhelming inertia and 'facticity' of existing social arrangements may inhibit even the consideration of any major transformation (Abercrombie, Hill and Turner, 1980, Chapter 6). Equally, there are forces of *compulsion* which reinforce integration. These include the compulsion of economic relations, which derives from the fact that people need to work in order to live and managers have power over employment and within the enterprise. They also include legal and political compulsions, exceptionally even the use of force, which contain any threats to system integration posed by the weakness of social integration.

The new working class

An argument popular outside Britain in the 1960s related variations in consciousness and action to the evolution of production technology and the structural differentiation of labour that follows. In America, Blauner (1964) suggested that automation would increase the social integration of workers. Mass production industry had created a type of worker who combined a generalised hostility to existing society with aggressive trade unionism and other forms of militant industrial action. Automation was thought to remove the sources of alienation in work, thus to abolish hostility and militant action. Mallet (1963 [1975]), in complete contrast, argued that automation in France led to new forms of class consciousness and action, which initially threatened the structure of the capitalist firm and then capitalist society itself. Once modern workers learned that they controlled the plant and were indispensable to its operations, and saw through the contradictions of capitalism, their objectives shifted from trade union-style economistic aspirations to demands for industrial control. High technology capitalism satisfied workers' material needs, allowing them to turn to issues of managerial control and private property. Thus members of the new working class came to see industrial relations in terms of the fundamental conflict between capital and labour, and established the goals of action as the control of economic decisions in companies and the economy as a whole.

Both views are wrong. Chapter 9 showed that advanced technology is not an important source of structural differentiation within the working class. The discussion of Blauner in Chapter 5 showed that technology does not determine integration within the enterprise and workers' consciousness. The evidence for Mallet's position is no more convincing. The illustrations used to substantiate his thesis show that the new working class posed little threat to French capitalism in the 1960s, contrary to what he claims. The control demands involved the sorts of limited restrictions on managerial prerogative in the workplace mentioned in Chapter 7 which British labour in advanced and traditional sectors of the economy had long enjoyed without seriously threatening capitalism or the individual firm. Indeed, it is more likely that it was because France remained for so long a relatively underdeveloped economy and society and had only in the postwar period completed the process of industrialisation that such labour relations issues seemed so radical. After all, trade unions in France have only legally existed inside the factory since 1968 and local collective bargaining has been recognised only since 1971 (Reynaud, 1978, pp. 108–14). To judge by Mallet's remarks, French managers retain very traditional notions about property rights and managerial prerogatives. His evidence points more to the old-fashioned nature of managerial ideology than to any modernity of the new working class, as Gallie (1978) has shown in his discussion of contemporary French industrial relations. Subsequently, in the 1970s, the new working class in France became quiescent: its industrial activity was low key and its demands were those of moderate trade unionism. At this time, the locus of industrial militancy shifted to the unskilled working class of the economically and technologically backward sectors, which deals a major blow to Mallet's thesis (Low-Beer, 1978, pp. 21–2). Investigation into new working class consciousness in France and Italy indicates that it has been exaggerated in both countries (Gallie, 1978; Low-Beer, 1978).

Intermediate and Upper Classes

Social class imagery

Investigations of the social class imagery and the perspectives of the old British middle class, following the traditional manual–non-manual division, found that middle-class members were better socialised into dominant values and had a less oppositional perspective than the working class (Mann, 1970). The reduced social coherence of the old middle class has been accompanied by the growth of a variety of distinct types of class awareness. The most widely-held image among the middle ranks of the male non-manual hierarchy, above the proletarianised segment, is that of the middle mass (K. Roberts *et al.*, 1977, pp. 135–7). This middle mass is positioned literally at the centre of the social hierarchy, between a small upper class of the rich and the powerful and a small lower class of the underprivileged. People who place themselves in this class are aware of material inequalities within the middle mass, but not of cleavage and conflict. They recognise no ideological splits, divisions of interest nor contrasts of life-style within the middle mass. Unlike the working class, they do not give class a relational aspect: the middle mass is amorphous and has no sense of its own collective identity or solidarity; nor does it refer to the relations between different classes, whether of conflict or otherwise. 'It is essentially a collection of individuals enjoying similar privileges and life-styles, rather than a class with a clear and distinctive sense of its interests and proper place in the world' (K. Roberts *et al.*, 1977, p. 138).

The middle-mass image is most commonly found among the organisation men who fill the central ranks of large-scale organisations, including managers, professionals and administrators, and among those in intermediate occupations who anticipate moving into these ranks. The remnants of the old middle class, that is the local bourgeoisies of small businessmen and self-employed professionals, and managers and administrators who have risen by the traditional means of long service, have a different image of society. They visualise a small middle class, to which they belong, that is squeezed between a much larger working class and an upper class of the more wealthy and powerful. They see themselves in an insecure position, their interests threatened by the more powerful working class (K. Roberts *et al.*, 1977, pp. 114–15). They appear to see class in relational terms, as one class 'doing' something to another, as well as a descriptive category. Furthermore, they have an awareness of shared class interests within the middle class. The other deviation from mainstream images is found in the intelligentsia. The social hierarchy here is seen as finely graded. Movement upwards reflects individual ability and achievement. Mistakenly, sociologists have in the past seen this as the *typical* form of non-manual social perspective. This 'ladder' model has two significant characterisitcs. No one stratum emerges as much larger than any other, nor is any stratum seen as a real group with a clear boundary and its own distinct class interests. Much of the educated and affluent professional section of the upper class subscribes to this image.

These three images of the class structure are of course ideal types, and their coherence and distinctiveness have deliberately been emphasised. Each type contains variations and ambiguities, but they are presented in order to give precise form to a blurred reality. They do approximate reality, however, and show how different intermediate and upper-class groups have different perceptions of the class system, their place in it, and the relations between classes.

It is noticeable that the characteristic perspective of management differs sharply from that of manual and clerical workers. The people who fill the bottom positions in firms have an awareness of class relationships. In varying degrees they see themselves as part of a corporate group whose members share interests and which stands in a relationship to other classes. Typically, inter-class relations are perceived in 'us' and 'them' terms, which at the very least highlight the differences between workers and managers and usually refer to the potential conflict between the two sides of industry. Managers do not see class or industry in these terms. This difference is part of the wider cultural separation of managerial and low-level employees in Britain which can also be found in other aspects of social consciousness and life-styles. Class has the effect of dividing British industry into substantially different worlds.

One may speculate about the consequences of this division for relations in industry. The anomic state of workplace industrial relations, marked by the weakness of shared values, reflects this deep cultural separation between workers and managers. Moreover, proletarian imagery creates an expectation among low-level employees that employment will bring them into conflict with their bosses and that collective unity will be necessary to defend their interests, whereas the managerial image emphasises unity and individualism. This difference is part of the explanation why managerial philosophy emphasises a harmony of interests (despite the concrete practice of management) which is denied by the labour force. At the most general level, one significant contribution to the suspicions and misunderstandings which are so often found in the conduct of British industrial relations is the different and class-specific perceptions of the world with which each side confronts the other.

Non-manual trade unionism

Non-manual employees provide the most rapidly growing section of the British trade union movement: between 1964 and 1974, the proportion of the unionised non-manual labour force grew by a third, from about 30 to about 40 per cent (Price and Bain, 1976). In certain areas, notably central and local government, teaching and banking, union densities are high even by manual trade union standards. Nor is unionism confined to the bottom of the hierarchy, to routine white-collar employees, for it occurs extensively among intermediate occupations and to a lesser extent in the upper reaches of the non-manual labour force. At the same time, some non-manual unions have begun to follow the tactics of manual unions and have become more aggressive or 'militant' in their methods. What are the implications of these developments for consciousness?

The starting point in most sociological analyses is an assumption that *manual* unionism is a class movement that indicates class attitudes. What then follows is a second assumption that trade unionism and class should be studied together, specifically that class imagery, union membership and union character are linked. Within this framework there are two different approaches. The one common in British sociology links unionism and proletarianism. In a study of clerical unionism, Lockwood (1958) suggested that the more the class situation of non-manual employees comes to resemble that of manual workers, the more likely is union density to increase and union behaviour to resemble that of manual workers. Professional associations have been separated from trade unions in sociological analysis, because they are seen as the characteristic middle-class organisations that reflect the allegedly typical image of society as a prestige hierarchy, a ranking of statuses rather than classes, through which people move by their own individual efforts (Prandy, 1965). Professional associations are status bodies which seek to enhance professional prestige. Unions are seen as class bodies that reflect their members' proletarian social image and engage in collective bargaining with employers. Their class ideology is held to be incompatible with the status ideology of the professions (Prandy, 1965). The other, American view suggests that non-manual employees unionise for different reasons and in different types of organisation than manual workers. Mills has claimed that they unionise for 'instrumental' reasons, as a simple economic calculation, and that their unions are solely economic instruments which advance their own sectional interests (1953, pp. 308–9). Unionism does not necessarily destroy the typical individualism and status awareness of the old middle class in this account, unlike the British view, though it does pose a trade-off problem. Non-manuals have to weigh the instrumental advantages of unionism against their own moral objections and the loss of prestige they will experience as unionists.

A model of what is called *unionateness* has been developed in order to capture what are believed to be differences among union types (Blackburn, 1967). This model specifies the major qualities of manual unionism, including collective bargaining, willingness to strike, affiliation to the Trades Union Congress and to the Labour Party. Non-manual unions are thought to have less of this 'unionate' quality and to show fewer of the class attributes of traditional unionism, being less likely to affiliate to other class agencies or to display militant industrial action. An international comparison shows that non-manual unions, except in Japan, strike less, rarely affiliate to manual union confederations (Britain is unusual in not having a separate non-manual confederation in parallel to the TUC), and do not recruit manual members (Sturmthal, 1966).

Non-sociologists specialising in the study of industrial relations criticise the linking of unionism and class (Bain *et al.*, 1973). They propose instead that all employees attempt to regulate their jobs and to influence the terms and conditions of their employment, and that some form of collective activity, which may involve conflict with employers, will be used to this end. It is an implication of this approach that sociologists have too restricted a definition of collective action when they concentrate on unions, because staff and professional associations are also agencies for the advancement of collective interests. 'Unionateness' can in fact cope with other forms of collective representation, and sociologists have used it in an attempt to show that staff and professional associations are different with respect to collective bargaining, militancy of actions, and affiliation to the TUC and Labour Party (Blackburn and Prandy, 1965; Blackburn, 1967). However, the union–non-union difference has been greatly overdrawn by sociologists. There are some staff associations, notably in banking, and professional associations, including that of doctors, which have for years bargained collectively and used sanctions against their employers (O. Robinson, 1969; Lumley, 1973). Doctors and university teachers in the 1970s affiliated to the TUC. Many staff associations have evolved into bodies that are more independent of employers and more militant: in some cases they have registered themselves as trade unions, in others they have merged with existing unions. In other words, traditional non-manual organisations have been capable of adopting collectivist strategies and pursuing industrial conflict.

The changing strategies of non-manual unions, staff and professional associations suggest that in practice the intermediate and upper classes are not always averse to 'class' actions of a collectivist and oppositional nature. In their survey, K. Roberts *et al.* found that non-manual respondents were no more likely to object on principle to trade unionism than the manual sample, and that nearly half of their 'middle mass' managers, administrators and professionals were indeed members of trade unions themselves (1977, p. 131). A study of unionised technicians found that the main impetus toward unionisation was the desire to maintain customary pay differentials over manual workers and to oblige managers to recognise technicians' aspirations for a career route into management (B. C. Roberts *et al.*, 1973). Technicians identified with management but felt that they had been unfairly treated. An investigation of airline pilots found a somewhat similar situation, in this case of professional employees reluctantly forced into collective action in order to defend themselves against their employer's failure to recognise their legitimate financial and control requirements (Blain, 1972). On social and political issues, pilots were conservative and typical of the professional stratum. However, both technicians and pilots are highly 'unionate', being TUC affiliates and with a reputation for militant trade unionism.

The 'industrial relations' approach correctly points to the difficulty of finding a clear relationship amongst class position, social class image and industrial relations activity, specifically trade unionism. Analytically, using the concepts of class theory, sociologists may see unionism as class action, as a solidaristic strategy used by subordinate classes to wrest something from those who control resources. However, this sociological description does not mean that unionists themselves therefore necessarily have a well-developed, class-conscious perspective or see unionism in terms of class struggle. This applies equally to non-manual *and* manual unionists. Unionism is by nature a form of collective organisation that reflects people's awareness of distinct collective interests and the need for collective action. It also embodies the understanding that interests conflict in employment. Instrumental collectivism is quite commonly the meaning that manual workers give to their unionism: a calculation that their own material interests are best served by collective organisation (Goldthorpe *et al.*, 1968a; S. Hill, 1976b; K. Roberts *et al.*, 1977). This has a long history in working-class culture. As Chapter 7 made clear, American and British workers have joined unions that represent the sectional, selfish interests of occupations and jobs and impede broader class organisation. Instrumentalism is also likely when trade unionism is so firmly established that membership becomes in effect a condition of employment, which is the case in many firms, and some manual workers with little commitment to broader union goals will have joined unions. Proletarian clerks, 'middle-mass' technicians and traditional middle-class airline pilots indicate that collective activity is a well-established strategy among the successors to the old middle class. 'Unionate' unionism is compatible with a variety of social perspectives, and on its *own* reveals only that collective action is seen to be useful and that employers and employees are not thought to have the same interests.

11 The state and the economy

A Politicised Economy

Modern capitalism works within a political economy. The state is directly involved in the internal workings of the economy; economic activity is bound up with politics rather than remaining separate; and the economic system is regulated from outside rather than regulating itself. The nature and extent of state involvement varies from society to society, however. In this chapter the link between the state and economic life is considered in the light of what has gone before, paying special attention to issues of industrial relations.

An influential but one-sided account of the history of capitalist industrialism suggests that nineteenth-century capitalism was based on *laissez-faire* principles, that these were progressively eroded in the second and third quarters of the twentieth century, and state-directed capitalism was well-established by the last quarter (Scott, 1979, pp. 145–50; Strinati, 1979). According to this account, early, *laissez-faire* capitalism was marked by an autonomous economy which was left alone to deal with its own crises, and to reproduce itself over time. Economic life was based on individualism, competition amongst large numbers of firms, and self-regulation of the economy by market mechanisms. This was a fragmented and anarchical economic system. Government had an economic role, which was to create an appropriate external environment for profitable business but not to intervene directly in economic processes. The state performed mainly 'allocative' functions (Offe, 1975), which meant allocating resources that it already controlled, such as taxation and public expenditure, but not taking a directly productive role in accumulation. The state promoted business activity in a variety of non-interventionist ways: by means of foreign policy and state purchasing that favoured domestic industry; by financing from public funds the social and physical infrastructures of industrialism that were essential for economic activity, but which private capital found too expensive or unprofitable (for example, public spending on education, roads and public health); by developing appropriate legal forms for business activity, such as joint-stock companies, limited liability and the legal regulation of industrial relations; and by preserving public order. The state occasionally did intervene more directly in economic processes, for example when factory legislation regulated the hours and conditions of employment in Britain. Characterisations of *laissez-faire* capitalism tend to ignore this type of interventionism.

Between the wars governments became more interventionist, according to this account imposing protective tariffs against outside competition, using state expenditure on public works or armaments in order to manipulate the level of economic activity, and after the Second World War developing budgetary techniques for 'fine tuning' the economy. Indirect regulation by means of demand management then shaded gradually into direct state regulation, whereby governments took on a new role for themselves. This involved planning the economy. It also involved restructuring and regenerating private business, so as to give the state directly productive functions in the process of capital accumulation. The state achieved this by using its power as a purchaser of goods and services, by means of state investment, subsidisation, or even public ownership, by directing private investment, and by regulating company formation (by controlling mergers and take-overs and sponsoring new firms for example). The new role further involved the state in controlling wages, salaries and prices. In these ways the economy became politically organised.

This account generalises from the experiences of a small number of capitalist economies that indeed went through a liberal or *laissez-faire* phase, America, Britain and Sweden being notable examples. It does *not*, however, describes the more common type of capitalist industrialism where the economy was politicised from the outset. It is a one-sided history of economic development. Capitalist industrialism in Japan and most of continental Europe, for example, was always marked by state interventionism and close control of all aspects of economic life (Landes, 1965; Henderson, 1975; Sumiya and Taira, 1979). Within Europe, the French, German and Italian governments are clear examples of how the state in the nineteenth and twentieth centuries controlled and sponsored the capitalist economy. The state was involved in the following activities: directly subsidising private entrepreneurs; directing and often controlling credit and investment capital; setting up state-owned firms (notably in Germany and Italy); regulating labour and product markets by political means; establishing protective tariffs; granting monopoly rights to produce certain goods or to sell in certain markets; granting government contracts. Detailed control of economic life was regarded as essential, for reasons of national power, state revenues and social order (Landes, 1965).

Despite this evidence to the contrary, there was long a *belief* that the natural form of capitalism involved an autonomous economy, self-regulation by means of the market forces of competition amongst units of capital, and individualistic values. This belief lay behind the institutionalisation of conflict thesis discussed in earlier chapters. It explains why pluralists and others greatly exaggerated the extent to which the political and economic realms were separated, and the faith such writers had about the neutrality of government between different interests on those occasions when they conceded that intervention occurred. Germany has developed a more independent economy with less state intervention since the Second World War (Küster, 1974), but with this exception the tendency has been the other way. The growing scale and changing nature of state involvement in the old *laissez-faire* economies in the postwar era, together with the new intellectual justification of this role (initially in Keynesian economics), has highlighted the real role of the state rather than concealing it. There is now a growing interest in the role of state activity in a politicised rather than a nominally autonomous economy. The sociological analysis of government's economic role has been heavily influenced by the Marxist perspective, that the state is 'capitalist'. This suggests that state activity is not neutral in the economy between the interests of capital and labour, nor in the struggle between the social classes that form around economic interests. Crouch (1979) contends that the pluralist view of the state has largely disappeared from contemporary discussion. This chapter looks at the modern accounts of the linkage between the state and the economy and the evidence for these. Industry is greatly influenced by state activity and the profitability of private enterprise depends to a large extent on government. Moreover, the state may have an effect on the structure of social relations and the balance of power within individual firms themselves. Several instances have been noticed before. The totality of government's economic and social policies creates an environment which favours one side or other of industry, while policy in the specific area of industrial relations has a more direct influence on the manner in which conflicting interests are resolved. In the course of this discussion the modern approach to the state will be shown to have various shortcomings and the range of different forms of the state to be considerable.

The Theory of the Capitalist State

The state can be described as a set of institutions or apparatuses comprising the legislature, the executive, central administration (the civil service), the judiciary, the police and local government. The variety of institutions indicates that the state may not be a unitary or homogeneous body. The state is the institutional system of political domination (Jessop, 1978), with a monopoly over the legitimate use of violence and over taxation and money supply. The state is not by definition capitalist, but becomes so, according to Marxist theory, when its role becomes to organise structures indispensable for the functioning of a capitalist economy and when it acts to promote capital accumulation (Strinati, 1979).

Instrumentalism and structuralism

Marxists at one time regarded the state as an instrument of the capitalist class (Miliband, 1969). The instrumentalist perspective is that the state acts in the interests of capital because the personnel of state apparatuses come from the same social origins as capitalists, or are more receptive to pressure from business interests than from other social groups. In addition, instrumentalism mainly refers to the conscious intentions of actors in order to explain how the connection between state personnel and capitalism operates. This perspective provides a simple, direct and clearly comprehensible link between state and economy which, if true, would account for why state activity is likely to support capital.

In two well-documented examples, America and Britain, there is evidence that may perhaps support the instrumentalist case. Mills once claimed that a business 'power élite' dominated the executive organs of American government and filled the 'command posts' of the state (1956, p. 267). The factual basis of this view has been endorsed by modern studies, which show that in every administration this century at least 60 per cent of U.S. cabinet members have come from a business background (Freitag, 1975; Mintz, 1975). The proportion has increased in the postwar era. A similar link between state personnel and business or propertied interests has been found in Britain (Guttsman, 1963 and 1974; Miliband, 1969; Roth, 1973). But instrumentalism does *not* explain state policies elsewhere. It does not explain why in Sweden, for example, where working-class interests are well-represented in the state's power-élite (Scase, 1977, pp. 72–5), and where organised labour is the major interest group within the political system, the state should for so long have supported the capitalist economy. From 1932 until the late 1960s, the Social Democratic Party (SAP) when in office had a policy of creating a profitable economic environment for private business. The 'historic compromise' between private ownership of the economy and socialist control of politics was the understanding that the state would work for economic growth and the maturation of capitalism (Korpi, 1978, pp. 80–6). In the early 1970s, after four decades of social democratic government, only 5 per cent of the Swedish industrial base was publicly owned (Ohlin, 1974).

A second Marxist account of state activity is now more fashionable: the structuralist perspective. The relationship between capital and the state is expressed in terms of structures rather than the class origins of élites. Structuralism suggests that capitalism has certain economic, political and ideological requirements that are to be met in part by the state. Regardless of the conscious intentions of individual members of the state apparatus, the effects of state activity are to support capital. Cases such as Sweden which do not fit the older model should in theory be more adequately explained in this account. In addition, the unwarranted tendency of instrumentalism to fuse into one totality the state and capital, or politics and economics, is avoided. A key feature of structuralism is to treat the state as *relatively autonomous* of the economy. One of the reasons for this is that the state is now correctly seen as a balancer of political forces rather than as an instrument. It is asserted that the state can serve the collective purposes of capitalists and the functional needs of the capitalist system without acting as the direct representative of the capitalist class (Parkin, 1979, p. 192). The state needs relative autonomy of economic interests precisely because it has to take actions designed to preserve capitalism as a total system. Some long-term policies may conflict with the short-term interests of businessmen. Moreover, capital is fragmented into segments (for example, into large- and small-scale capital, industrial, financial and landed capital) whose interests conflict, and the state must promote collective rather than sectional ends (Poulantzas, 1973). Another feature of some structuralist accounts is to suggest that the state itself may depend on the capitalist mode of production, because it relies on taxation and borrowing for its own existence (O'Connor, 1973).

This approach has its merits, notably the insistence that state policies are constrained, whatever the backgrounds or intentions of state personnel, and the state is not simply an outpost of a dominant class. But several substantial criticisms can be levelled at it. It does not adequately explain *why* the state is capitalist, because it does not specify the mechanisms linking the state to the requirements of capitalism. The functionalist assumption, that the state is capitalist because the economy is capitalist and makes certain demands on the state, is hardly satisfactory. In order to break entirely with instrumentalism, structuralism mistakenly denies the significance of action and the role of the human subject (Poulantzas, 1976). This means that no account is given of why political actors end up supporting capitalism, apart from ill-defined, vague notions of the logic of capitalism and the systemic links between state and economy. However if state activity is a political balance, a compromise among different interests (including labour) that are represented politically, and if the state has some autonomy to determine how this balance is struck, then more weight must be given to action explanations of why the state is capitalist.

'Relative autonomy' is ambiguous. One interpretation is that the state may become an independent institution with its own corporate group which is largely or perhaps entirely divorced from any dominant class. If this is the case, then the state will have its own independent effectiveness and the state bureaucracy will be an autonomous political actor. This raises interesting possibilities which modern Marxists appear unwilling to consider: namely, that the state and its bureaucracy may come to dominate society as Weber predicted; or that in democratic political systems non-capitalist interests may come to control state power, even to use this against the interests of capital. As presently used, 'relative autonomy' conveys the Marxist belief that real autonomy of this sort is not possible. As Parkin remarks, if such developments are ruled out then it is difficult to see that relative autonomy is a useful notion (1979, pp. 119–41). It in fact disguises a covert form of instrumentalism, if all that it means is that the state represents a functional differentiation of the 'executive committee' of the bourgeoisie from the wider body, as the result of a simple division of labour. Parkin prefers an openly instrumentalist perspective, in which state activity is the outcome of struggle between the different sections of capital and between capital and labour. Thus, if the state promotes working-class interests (for example, in trade union legislation), this is not to be explained as a relatively autonomous state acting in the long-term collective interests of capital, buying industrial peace at the cost of the immediate interests of business, but as the result of the struggle between labour and capital, each striving to use the state as its own instrument. Parkin believes that class conflict and the balance of class advantage are sufficient to explain state policies (1979, pp. 119–41).

A satisfactory account therefore must do four things. In the first place it requires an action element, because the capitalist state is ultimately the outcome of people acting to maintain capitalism. This outcome may result, for example, from an autonomous state bureaucracy finding itself under environmental constraints, such as the requirement to promote a profitable economy in order to finance state expenditure, which is one plausible account of the links between structure and action. It may also be an outcome because some particular state has in fact become the instrument of its bourgeoisie. Secondly there needs to be a proper account of the state realm. Assumptions about the state simply being a cipher run by the instruments of capital or responding to functional imperatives ignore the character of the state as a separate institution with its own actors and decision-making rules. Autonomy from the capitalist class and economy must in principle be possible, or there is in fact no need for a separate state theory. The state can have its *own* influence on the economy and class relations. For example, when industrial relations policy supports one side of industry against the other. Analysis of the state realm shows that the state does not function as a unit but contains a variety of apparatuses with different personnels and responsive to different interests. Typically, some parts of the state are more responsive to popular interests than others. In Britain, for example, parliament has been more responsive to trade unionism than has the judiciary, which has tended to support property (W. Wedderburn, 1971). The pattern of differentiation varies from state to state. The third feature is an explanation of how capitalist states flourish in political systems that are based on universal suffrage. A fundamental issue for Marxist state theory is why the mass electorate does not reject a political system that favours capitalism. The fourth derives from the others. This is the recognition that the modern state, like the economy, may also be an arena of conflict between business and labour. Such conflict becomes manifest in political struggles within the state itself. Politics are concerned to contain the conflict and the political realm develops its own procedures for this task.

The fact that democratic political systems regularly produce states which support capitalism suggests that mass electorates and government bureaucracies at least tolerate the capitalist state. Toleration need imply no endorsement, but while the economy is capitalist and while both the state personnel and the mass electorate depend on the prosperity of the existing economic system for their own material welfare, then the link is likely to survive. Chapter 10 mentioned various reasons why people tend not to work for major, systemic transformations but acquiesce in the status quo, including the costs of change and uncertainty whether an alternative form of economic organisation would in practice be significantly better. Given capitalism, governments depend for their own survival on it being prosperous. They need to raise finance to pay for the state apparatus and to provide employment for state personnel. They also depend on being voted into office, and depressed economies lose votes. Likewise the electorate expects the state to maintain economic prosperity. There is some commonality of interest here between capital and labour, because a prosperous capitalism may also enhance the material welfare of labour. The interests of autonomous state apparatuses, the way the political markets for votes work in democracies, and the absence of any serious popular pressure for political initiatives fundamentally to transform the economy are all explanations which refer to *political actors*. They are all important reasons *why* there is a systemic link between state and economy.

This is not to say that states always manage successfully to promote business interests. The conflict of interests in the economy means that popular demands reflected in state policy may be more than the economic system can tolerate, even though the destruction of the system may not be an issue for the electorate. This is especially true of the cumulative effect of popular demands. The success with which different states resolve this dilemma depends both on the amount of popular acquiescence in the existing form of economic organisation, which in turn is influenced by the material prosperity that the economy generates, and the manner in which labour interests are politically represented.

The political mediation of interests

The representation of interests is a vitally important variable. Nevertheless this has largely been ignored in the modern account of the state. Political parties have a central role in connecting state action and the various political forces in society at large. The role of parties is to give organised expression to interests and make them politically effective. They mediate the linkage between democratic pressures and the policy outcomes of state activity. Moreover, parties in turn do not passively reflect interests but help to structure the way interests are perceived. Labour interests are represented in different ways in different societies and the influence of the working class on state policies varies widely. At one extreme the working class is effectively outside the state. At the other, its interests are politically very influential. This variability explains why the theory of the capitalist state may perhaps establish broad generalisations but does not account for specific instances.

Sweden and Britain show how the political mediation of democratic pressures has so far sustained capitalism. In both states working-class interests are politically influential, more so in Sweden than Britain. The working class and organised labour in Sweden is politically the most important interest and others have far less access to the state. For most of the period since 1932 the Social Democratic Party has been in office, sometimes in coalition with other parties representing non-labour interests. Despite a firm ideological commitment to socialism, the political strategy of the party from the 1930s at least until the late 1960s was deliberately and consciously reformist (Korpi, 1978, pp. 80–5): to use state power to transform society gradually, first destroying the political power of capital and then socialising the realm of distribution by means of regressive taxation, redistributive social welfare expenditure and greater social equality. In the long term the state would socialise the means of production. In the meantime, private capitalism was to be encouraged to become more efficient in order to improve the material prosperity of labour, finance the welfare state, and accelerate the 'maturation' of capitalism prior to its socialisation. Socialisation still remains far off, but from the late 1960s onwards the state began to intervene more in the economy in order to reduce the power of capital to control economic activity in its own private interests, in particular dealing with the problems of regional development and structural change. The specific policy aims that the government has pursued have scarcely differed from those pursued elsewhere (Ohlin, 1974). Intervention in the social relations of production within the business enterprise has now established an element of economic democracy, by providing workers with the legal right to participate in decision-making at the workplace and company levels and restricting managers' right to hire and fire. In the unions there is now the feeling that the limits of reformism may have been reached, that the way private capitalist firms are run involves unacceptable human costs and that production in mature capitalism is social in nature (Korpi, 1978, p. 310). Therefore the union wing of the labour movement advocates the gradual socialisation of the economy (see Chapter 8). The political party has not yet endorsed this policy, but there is obviously the possibility that some future Social Democratic government may come to office with this commitment and act on it. Should this happen, it would indicate that under specific conditions state power may be used to destroy as well as protect a capitalist economy.

It is important to appreciate that political processes may in turn react back on how the working class perceives its interests. The anti-capitalist ideology of the labour movement fosters an oppositional consciousness among Swedish workers, but at the same time the success of the party in capturing the state and the claim that it has used state power to make society more equal reduce the popular pressure to destroy capitalism in the economy (Scase, 1977, pp. 168–9).

The Labour Party in Britain can be seen as an integrative party which has worked to prevent economic conflict from creating class-based schisms in society at large (Panitch, 1976). The integrative core of Labour's ideology means that its political objectives are not defined as in Sweden as the conquest of power by the working class, but as the preservation of 'social harmony and class collaboration' (Panitch, 1976, p. 1). The Labour Party is a *national* rather than a class party. It integrates organised labour into the national political system, and the two wings of the labour movement have promoted social stability. Working-class gains appear to have been less substantial in Britain than Sweden. In the areas of social welfare, income redistribution, employee and trade union rights, where the Labour Party has attempted to promote popular interests, the Social Democrats in Sweden have achieved more. The effect of Labour's political philosophy has been to support the status quo, though in Britain as elsewhere the cumulative effect of policies designed to reconcile labour to the existing economic system may have caused some unintentional damage to business, as noted in Chapter 8. The integrative and national role has been opposed at various times by factions within the labour movement, but the internal structure of power has favoured the integrationist view against more radical challenges (Panitch, 1976). This political stance can be seen in part as a de-radicalisation of labour, resulting from the number of middle-class members and leaders, the workings of the iron law of oligarchy, and the need to make compromises in office given the balance of political forces (Parkin, 1972). But in fact a radical socialist ideology was never as central to the British Labour Party as it was to the Swedish party, and reformism has been the dominant characteristic.

The Swedish and British cases contrast sharply with the American and show the *range* of political forms that exist within modern capitalism. A small and contracting trade union movement and the absence of a political party that specifically represents labour in America mean that the labour interest has little effect as a political force that is linked to state action (Wilson, 1979). As a result, the American state appears less responsive to organised labour than are Western European social democracies.

Interventionism

In the second half of the twentieth century, state interventionism grew in what were once *laissez-faire* economies and interventionism assumed more direct forms everywhere. These developments have been explained in two ways: either as a response to the new economic problems of late capitalism, or as the product of social problems that are generic to capitalism and have assumed particularly serious forms in modern democratic political systems.

The economic stimulus to interventionism arises partly from the growth of 'monopoly' capitalism. There is the familiar argument that large corporations require stable environments that minimise uncertainty (Kidron, 1968, pp. 17–44). The state attempts to plan the economy in order to provide this predictable environment. Economic management ultimately may involve the state in the affairs of individual industries and companies, because the decisions made by private enterprise need to mesh with national plans. Some Marxists argue a different case. They claim that oligopolistic competition in 'monopoly' capitalism, replacing the old system of competition between a multiplicity of economic units, destroyed the mechanism whereby profits were distributed fairly equally across different units of capital, so that most tended toward average profits. Oligopoly allows some firms to earn 'super' profits which, in turn, cause other firms to stagnate. State intervention follows since it alone has the independence which allows it to discriminate amongst sectors of capital in order to favour the less profitable (Urry, 1977). Both arguments suggest that capitalism becomes more 'organised' because indigenous mechanisms of self-regulation such as market competition fail to provide sufficient equilibrium. A different line of reasoning has suggested that it is not so much monopoly capitalism as the politically-inspired postwar movement for free trade which provides the stimulus: the ending of tariffs has denied governments their traditional means of protecting their economies against more powerful nations, and new instruments have had to be found (Ohlin, 1974).

Another way of viewing intervention is as a response to class conflict and the need to maintain social equilibrium: the state preserves social peace by making concessions to working-class interests. A position commonly encountered within recent accounts is that concessions are made by a state that represents only capital to a class that is outside the state (see for example, Gough, 1975). An alternative and more convincing position is the one taken here, that if class struggle is reflected in state policies this is because *both* capital and labour are politically represented in the state rather than one being outside. Unregulated competitive capitalism was marked by a business cycle with periodic crises which interrupted accumulation.

These in turn gave rise to social crises, when recession led to the greater exploitation of labour or to people being made unemployed. State action has been designed to avert social crises at the same time that it aims to help business interests. Keynesian economic regulation, economic planning and direct state involvement are techniques which aim to secure simultaneously the material interests of capital and labour: stable economic growth suits both parties.

One important aspect of concessionary state policy in Western European societies has been the *welfare compromise.* The state compromises between business and other interests in order to protect people from the worst effects of a free market economy and redress some of imbalance of power between the two sides of industry. In fact, three of the basic elements of the compromise – increased employment, more state expenditure and rising money wages – are concessions to organised labour that may also help business in the short term. Full employment in the two postwar decades significantly reduced the pre-war threats to social stability. Part of state expenditure in these economies has been used directly to help private enterprise by distributing some of the revenue raised from taxation into corporate profits by means of investment grants, cheap loans, tax concessions, government contracts, etc. Even purely 'social' expenditure has indirectly benefited business, to the extent that it has created the social infrastructure appropriate to an advanced industrial society (for example, the supply of highly trained manpower). Rising money wages have overcome a traditional problem of capitalist economies: lack of effective demand. Interventionism can therefore be seen as a political strategy whereby governments try to promote profitable business and social stability and integration at the same time.

The strategy was fairly successful in the 1950s and 1960s, resolving the pre-war tendency toward recurrent crises and creating the appropriate environment for the newly-emerging 'monopoly' capitalism. But in the longer term it has had definite limitations. The welfare compromise became increasingly dysfunctional for business. Ever-increasing state expenditure meant heavier corporate taxation. This occurred at the moment when the strength of labour in the labour market and within the firm increased under the conditions of full employment and enhanced legal rights for employees. These developments contributed to the squeeze on corporate profits and price inflation after the mid-1960s. This shows how difficult it is for the state to resolve by political actions those conflicts of interest that are economically generated. Moreover, it demonstrates how state intervention may end up impeding the smooth working of the economy and harming business interests.

The explanation of why some states should have difficulty promoting business interests satisfactorily can be found in the points made in the previous section. The crucial one is that relative autonomy allows the state to be responsive to popular demands and to develop its own decision-making rules. Whereas effective economic planning requires technocratic procedures that follow the criteria of economic rationality, governments provide bureaucratic procedures whose goals are determined by political ends (Offe, 1975). In a political system where labour is well represented, these political ends are influenced by working-class as well as business interests. For example, state financial support for industry in Britain in the 1970s was as much concerned with maintaining employment as with industrial profitability. As a consequence, much state investment was misdirected from the point of view of business. The relative autonomy of state personnel may heighten the problem, because their own vested interest in reducing political conflict and promoting stability leads them to policies that compromise among politically-represented interests. The rationality of planning is further limited to the extent that it is reactive to decisions made privately in the economy, given that there are limits to the state's power to direct capital in most modern economies (Mandel, 1972, pp. 233–6).

Divisions between sections of capital, the disunity of state apparatuses and the manner in which capital is politically represented are also relevant. What happens is that the state, or rather certain parts of the state apparatus, favour the limited interests of sections of capital at the cost of the wider, collective interest. Two aspects of the economic policies of British governments in the 1960s illustrate this point. At that time financial interests had more political influence than industrial (Longstreth, 1979), and large-scale capital as a whole was more influential than small-scale business (Gamble, 1974). The interest of the financial world in preserving a fixed exchange rate and the role of sterling as a world currency was represented in the state by two powerful economic agencies, the Treasury and the Bank of England. One consequence of this political strength was to delay the devaluation of sterling that other sections of capital, represented by other parts of the administration and with political allies in the executive, needed in order to preserve *their* interests (Longstreth, 1979). The second illustration is to be found in the way that it was intended to reconcile profitable business and social stability. The policy of Conservative and Labour governments in the early 1960s was to favour large-scale industry at the cost of small businesses: to rationalise industry by creating larger capital units and to stimulate competition which would drive out small or inefficient firms. The welfare compromise also imposed costs, such as job security, fair wages, trade union recognition, health and safety regulations, that large firms could bear but which hurt smaller businesses. These policies produced divisions *within* the Conservative Party, which represented politically both large and small capital: the small businessmen who constituted the rank and file of the party were unable to ensure that their interests were politically effective when the party's leadership acted on behalf of large business (Harris, 1972, pp. 235–40).

A third set of problems derives from popular perceptions of the state. The state has an important role in generating social legitimation of the existing order, and to this end the claim is made that governments are not tied to the preservation of private interests but preserve the interests of all citizens and groups equally. This in turn leads to heightened popular expectations that the state can provide political solutions to economically-generated problems; for example, that the state can abolish inequalities of wealth and income or restore the control that people lack at work. But these sorts of problems are really beyond the capability of the political realm to solve, because they are basic to the form of economic organisation that the state in fact protects. The more the state is expected politically to settle irreconcilable economic conflicts, the clearer it becomes that the state is the locus, indeed the crystallisation, of the antagonisms within civil society (Offe, 1975). Marxists suggest that this provokes a crisis in the legitimation of the existing economic and political order (Habermas, 1976). Pluralists describe the same process as the crisis of 'overloaded' government, when popular demands become excessive and cannot be satisfied without destroying the economy (Crouch, 1979).

The State and Industrial Relations

Intervention in industrial relations has become a significant aspect of the state's economic role in Western Europe. Historically, the weakness of labour was usually sufficient to ensure that it was subordinated at work. Market forces and repressive laws restricting the right to join unions or to strike supported the power of owners and their managers. These factors no longer hold good, now that the welfare compromise has weakened the pressure of market forces on labour and the law no longer supports managerial prerogative to the same extent. The greater strength of labour has become a threat to business profitability, and a central issue for the modern state is how to contain this threat. Weakening labour by leaving it prey to unregulated market forces, for example by allowing unemployment to rise unchecked and systematically reducing the scope of the welfare compromise in other ways, is not politically feasible for long, nor a strategy which will necessarily work given the amount of union influence in the modern labour market. Direct coercion comes up against the same problem of political acceptability where popular interests are influential in the political system. In the search for an alternative strategy of containment, *corporatism* has been a favoured policy (Crouch, 1979).

Corporatism tries to bind workers to the state and its policies through their own organisations. The essence of the strategy is to use the leaders of labour organisations to control their members in the state's interest. Trade union leaders are brought within the state's orbit, to participate in state institutions and influence policy formulation (in a consultative rather than decision-making role), and mix regularly with state personnel. Corporatism has constitutional implications: popular interests are politically represented by the leaders of labour organisations in interaction with state personnel, rather than by the institutions of parliamentary democracy. The pluralism of a system based on diverse and fragmented interest groups and political parties, including popular interests that are outside organised labour, working independently of state control and opposed to state interference in their affairs, is rivalled by a centralised, state-directed system that attempts to evade the pressures of parliamentary democracy (Strinati, 1979). If this strategy is to succeed, there are two essential ingredients: hierarchy and consensus (Crouch, 1979). Hierarchical control within labour organisations is necessary if these are to regulate their memberships. Normative consensus is necessary if hierarchy is to be accepted as legitimate and if the membership is to be mobilised behind their leaders' policies. In addition corporate states aim for a wider form of consensus that extends to the economic and social system as a whole. Corporatism as an industrial relations strategy suits the interventionist state well, because it extends to labour the same centralising and organising principles that have been applied to capital. Indeed, the means the state chooses to regulate labour and capital are often symmetrical, as when the interventionist state tries to influence the conduct of individual units of capital by means of their collective organisations (for example, employers' associations).

Corporatist strategies can be found in several Western European nations. Swedish industrial relations have corporatist elements:

trade union leaders have co-operated with the state to maintain business prosperity and increase efficiency since 1932; trade union organisation has been centralised and hierarchically structured in this period, allowing leaders to control members; there is a high degree of consensus about the ultimate goals of the political and industrial wings of the labour movement (Korpi, 1978). Corporatist strategies that bind *both* capital and labour are highly developed in Belgium and the Netherlands, and to a lesser extent in Germany.

The decade of postwar reconstruction was important for Belgian and Dutch corporatism. The Dutch government established a centralised consultative system which drew together government, trade union leaders and employers' representatives into an advisory council. Tripartite consultation amongst government, unions and business on all aspects of national economic policy became the normal means of policy determination (Akkermans and Grootings, 1978). Collective bargaining after 1945 was controlled by a board of mediators, which included trade unionists, with the right to approve, modify or reject collective agreements. This became the central agency for enforcing government incomes policy (Malles, 1973, p. 130). Dutch unions are centralised and their leaders have been well insulated from rank-and-file pressure (Akkermans and Grootings, 1978). The right to strike does not extend to unofficial action and even unions have virtually lost this right after a series of court decisions. Workplace representation after 1950 was entrusted to works councils chaired by the employer, weakening the independent power of labour at the workplace. The position of trade union leaderships has thus been both protected and restricted by state action, and they have derived their strength from their integration into the state rather than the industrial power of their members (Crouch, 1978). The Dutch system has begun to change, however, in recent years as the earlier discussion of unionism showed: unofficial, illegal strikes have become fairly common since the 1960s as workers have organised independently of their unions; unions have moved into the workplace in order to contain this threat and have begun to establish plant organisations for the first time since the war; the co-operative, accommodative position of unions has changed to a more contestive stance in negotiations.

Belgian governments after the war incorporated trade unions and employers' associations into the structure of national decision-making in economic and social spheres. Lorwin (1975) suggests that unions and employers' associations have effectively replaced political parties as the agents of national unity, such is their influence: for example, the Government's 1975 economic recovery plan was first discussed, modified and approved by these outside bodies before being presented to Parliament. Unions participate in a wide variety of advisory and even decision-making state bodies concerned with economic and social policy, and sit on the management committees of various industries (gas, steel, electricity, petroleum) and public economic institutions (the National Bank, public investment and regional development companies). In return for this incorporation, unions after the war largely gave up using their bargaining strength and accepted the state's criteria of acceptable wage levels. As in the Netherlands, unions have benefited from a range of legal rights conceded by the state that have served to integrate further the leadership and divorce them from popular pressures or dependence on the rank and file. But, again as in the Netherlands, corporatism has begun to crack in the face of rank-and-file action on the shop floor, plant-level bargaining, unofficial strike action, and the difficulty that union leaders find in delivering their side of the bargain with the state (Molitor, 1978).

German corporatism derives more from the legal state apparatus than from government (Crouch, 1978). The postwar reconstruction imposed by the occupying forces replaced the corporate, fascist state with a pluralistic political system, an autonomous, free market economy, and unions and employers' associations that remained outside politics. The law, however, fostered corporatism in its assumptions that trade unions derived their rights to exist and their powers from the state, and that the right to take industrial action such as striking is a corporate right belonging to a legally-sanctioned trade union rather than the right of individual employees. This is in contrast to English common law, which found it difficult to accept the right to combine collectively in trade unions and the existence of unions as corporate bodies (Crouch, 1978). Trade union activity in Germany is therefore minutely regulated by law. This law embodies two important principles: unions share with management the duty of preserving industrial peace and should collaborate to this end, and striking is only an act of last resort. Both emphasise the role of trade unions in minimising conflict by controlling the threat that their members might otherwise pose to business. The law has supported the rights of leaders against union members, notably by outlawing unofficial action and standing in the way of autonomous workplace organisation. In the 1960s, government itself became involved in a corporatist strategy when it initiated a policy of tripartite negotiation with unions and employers' organisations. This policy of 'concerted action' involved the three parties agreeing on the economic policy objectives to be pursued by government and industry, and defined acceptable wage rises that the unions would enforce. 'Concerted action' was similar to the Belgian and Dutch form of corporatism.

There have been less systematic attempts to introduce elements of corporatism elsewhere. France has no corporatist tradition, despite more than a century of state intervention in the economy which has extended to such detailed matters as the pricing policies of individual firms. But in the 1970s the government attempted to control labour by corporatist means. The 1968 crisis had led to a feeling that social and economic stability could best be preserved if labour were incorporated. There was some dialogue between government and unions on economic and industrial relations policy in the 1970s, but more commonly the state encouraged bipartite discussions between unions and employer federations with legislative support for any outcomes. Reynaud (1975) suggests that bipartite discussions with the state as the third party behind the scenes provided unions with real influence: in the area of economic planning the state took account of union views about policy, while in the area of industrial relations the bipartite forum in effect *determined* the government's legislative programme. Unions established their legal rights within the enterprise, established collective bargaining at the same level, improved the age and conditions of retirement and improved conditions of work. Union leaders, however, refused to be incorporated despite these concessions, maintained their oppositional stance within industry, and in any event lacked the means to control their members. In 1976, the French government effectively ended its flirtation with corporatism and returned to an older strategy, which was to allow the discipline of the market to deal with labour power and the legal system to cope with any consequential unrest.

The industrial relations tradition in Britain has been non-corporatist and both sides of industry were long committed to free collective bargaining and autonomy in their dealings with each other. But in the late 1960s and during the 1970s, different sections of industrial capital developed different conceptions of what sort of industrial relations system would best promote their interests (Strinati, 1979). Multinational firms in the 'monopoly' capital sector, excluding those in the motor industry, were content to deal with labour at the local level without any state interference. Being capital-intensive they were able and willing to buy off labour trouble in order to maintain uninterrupted production. Indeed, they contributed to an acceleration of wage rates and a decentralisation of bargaining which was criticised by other employers (Strinati,

1979). Small-scale capital resisted the directly interventionist state and corporate industrial relations strategies, but advocated that government create an appropriate, highly restrictive legal framework which would weaken labour power and keep unions out of their firms (Strinati, 1979). Large firms in the national 'monopoly' capital sector and the British subsidiaries of multinationals in the motor industry reacted to the growing anarchy of industrial relations in this period by demanding that the state secure the corporatist reorganisation of the trade unions (Strinati, 1979).

The late 1960s and the 1970s were marked by tension and shifts in the state's industrial relations' policy as it tried to grapple with the consequences of the failure of the welfare compromise to secure industrial peace. There was a conflict within the state, just as within industry, about the appropriate strategy. The judiciary rejected corporatism, emphasised individual and property rights against the collective rights of trade unions and the diminution of property rights which successive trade union legal immunities had conferred, rejected the intervention of the state except to secure an appropriate legal framework, and favoured a legally repressive control of trade unionism and trade disputes that would reverse the immunities gained over the previous half century (W. Wedderburn, 1971, pp. 324–84; Griffith, 1977). This judicial perspective was congruent with the interests of small-scale capital. The legislature and executive were disposed more toward corporatism, since they were exposed to popular pressures and the effective political campaigning of large-scale national capital. The tension can be seen in the 1971 Industrial Relations Act, whose underlying principles were simultaneously restrictive, individualistic and corporatist (Simpson and Wood, 1973, pp. 22–71): it tried to weaken the power of employees at work and regulate the expression of industrial conflict; it gave individual employees and employers greater redress against trade unions; at the same time, it attempted to centralise unions and turn them into hierarchically-structured organisations which would control their members and to permit state regulation of the internal management of trade unions. The 1971 Act survived only for three years before it was repealed by the incoming Labour government in 1974. Its restrictive provisions were used primarily by small employers during this period, for multinationals and large national firms refused to have anything to do with it for fear of damaging industrial relations and provoking union hostility (Weekes *et al.*, 1975). For a brief period in the middle and late 1970s Britain did adopt a systematically corporatist strategy: the 'social contract' between the union movement and the Labour administrations of 1974–9 was a deal whereby the unions delivered industrial peace and greatly moderated wage demands in exchange for legislation that extended trade union rights in industry and for the government considering union proposals in the social and economic policy areas. The collapse of this strategy in 1978, when union leaders were unable any longer to contain strikes or pay demands, followed by the accession of a Conservative administration in 1979, marked the end of the corporatist experiment. There was a return to a more restrictive trade union law and greater use of unemployment and market forces to control labour.

In conclusion, it should be noted that the corporatist solution to the labour problem has *not* been particularly successful in the long term, and industrial conflict and excessive wage demands have increasingly broken through corporatist regulation (Crouch, 1978). As was noted in Chapter 7, shopfloor militancy in Belgium, Holland and Sweden demonstrated the fragility of corporatism in the early 1970s, while the new radicalism of the Swedish trade union movement's economic programme threatens to replace corporatism with an entirely new type of political economy. At the same time the Dutch have moved away from corporatism toward a more 'liberal' form of bargaining and industrial relations (Akkermans and Grootings, 1978). A basic flaw is that corporatism cannot by itself bridge the opposition of interests within industry. It needs an element of normative consensus, and this is precisely what is so often missing in industrial relations. Where the opposition between the two sides of industry has been sufficiently subdued to make corporatism work, principally in Germany, this has resulted more from affluence than anything else. Affluence may work as a functional alternative to normative consensus and contain the disruptive potential of divergent interests as Chapter 10 showed. Corporatism is successful in precisely those industrial relations systems which may in any event have been peacefully regulated because it relies on the prior existence of some degree of harmony. A second problem is that unions find it difficult to deliver their side of the bargain, because there are limits to the power of trade union leaders over their members, even in hierarchical and centralised organisations where leadership power is buttressed by the law, as Chapter 7 demonstrated. A third issue is that modern corporatism is a bargained relationship, in which unions exchange industrial peace or wage restraint for concessions from government. The relationship is therefore inherently unstable. Moreover, in its illustrating the link that exists between the state and the economy, the corporatist relationship encourages unions to make new demands. Unions realise that the state can grant them reforms that they would never achieve by their own industrial strength alone, and with this realisation their aspirations expand to embrace broader themes of economic and social policy and issues such as the redistribution of power and control in industry, rather than remain with limited concerns such as trade union law. As the demands become more ambitious, however, they become more difficult to satisfy.

12 Conclusion

I have set out to investigate the nature of industrial conflict and to chart its manifestations. The starting point of this venture remains employment and the social relations involved in production. These have always been the concerns of industrial sociology, but to understand these issues fully the analysis must be extended to cover managerial organisation and the behaviour of firms, social stratification, and the link between the economy and the state. The modern study of industry thus breaks the confines within which previous generations of sociologists chose to work, to become the political economy of industrial relations.

The most obvious manifestations of the underlying structure of conflict are to be found in employer strategies toward labour and the resistance of workers. Braverman's description of the relationship among profitability, labour control and work degradation may be endorsed as an accurate but limited statement about the world of work. The analysis carried out here shows that there is currently a wider range of managerial strategies: these include work redesign, delegated control, corporate paternalism in addition to the simple form of rationalisation which Braverman described. The variety of employer strategies may be explained by the inadequacy of the dominant Western managerial strategy deriving from Taylor to provide an optimal solution to the human and technical problems of production.

In this context, it is significant that labour resistance is more pronounced and has greater effect than has been acknowledged. Resistance takes the two characteristic forms of autonomous shopfloor organisation and official trade union action through the formal channels of conflict regulation such as collective bargaining. The effectiveness of shopfloor and union resistance has always depended on the state of product and labour markets, fluctuating according to the economic environment. But in the postwar era in Western Europe political processes have assumed more significance for the resolution of the competition between labour and capital. The state is obviously involved in economic conflict in ways which were in the past ignored by those who subscribed to the belief that the economy and polity were essentially separate spheres. But this involvement is not straightforwardly on the side of capital as modern accounts of the state assert, because the balance of power in the economy does not simply determine the outcome of the political process. The political realm in fact has some degree of influence over the economy which, when the political system provides the mass electorate with real political influence, allows labour to modify the distribution of power within industry by political means. Differences in the amount of labour's influence help explain why the effect of government on the outcome of industrial conflicts varies so much among societies. It is notable that however much some governments may have reduced labour's disadvantage, none has yet *overturned* the traditional power distribution which favours employers. There are indeed certain conditions necessary for the existence of the typical form of modern economic organisation, one of which is an asymmetrical distribution of power in industry so that the recalcitrance of labour may be controlled. In the absence of any clear resolve in the electorate and the organs of the state that the present economic order should be replaced, governments have to maintain the minimum conditions necessary to sustain the existing machinery of wealth creation.

Economic conflicts have implications for social stratification. Classes are constituted economically and the major divisions of economic condition can be conceived as class boundaries. The degree to which the classes so formed are structured and assume an identity varies. Changes in the organisation of the economy, notably the homogenisation of work and market conditions among the lower levels of the employed population, produce an increasingly well-structured working class. Conversely, higher classes increasingly fragment as the result of occupational change. Many industrial sociologists ignore the close conceptual and substantive links between their customary concerns with productive activity and the system of social stratification, and in the discussion in Chapters 9 and 10 I tried to show the real gains in understanding which follow the integration of these areas. An implication of viewing classes as economically determined and crystallising around major economic divisions is that industrial relations involve relations between classes. To say this is not to suggest that workers and managers themselves regard their relationships as class-based, let alone as ones of class conflict. It is simply to point to a theoretical link which logically exists between analytical concepts. As it happens, however, investigation of class awareness shows that the British working class does view industrial relations in class terms and does have a conception of class conflict, although these views remain poorly developed. This proletarian class awareness has industrial rather than political implications, which are demonstrated in the anomic disorder of British industrial relations. The dominant value system fails to integrate British workers. Class analysis in addition highlights the different cultural worlds which the two sides of industry inhabit and explains the huge gulf in perception which separates managers and others.

Examination of the structure of economic competition reveals that interests are opposed in both the distributive and productive spheres. In other words, employees' interests conflict with those of their employers even at the moment that they produce goods and services and not just at the end of the day when the fruits of their productive activity are distributed amongst the different factors of production. This means that a common assumption, that industrial conflict concerns the distribution of the surplus while the actual process of production is both co-operative and essentially harmonious, cannot be justified. Nor is it legitimate to separate economic and control issues and assert that economism is the arena of conflict. These approaches assume that conflict may easily be resolved to the satisfaction of each contender because competition over financial resources need not be a zero-sum struggle in which one party benefits only at the cost of the other. Control conflicts which mark the production system are likely to have a zero-sum quality, however, which greatly diminishes the possibility of an outcome that satisfies all parties. The link between economism and control is to be seen at all the levels in which economic competition is manifest: in autonomous workplace activity, in trade union action, and in the policies pursued by governments in response to pressures from business or labour interests.

Within the social sciences the issue of distributive and productive conflicts marks a major divide between rival interpretations of industrial relations. The institutionalisation of conflict thesis simply assumed that industrial conflict represented the competition between labour and capital in the realm of distribution and was oriented around economistic issues. Because these conflicts in principle were capable of resolution with some degree of mutual satisfaction, commentators believed that industrial peace required only the creation of appropriate institutional forms to regulate and resolve such disputes. These were trade unionism and collective bargaining. This interpretation has foundered with the resurgence of unregulated, non-institutionalised social conflict. I have shown the case for taking the alternative position, that the conditions under which surpluses are produced are as much a source of competition as their distribution. This assumption is what makes sense of the actions of management and labour in modern organisations.

The modified classical economic and sociological models of the conditions of production prove useful. They integrate the separate discussions of managerial control strategies, the patterns of industrial relations in the modern economy, the structure of co-operative enterprises, class relations, even alienation, within a single universe of discourse. The modern forms of these classical traditions explain why alternative systems of economic organisation are inherently less prone to disruptive conflicts and remove a major source of alienation, but may still operate efficiently. There is an important distinction between the coercion of low-trust patterns of managerial control, which reflect a lack of fit between the interests of employers and employees stemming from appropriation and exploitation, and the pressures of the market place. The latter also have a coercive force, but this does not produce the structured opposition within the fabric of industrial organisation which is found in most modern economies. There are compelling reasons for believing that a co-operative organisational form is *inherently* more efficient than those which presently dominate economic life. Conventional capitalism and state socialism contain a significant and continuing source of inefficiency, because they squander costly resources to control recalcitrant employees. This internal control function directly inflates salary costs by the number of supervisory and managerial staff needed for the purpose, diverts the attention of all levels of management away from other aspects of the business, and distorts the evolution of production technology. Co-operative organisation avoids these negative costs and draws positive benefits from the release of members' energies to promote the welfare of the organisation, benefits which are unavailable to modern capitalism. Meanwhile the market continues to exert the discipline which accounts for whatever level of productive efficiency contemporary capitalism has attained. There are sound economic reasons for preferring co-operation: it can be a highly efficient way of organising economic activity, as the Yugoslavian and Mondragon enterprises demonstrate. It can be efficient precisely because it does away with the counter-productive conflicts of other organisational forms.

A solution commonly advocated to resolve the industrial relations problems which stem from divergent interests is the creation of a moral community at work. In sociology this solution is associated with the Durkheimian tradition and specifically the human relations school of industrial sociologists. It remains a persuasive argument among managers and forms part of the high-trust philosophy characteristic of managerial thought. Despite the length of time the solution has been advocated and its widespread endorsement in management, it has been of little practical consequence. Managers have not tried to generate social cohesion in any meaningful or systematic manner and worker activity has remained unaffected. The exception is to be found in the management of large-scale Japanese corporations, which provides a measure of how half-heartedly managers have pursued the ideal of community elsewhere. Large private enterprises in Japan have remarkably peaceful industrial relations and a contributory factor is undoubtedly the form of moral cohesion instituted in corporate paternalism. This suggests that the social conflicts arising out of economic competition can be contained by enlightened policies. Even in Japan, however, the system contains certain pressures which contribute to industrial peace. The central problem facing modern business is the impossibility of abolishing the conditions which create conflict without destroying the present form of the economy. Managers have to hope to find a palliative to suppress the symptoms of conflict and thus 'solve' the problems of industrial relations without curing the basic ailment. Suppression may be primarily coercive, which has been the most common though not the sole strategy in Western business since Taylor, or it may assume the form of the more sophisticated blend of cohesion and compulsion found in Japan.

Bibliography

Aaronovitch, S. and Sawyer, M. C. (1975), *Big Business*, London.

Abercrombie, N. and Hill, S. (1976), 'Paternalism and patronage', *British Journal of Sociology*, Vol. 27, No. 4.

Abercrombie, N., Hill, S. and Turner, B. S. (1980), *The Dominant Ideology Thesis*, London.

Acker, J. (1973), 'Women and social stratification: a case of intellectual sexism', *American Journal of Sociology*, Vol. 78, No. 4.

Adams, R. J. (1975), *The Growth of White-Collar Unionism in Britain and Sweden: A Comparative Investigation*, University of Wisconsin.

Aguren, S. *et al.* (1976), *The Volvo Kalmar Plant*, The Rationalization Council SAF-LO, Stockholm.

Akkermans, T. and Grootings, P. (1978), 'From corporatism to polarisation: elements of the development of Dutch industrial relations', in C. Crouch and A. Pizzorno (eds.) (1978) *The Resurgence of Class Conflict in Western Europe since 1968*, London.

Anderson, P. (1964), 'Origins of the present crisis', *New Left Review*, No. 23.

Anthony, P. D. (1977), *The Ideology of Work*, London.

Bain, G. S. *et al.* (1973), *Social Stratification and Trade Unionism*, London.

Baldamus, W. (1961), *Efficiency and Effort*, London.

Barron, R. and Norris, G. (1976), 'Sexual divisions in the dual labour market', in D. L. Barker and S. Allen (eds.) (1976) *Dependence and Exploitation in Work and Marriage*, London.

Batstone, E. *et al.* (1977), *Shop Stewards in Action*, Oxford.

Batstone, E. *et al.* (1978), *The Social Organisation of Strikes*, Oxford.

Baudouin, T., Collin, M. and Guillerm, D. (1978), 'Women and immigrants: marginal workers?', in C. Crouch and A. Pizzorno (eds.) (1978) *The Resurgence of Class Conflict in Western Europe since 1968*, London.

Bell, C. (1968), *Middle Class Families*, London.

Bellas, C. J. (1975), 'Industrial democracy through worker ownership: an American experience', in J. Vanek (ed.) (1975) *Self-Management*, Harmondsworth.

Bendix, R. (1964), *Nation-Building and Citizenship*, New York.

Bendix, R. (1966), *Work and Authority in Industry*, New York.

Benson, J. K. (1977), 'Organizations: a dialectical view', *Administrative Science Quarterly*, Vol. 22.

Benson, L. (1974), 'Market socialism and class structure: manual workers and managerial power in the Yugoslav enterprise', in F. Parkin (ed.) (1974) *The Social Analysis of Class Structure*, London.

Berle, A. and Means, G. C. (1932), *The Modern Corporation and Private Property*, Chicago.

Beynon, H. (1973), *Working for Ford*, London.

Beynon, H. and Blackburn, R. M. (1972), *Perceptions of Work*, Cambridge.

Blackburn, R. M. (1967), *Union Character and Social Class*, London.
Blackburn, R. M. and Mann, M. (1979), *The Working Class in the Labour Market*, London.
Blackburn, R. M. and Prandy, K. (1965), 'White-collar unionization: a conceptual framework', *British Journal of Sociology*, Vol. 16, No. 2.
Blain, A. J. N. (1972), *Pilots and Management*, London.
Blauner, R. (1964), *Alienation and Freedom*, Chicago.
Bonham, J. (1954), *The Middle Class Vote*, London.
Bottomore, T. B. (ed.) (1964), *Karl Marx, Early Writings*, New York.
Bowen, P. (1976), *Social Control in Industrial Organisations*, London.
Boyd, D. (1973), *Elites and their Education*, Windsor.
Bradley, K. and Gelb, A. (1979), 'The political economy of "radical" policy', *British Journal of Political Science*, Vol. 9, No. 1.
Brannen, P. and Caswill, C. (1978), 'Changes in law and values', in D. Gregory (ed.) (1978) *Work Organisation*, proceedings of an SSRC (Social Science Research Council) Conference, London.
Braverman, H. (1974), *Labor and Monopoly Capital*, New York.
Bright, J. R. (1966), 'The relationship of increasing automation and skill requirements', in *The Employment Impact of Technological Change*, National Commission on Technology, Automation, and Economic Progress, Washington, D. C.
Brown, R. *et al.* (1972), 'The contours of solidarity: social stratification and industrial relations in shipbuilding', *British Journal of Industrial Relations*, Vol. 10, No. 1.
Brown, W. (1973), *Piecework Bargaining*, London.
Brown, W. *et al.* (1978), 'Factors shaping shop steward organisation in Britain', *British Journal of Industrial Relations*, Vol. 16, No. 2.
Burch, P. H. (1972), *The Managerial Revolution Reassessed*, Lexington, Mass.
Burnham, J. (1941), *The Managerial Revolution*, Harmondsworth.
Burns, T. and Stalker, G. M. (1961), *The Management of Innovation*, London.
Carchedi, G. (1975), 'On the economic identification of the new middle class', *Economy and Society*, Vol. 4, No. 1.
Carew, A. (1978), *Democracy and Government in European Trade Unions*, London.
Carey, A. (no date), *A Sociological Critique of Industrial Psychology and Sociology*, mimeo., University of New South Wales.
Castles, S. and Kosack, G. (1973), *Immigrant Workers and the Class Structure in Western Europe*, London.
Chamberlain, N. W. (1961), 'Determinants of bargaining structures', in A. R. Weber (ed.) (1961) *The Structure of Collective Bargaining*, New York.
Chandler, M. K. (1964), *Management Rights and Union Interests*, New York.
Chaplin, P. and Cowe, R. (1977), *A Survey of Contemporary British Worker Co-operatives*, Manchester Business School.
Cherns, A. (1973), 'Better working lives – a social scientist's view', *Occupational Psychology*, Vol. 47, No. 1.
Child, J. (1969), *British Management Thought*, London.
Child, J. (1972), 'Organisational structure, environment and performance: the role of strategic choice', *Sociology*, Vol. 6, No. 1.
Chinoy, E. (1955), *Automobile Workers and the American Dream*, New York.
Clark, R. (1979), *The Japanese Company*, New Haven, Conn.
Clarke, D. (1966), *The Industrial Manager*, London.

Clegg, H. (1976), *Trade Unionism under Collective Bargaining*, Oxford.
Clements, R. V. (1958), *Managers: a study of their careers in industry*, London.
Cole, R. E. (1971), *Japanese Blue Collar: the Changing Tradition*, Berkeley, Calif.
Cole, R. E. (1979), *Work, Mobility and Participation*, Berkeley, Calif.
Cooley, M. J. E. (1977), 'Taylor in the office', in R. N. Ottoway (ed.) (1977) *Humanising the Workplace*, London.
Cooper, R. (1972), 'Man, task and technology', *Human Relations*, Vol. 25, No. 2.
Copeman, G. H. (1955), *Leaders of British Industry*, London.
Crompton, R. (1976), 'Approaches to the study of white-collar unionism', *Sociology*, Vol. 10, No. 3.
Crouch, C. (1978), 'The changing role of the state in industrial relations in Western Europe', in C. Crouch and A. Pizzorno (eds.) (1978) *The Resurgence of Class Conflict in Western Europe since 1968*, London.
Crouch, C. (1979), 'The state, capital and liberal democracy', in C. Crouch (ed.) (1979), *State and Economy in Contemporary Capitalism*, London.
Crouch, C. and Pizzorno, A. (eds.) (1978), *The Resurgence of Class Conflict in Western Europe since 1968*, London.
Crossick, G. (1976), 'The labour aristocracy and its values', *Victorian Studies*, Vol. 19, No. 3.
Crozier, M. (1964), *The Bureaucratic Phenomenon*, London.
CSO (Central Statistical Office) (1975; 1978), *Social Trends*, nos. 6 and 9, London.
Cunnison, S. (1966), *Wages and Work Allocation*, London.
Dahrendorf, R. (1959), *Class and Class Conflict in Industrial Society*, London.
Davis, L. E. (1972), 'The design of jobs', in L. E. Davis and J. C. Taylor (eds.) (1972) *Design of Jobs*, Harmondsworth.
Davis, R. L. and Cousins, J. J. (1975), 'The "new working class" and the old', in M. Bulmer (ed.) (1975) *Working Class Images of Society*, London.
Diamond Report (1979), *Report No. 8*, Royal Commission on the Distribution of Income and Wealth, London.
Dickson, D. (1974), *Alternative Technology*, Glasgow.
Doeringer, P. B. and Piore, M. J. (1971), *Internal Labour Markets and Manpower Analysis*, Lexington, Mass.
Donovan Report (1968), *Report*, Royal Commission on Trade Unions and Employers' Associations 1965–1968, London.
Dore, R. (1973), *British Factory–Japanese Factory*, London.
Drucker, P. F. (1955), *The Practice of Management*, London.
Dubois, P. (1978), 'New forms of industrial conflict', in C. Crouch and A. Pizzorno (eds.) (1978) *The Resurgence of Class Conflict in Western Europe since 1968*, London.
Dubois, P. *et al.* (1978), 'The contradictions of French trade unionism', in C. Crouch and A. Pizzorno (eds.) (1978) *The Resurgence of Class Conflict in Western Europe since 1968*, London.
Edelstein, J. D. and Warner, M. (1975), *Comparative Union Democracy*, London.
Eldridge, J. E. T. (1971), *Sociology and Industrial Life*, London.
Elliott, D. and Elliott, R. (1976), *The Control of Technology*, London.
Elliott, J. (1978), *Conflict or Co-operation?*, London.
Emery, F. E. and Trist, E. L. (1960), 'Socio-technical systems', in

C. W. Churchman and M. Verhulst (eds.) (1960) *Management Science, Models and Techniques*, Oxford.

Erritt, M. J. and Alexander, J. C. D. (1977), 'Ownership of company shares: a new survey', *Economic Trends*, No. 287.

Flanders, A. (1964), *The Fawley Productivity Agreements*, London.

Flanders, A. (1970), *Management and Unions*, London.

Forsebäck, L. (1976), *Industrial Relations and Employment in Sweden*, Stockholm.

Fox, A. (1971), *A Sociology of Work in Industry*, London.

Fox, A. (1974), *Beyond Contract: Work, Power and Trust Relations*, London.

Fox, A. (1975), 'Collective bargaining, Flanders and the Webbs', *British Journal of Industrial Relations*, Vol. 13, No. 2.

Fox, A. and Flanders, A. (1969), 'The reform of collective bargaining: from Donovan to Durkheim', *British Journal of Industrial Relations*, Vol. 7, No. 2.

Francis, A. (1980), 'Families, firms and finance capital', *Sociology*, Vol. 14, No. 1.

Freitag, P. J. (1975), 'The cabinet and big business: a study of interlocks', *Social Problems*, Vol. 23, No. 2.

Friedman, A. (1977), *Industry and Labour: Class Struggle at Work and Monopoly Capitalism*, London.

Friedmann, G. (1961), *The Anatomy of Work*, London.

Galbraith, J. K. (1967), *The New Industrial State*, London.

Gallie, D. (1978), *In Search of the New Working Class*, Cambridge.

Gamble, A. (1974), *The Conservative Nation*, London.

Garnsey, E. (1978), 'Women's work and theories of class stratification', *Sociology*, Vol. 12, No. 2.

George, K. D. and Ward, T. S. (1975), *The Structure of Industry in the EEC*, Cambridge.

Giddens, A. (1973), *The Class Structure of the Advanced Societies*, London.

Glass, D. V. (ed.) (1954), *Social Mobility in Britain*, London.

Glyn, A. and Sutcliffe, R. (1972), *British Capitalism, Workers and the Profits Squeeze*, Harmondsworth.

Goldstein, J. (1952), *The Government of British Trade Unions*, London.

Goldthorpe, J. H. (1974), 'Industrial relations in Great Britain: a critique of reformism', *Politics and Society*, Vol. 4, No. 3.

Goldthorpe, J. H. (1978), 'The current inflation; towards a sociological account', in F. Hirsch and J. H. Goldthorpe (eds.) (1978) *The Political Economy of Inflation*, Oxford.

Goldthorpe, J. H. and Llewellyn, C. (1977a), 'Class mobility in modern Britain: three theses examined', *Sociology*, Vol. 11, No. 2.

Goldthorpe, J. H. and Llewellyn, C. (1977b), 'Class mobility: intergenerational and worklife patterns', *British Journal of Sociology*, Vol. 28, No. 3.

Goldthorpe, J. H. *et al.* (1968a), *The Affluent Worker: Industrial Attitudes and Behaviour*, Cambridge.

Goldthorpe, J. H. *et al.* (1968b), *The Affluent Worker: Political Attitudes and Behaviour*, Cambridge.

Goldthorpe, J. H. *et al.* (1969), *The Affluent Worker in the Class Structure*, Cambridge.

Goldthorpe, J. H., Payne, C. and Llewellyn, C. (1978), 'Trends in class mobility', *Sociology*, Vol. 12, No. 3.

Goodrich, C. L. (1920), *The Frontier of Control*, London.

Gorz, A. (1967), *Strategy for Labor*, Boston, (translation of original French edition published Paris, 1964).

Gorz, A. (1976), 'Technology, technicians and class struggle', in A. Gorz (ed.) (1976) *The Division of Labor*, Hassocks, (translation of original French edition published Paris, 1973).

Gough, I. (1975), 'State expenditure in advanced capitalism', *New Left Review*, No. 92.

Gray, R. Q. (1976), *The Labour Aristocracy in Victorian Edinburgh*, Oxford.

Griffith, J. A. G. (1977), *The Politics of the Judiciary*, London.

Gutman, H. G. (1977), *Work, Culture and Society in Industrializing America*, Oxford.

Guttsman, W. L. (1963), *The British Political Elite*, London.

Guttsman, W. L. (1974), 'The British political élite and the class structure', in P. Stanworth and A. Giddens (eds.) (1974) *Elites and Power in British Society*, London.

Habermas, J. (1976), *Legitimation Crisis*, London.

Hadley, R. (1975), 'Rowen, South Wales: notes on an experiment in workers' self-management', in J. Vanek (ed.) (1975) *Self-management*, Harmondsworth.

Hannah, L. and Kay, J. A. (1977), *Concentration in Modern Industry*, London.

Haraszti, M. (1977), *A Worker in a Worker's State*, Harmondsworth.

Harris, N. (1972), *Competition and the Corporate State*, London.

Henderson, W. O. (1975), *The Rise of German Industrial Power*, London.

Herding, R. (1972), *Job Control and Union Structure*, Rotterdam.

Hill, P. (1971), *Towards a New Philosophy of Management*, London.

Hill, S. (1974), 'Norms, groups and power: the sociology of industrial relations', *British Journal of Industrial Relations*, Vol. 12, No. 2.

Hill, S. (1976a), 'The new industrial relations?', *British Journal of Industrial Relations*, Vol. 14, No. 2.

Hill, S. (1976b), *The Dockers*, London.

Hinton, J. (1973), *The First Shop Stewards Movement*, London.

Hobsbawm, E. J. (1964), *Labouring Men*, London.

Hobsbawm, E. J. (1968), *Industry and Empire*, London.

Hobsbawm, E. J. (1975), *The Age of Capital 1848–1875*, London.

Homans, G. C. (1950), *The Human Group*, New York.

Huber, J. and Form, W. H. (1973), *Income and Ideology: An Analysis of the American Political Formula*, New York.

Hyman, R. (1971), *Marxism and the Sociology of Trade Unionism*, London.

Hyman, R. (1978a), 'Pluralism, procedural consensus and collective bargaining', *British Journal of Industrial Relations*, Vol. 16, No. 1.

Hyman, R. (1978b), 'Occupational structure, collective organisation and industrial militancy', in C. Crouch and A. Pizzorno (eds.) (1978b) *The Resurgence of Class Conflict in Western Europe since 1968*, London.

Hyman, R. and Brough, I. (1975), *Social Values and Industrial Relations*, Oxford.

ILO (International Labour Office) (1966), 'Technological change and manpower in a centrally planned economy', *Labour and Automation*, Bulletin no. 3, Geneva.

Ingham, G. K. (1974), *Strikes and Industrial Conflict*, London.

Janérus, I. (1978), 'Trade union approach to work organisation and democracy', in D. Gregory (ed.) (1978) *Work Organisation*, proceedings of an SSRC (Social Science Research Council) Conference, London.

Jessop, B. (1978), 'Capitalism and democracy', in G. Littlejohn *et al.* (eds.) (1978) *Power and the State*, London.

Johnson, G. E. (1975), 'Economic analysis of trade unionism', *American Economic Review*, Vol. 65, No. 2.

Jones, D. C. (1980), 'Producer co-operatives in industrialised Western economies', *British Journal of Industrial Relations*, Vol. 18, No. 2.

Kerr, C. (1964), *Labor and Management in Industrial Society*, New York.

Kerr, C. *et al.* (1960), *Industrialism and Industrial Man*, Cambridge, Mass.

Kidron, M. (1968), *Western Capitalism since the War*, London.

Kirkwood, T. and Mewes, H. (1976), 'The limits of trade union power in the capitalist order: the case of West German labour's quest for codetermination', *British Journal of Industrial Relations*, Vol. 14, No. 3.

Korpi, W. (1977), *Strikes, Industrial Relations and Class Conflict: the Case of Sweden*, mimeo., University of Stockholm.

Korpi, W. (1978), *The Working Class in Welfare Capitalism*, London.

Kuhn, J. W. (1961), *Bargaining in Grievance Settlement*, New York.

Kuhn, J. W. (1968), 'Business unionism in a laboristic society', in I. Berg (ed.) (1968) *The Business of America*, New York.

Küster, G. H. (1974), 'Germany', in R. Vernon (ed.) (1974) *Big Business and the State*, Cambridge, Mass.

Landes, D. S. (1965), 'Technical change and development in Western Europe, 1750–1914', in M. M. Postan and H. J. Habbakuk (eds.) (1965) *The Cambridge Economic History of Europe*, Vol. VI, Part I, Cambridge.

Lash, S. M. (1980), *Socialization and Subjective Social Class: Determinants of Political and Industrial Radicalism among French and American Workers*, unpublished University of London Ph.D. thesis.

Lenin, V. I. (1961), 'What is to be done?' (1902) in *Collected Works*, Vol. V, Moscow.

Levine, A. L. (1967), *Industrial Retardation in Britain, 1880–1914*, London.

Lewis, H. G. (1963), 'Relative employment effects of unionism', *Industrial Relations Research Association Proceedings*.

Lewis, R. and Maude, A. U. E. (1949), *The English Middle Classes*, London.

Lindholm, R. (1978), 'On success and failure', in D. Gregory (ed.) (1978) *Work Organisation*, proceedings of an SSRC (Social Science Research Council) Conference, London.

Lipset, S. M., Trow, M. A. and Coleman, J. S. (1956), *Union Democracy*, Glencoe, Illinois.

Littler, C. R. (1978), 'Understanding Taylorism', *British Journal of Sociology*, Vol. 29, No. 2.

Littler, C. R. (1980), *The Bureaucratisation of the Shop Floor: the Development of Modern Work Systems*, unpublished University of London Ph.D. thesis.

Lockwood, D. (1958), *The Blackcoated Worker*, London.

Lockwood, D. (1964), 'Social integration and system integration', in G. K. Zollschan and W. Hirsch (eds.) (1964) *Explorations in Social Change*, London.

Lockwood, D. (1966), 'Sources of variation in working class images of society', *Sociological Review*, Vol. 14, No. 3.

Lockwood, D. (1975), 'In search of the traditional worker', in M. Bulmer (ed.) (1975) *Working Class Images of Society*, London.

Longstreth, F. (1979), 'The city, industry and the state', in C. Crouch (ed.)

(1979) *State and Economy in Contemporary Capitalism*, London.

Lorwin, V. R. (1975), 'Labour unions and political parties in Belgium', *Industrial and Labour Relations Review*, Vol. 28, No. 2.

Lösche, P. (1973), 'Stages in the evolution of the German labor movement', in A. Sturmthal and J. G. Scoville (eds.) (1973) *The International Labor Movement in Transition*, Urbana, Illinois.

Low-Beer, J. R. (1978), *Protest and Participation*, Cambridge.

Lumley, R. (1973), *White-Collar Unionism in Britain*, London.

Lupton, T. (1963), *On the Shop Floor*, Oxford.

Maccio, M. (1976), 'Party, technicians and the working class in the Chinese revolution', in A. Gorz (ed.) (1976) *The Division of Labor*, Hassocks, (translation of original French edition published Paris, 1973).

Mackay, D. I. *et al.* (1971), *Labour Markets under Different Employment Conditions*, London.

Mackenzie, G. (1973), *The Aristocracy of Labour*, Cambridge.

Mackenzie, G. (1974), 'The "Affluent Worker" study: an evaluation and critique', in F. Parkin (ed.) (1974) *The Social Analysis of Class Structure*, London.

McKenzie, R. and Silver, A. (1968), *Angels in Marble*, London.

Malles, P. (1973), *The Institutions of Industrial Relations in Continental Europe*, Ottawa.

Mallet, S. (1975), *The New Working Class*, Nottingham, (translation of 4th French edition (1969); first published in Paris, 1963).

Mandel, E. (1972), *Late Capitalism*, London.

Mann, M. (1970), 'The social cohesion of liberal democracy', *American Sociological Review*, Vol. 35, No. 3.

Mann, M. (1973a), *Workers on the Move*, Cambridge.

Mann, M. (1973b), *Consciousness and Action among the Western Working Class*, London.

Marcuse, H. (1968), *One Dimensional Man*, London.

Marglin, S. A. (1976), 'What do bosses do?', in A. Gorz (ed.) (1976) *The Division of Labor*, Hassocks, (translation of original French edition published Paris, 1973).

Marris, R. (1964), *The Economic Theory of 'Managerial' Capitalism*, London.

Marsden, D. (1978), *Industrial Democracy and Industrial Control in West Germany, France and Great Britain*, Department of Employment, London.

Martin, R. (1968), 'Union democracy: an explanatory framework', *Sociology*, Vol. 2, No. 2.

Martin, R. (1978), 'The effects of recent changes in industrial conflict on the internal politics of trade unions: Britain and Germany', in C. Crouch and A. Pizzorno (eds.) (1978) *The Resurgence of Class Conflict in Western Europe since 1968*, London.

Marx, K. (1970), *Capital*, London (Volume 1 originally published in 1867).

Marx, K. and Engels, F. (no date; originally 1848), *Manifesto of the Communist Party*, Moscow.

Mathias, P. (1978), 'Economists, trade unions and wages', in *Trade Unions: Public Goods or Public 'Bads'?*, Institute of Economic Affairs (ed.) (1978), London.

Mayhew, K. and Rosewell, B. (1978), 'Immigrants and occupational crowding in Great Britain', *Oxford Bulletin of Economics and Statistics*, Vol. 40, No. 3.

Meek, R. L. (1977), *Smith, Marx, and After*, London.
Meissner, M. (1969), *Technology and the Worker*, San Fransisco.
Mercer, D. E. and Weir, D. T. H. (1972), 'Attitudes to work and trade unionism amongst white-collar workers', *Industrial Relations Journal*, Vol. 3, No. 2.
Merton, R. K. (1957), 'Bureaucratic structure and personality', in *Social Theory and Social Structure*, New York.
Metcalf, D. (1977), 'Unions, incomes policy and relative wages in Britain', *British Journal of Industrial Relations*, Vol. 15, No. 2.
Michels, R. (1915), *Political Parties*, New York.
Miliband, R. (1969), *The State in Capitalist Society*, London.
Mill, J. S. (1848), *Principles of Political Economy*, London.
Mills, C. W. (1948), *The New Men of Power: America's Labor Leaders*, New York.
Mills, C. W. (1953), *White Collar: the American Middle Classes*, New York.
Mills, C. W. (1956), *The Power Elite*, New York.
Mintz, B. (1975), 'The president's cabinet, 1897–1972', *Insurgent Sociologist*, Vol. 5, No. 3.
Molitor, M. (1978), 'Social conflicts in Belgium', in C. Crouch and A. Pizzorno (eds.) (1978) *The Resurgence of Class Conflict in Western Europe since 1968*, London.
Moorhouse, H. F. (1976), 'Attitudes to class and class relationships in Britain', *Sociology*, Vol. 10, No. 3.
Moorhouse, H. F. and Chamberlain, C. W. (1974), 'Lower class attitudes to property: aspects of the counter ideology', *Sociology*, Vol. 8, No. 3.
Morishima, M. (1973), *Marx's Economics: a Dual Theory of Value and Growth*, Cambridge.
Mouzelis, N. (1967), *Organisation and Bureaucracy*, London.
Müller-Jentsch, W. and Sperling, H-J. (1978), 'Economic development, labour conflicts and the industrial relations system in West Germany', in C. Crouch and A. Pizzorno (eds.) (1978) *The Resurgence of Class Conflict in Western Europe since 1968*, London.
NEDO (National Economic Development Office) (1975), *Finance for Investment: a Study of Mechanisms Available for Financing Industrial Investment*, London.
Nelson, D. (1975), *Managers and Workers*, Madison, Wisconsin.
Newby, H. (1977), *The Deferential Worker*, London.
Newby, H. *et al.* (1978), *Property, Paternalism and Power*, London.
Nichols, T. (1969), *Ownership, Control, and Ideology*, London.
Nichols, T. and Armstrong, P. (1976), *Workers Divided*, Glasgow.
Nichols, T. and Beynon, H. (1977), *Living with Capitalism*, London.
National Institute of Industrial Psychology (1951), *The Foreman*, London.
Nordhaus, W. (1974), 'The falling share of profits', in A. Okun and L. Perry (eds.) (1974) *Brooking Papers in Economic Activity*, No. 1, Washington, DC.
Nyman, S. and Silberston, A. (1978), 'The ownership and control of industry', *Oxford Economic Papers*, Vol. 30, No. 1.
Oakeshott, R. (1978), *The Case for Worker Co-ops*, London.
OECD (Organisation for Economic Co-operation and Development) (1965), *Wages and Labour Mobility*, Paris.
O'Connor, J. (1973), *The Fiscal Crisis of the State*, New York.
Offe, C. (1975), 'The theory of the capitalist state and the problem of policy

formation', in L. N. Lindberg *et al.* (eds.) (1975) *Stress and Contradiction in Modern Capitalism*, Lexington, Mass.

Offe, C. (1976), *Industry and Inequality*, London.

Ohlin, G. (1974), 'Sweden', in R. Vernon (ed.) (1974) *Big Business and the State*, Cambridge, Mass.

Okochi, K. *et al.* (1973), 'The Japanese industrial relations system', in K. Okochi *et al.* (eds.) (1973) *Workers and Employers in Japan*, Princeton.

OPCS (Office of Population and Census Surveys) (1973), *The General Household Survey, Introductory Report*, London.

Pahl, J. M. and Pahl, R. E. (1971), *Managers and their Wives*, London.

Pahl, R. E. and Winkler, J. T. (1974), 'The economic élite: theory and practice', in P. Stanworth and A. Giddens (eds.) (1974) *Elites and Power in British Society*, London.

Palmer, B. (1975), 'Class, conception and conflict', *The Review of Radical Political Economy*, Vol. 7, No. 2.

Panitch, L. (1976), *Social Democracy and Industrial Militancy*, London.

Parkin, F. (1968), *Middle Class Radicalism*, Manchester.

Parkin, F. (1972), *Class Inequality and Political Order*, London.

Parkin, F. (1974), 'Strategies of social closure in class formation', in F. Parkin (ed.) (1974) *The Social Analysis of Class Structure*, London.

Parkin, F. (1978), 'Social stratification', in T. Bottomore and R. Nisbet (eds.) (1978) *A History of Sociological Analysis*, New York.

Parkin, F. (1979), *Marxism and Class Theory: a Bourgeois Critique*, London.

Perrow, C. (1970), 'Bureaucracy, structure and technology', in *Organizational Analysis*, London.

Phelps-Brown, E. H. (1966), 'Minutes of evidence 38', Royal Commission on Trade Unions and Employers' Associations, London.

Pignon, D. and Querzola, J. (1976), 'Dictatorship and democracy in production', in A. Gorz (ed.) (1976) *The Division of Labor*, Hassocks, (translation of original French edition published Paris, 1973).

Pollard, S. (1965), *The Genesis of Modern Management*, London.

Poulantzas, N. (1973), *Political Power and Social Classes*, London.

Poulantzas, N. (1975), *Classes in Contemporary Capitalism*, London.

Poulantzas, N. (1976), 'The capitalist state: a reply to Miliband and Laclau', *New Left Review*, No. 95.

Prandy, K. (1965), *Professional Employees*, London.

Price, R. and Bain, G. S. (1976), 'Union growth revisited', *British Journal of Industrial Relations*, Vol. 14, No. 3.

Ramondt, J. (1979), 'Workers self-management and its constraints: the Yugoslav experience', *British Journal of Industrial Relations*, Vol. 17, No. 1.

Reeves, T. K. and Woodward, J. (1970), 'The study of managerial control', in J. Woodward (ed.) (1970) *Industrial Organisation: Behaviour and Control*, London.

Rex, J. (1974), 'Capitalism, élites and the ruling class', in P. Stanworth and A. Giddens (eds.) (1974) *Elites and Power in British Society*, London.

Reynaud, J. D. (1975), 'Trade unions and political parties in France: some recent trends', *Industrial and Labour Relations Review*, Vol. 28, No. 2.

Reynaud, J. D. (1978), *Les Syndicats, les Patrons et l'Etat*, Paris.

Roberts, B. C. *et al.* (1973), *The Reluctant Militants*, London.

Roberts, K. *et al.* (1977), *The Fragmentary Class Structure*, London.

Robinson, D. (ed.) (1970), *Local Labour Markets and Wage Structures*, London.

Robinson, O. (1969), 'Representation of the white-collar workers: the bank staff associations in Britain', *British Journal of Industrial Relations*, Vol. 7, No. 2.

Roeber, J. (1975), *Social Change at Work*, London.

Ross, N. S. (1958), 'Organised labour and management: the U.K.', in E. M. Hugh-Jones (ed.) (1958) *Human Relations and Management*, Amsterdam.

Roth, A. (1973), 'The business background of M.P.s', in J. Urry and J. Wakeford (eds.) (1973) *Power in Britain*, London.

Rowthorn, B. (1976), 'Late capitalism', *New Left Review*, No. 98.

Sayles, L. R. (1958), *Behaviour of Industrial Work Groups*, New York.

Sayles, L. R. (1974), *Managerial Behaviour*, New York.

Scase, R. (1977), *Social Democracy in Capitalist Society*, London.

Schloss, D. F. (1898), *Methods of Industrial Remuneration*, London.

Scott, J. (1979), *Corporations, Classes and Capitalism*, London.

Sellier, F. (1973), 'The French workers' movement and political unionism', in A. Sturmthal and J. G. Scoville (eds.) (1973) *The International Labour Movement in Transition*, Urbana, Illinois.

Senker, S. *et al.* (1976), *Technological Change, Structural Change and Manpower in the U.K. Toolmaking Industry*, Electrical Engineering Training Board, Research Paper 2, Watford.

Sheppard, H. L. and Herrick, N. Q. (1972), *Where Have All the Robots Gone?*, New York.

Shonfield, A. (1965), *Modern Capitalism*, London.

Shorter, E. and Tilley, C. (1974), *Strikes in France 1830–1968*, Cambridge.

Simpson, R. C. and Wood, J. (1973), *Industrial Relations*, London.

Sisson, K. (1975), *Industrial Relations in Fleet Street*, Oxford.

Sofer, C. (1972), *Organizations in Theory and Practice*, London.

Sorge, A. (1976), 'The evolution of industrial democracy in the countries of the European Community', *British Journal of Industrial Relations*, Vol. 14, No. 3.

Speigelberg, R. (1973), *The City*, London.

Sraffa, P. (1960), *Production of Commodities by Means of Commodities*, Cambridge.

Stanworth, P. and Giddens, A. (1974), 'An economic élite: a demographic profile of company chairmen', in P. Stanworth and A. Giddens (eds.) (1974) *Elites and Power in British Society*, London.

Stanworth, P. and Giddens, A. (1975), 'The modern corporate economy', *Sociological Review*, Vol. 23, No. 1.

Stewart, A., Prandy, K., and Blackburn, R. M. (1980), *Social Stratification and Occupations*, London.

Stewart, M. (1974), *Trade Unions in Europe*, London.

Stinchcombe, A. L. (1959–60), 'Bureaucratic and craft administration of production: a comparative study', *Administrative Science Quarterly*, Vol. 4.

Strinati, D. (1979), 'Capitalism, the state and industrial relations', in C. Crouch (ed.) (1979) *State and Economy in Contemporary Capitalism*, London.

Strom, F. (1976), 'Direct participation in the decision making process', *Current Sweden*, Vol. 140.

Sturmthal, A. (1966), 'White-collar unions: a comparative essay', *White-Collar Trade Unions*, Urbana, Illinois.

Sturmthal, A. (1975), 'Worker participation in management: a review of the U.S. experience', *International Institute for Labour Studies*, Bulletin no. 6.

Sumiya, M. and Taira, K. (eds.) (1979), *An Outline of Japanese Economic History, 1603–1940*, Tokyo.

Szymanski, A. (1975), 'Trends in economic discrimination against blacks in the U.S. working class', *The Review of Radical Political Economy*, Vol. 7.

Taira, K. (1970), *Economic Development and the Labor Market in Japan*, New York.

Taylor, F. W. (1964), *Scientific Management*, London.

Touraine, A. (1955), *L'Evolution du Travail aux Usines Renault*, Paris.

Touraine, A. (1971), *The Post-Industrial Society*, New York, (translation of original French edition, published Paris, 1969).

Trist, E. L. and Bamforth, K. W. (1951), 'Some social and psychological consequences of the Longwall method of coal-getting', *Human Relations*, Vol. 4, No. 1.

TUC (Trades Union Congress) (1979), *Industrial Democracy*, London.

Turner, H. A. (1962), *Trade Union Growth, Structure and Policy*, London.

Turner, H. A. *et al.* (1967), *Labour Relations in the Motor Industry*, London.

Turner, H. A. and Wilkinson, F. (17 July 1975), 'The seventh pay policy', *New Society.*

Urry, J. (1977), 'Capital and the state', mimeographed paper to the B.S.A. conference, Sheffield.

Vanek, J. (1975), 'The worker-managed enterprise as an institution', in J. Vanek (ed.) (1975) *Self-Management*, Harmondsworth.

Walker, C. R. *et al.* (1956), *The Foreman on the Assembly Line*, Cambridge, Mass.

Walker, C. R. and Guest, R. H. (1952), *The Man on the Assembly Line*, Cambridge, Mass.

Watson, J. (1977), 'New management attitudes to the humanisation of work', in R. N. Ottoway (ed.) (1977) *Humanising the Work Place*, London.

Watson, T. (1977), *The Personnel Managers*, London.

Weber, M. (1946), 'Bureaucracy', in H. H. Gerth and C. W. Mills (eds.) (1946) *From Max Weber: Essays in Sociology.*

Weber, M. (1964), *The Theory of Social and Economic Organization*, New York (translated and edited by A. M. Henderson and Talcott Parsons; originally published as Volume 1, Part 1 of *Wirtschaft und Gesellschaft* [*Economy and Society*], 1922).

Wedderburn, D. (1978), 'Swedish experiments in work organisation', in D. Gregory (ed.) (1978) *Work Organisation*, proceedings of an SSRC (Social Science Research Council) Conference, London.

Wedderburn, D. and Craig, C. (1974), 'Relative Deprivation in work', in D. Wedderburn (ed.) (1974) *Poverty, Inequality and Class Structure*, Cambridge.

Wedderburn, D. and Crompton, R. (1972), *Workers' Attitudes and Technology*, Cambridge.

Wedderburn, W. (1971), *The Worker and the Law*, Harmondsworth.

Weekes, B. *et al.* (1975), *Industrial Relations and the Limits of Law*, Oxford.

Weir, M. (1977), 'Are computer systems and humanised work compatible?', in R. N. Ottoway (ed.) (1977) *Humanising the Workplace*, London.

Westergaard, J. and Resler, H. (1975), *Class in a Capitalist Society*, London.

Whitley, R. (1974), 'The city and industry: the directors of large companies, their characteristics and connections', in P. Stanworth and A. Giddens (eds.) (1974) *Elites and Power in British Society*, London.

Whyte, W. H. (1956), *The Organisation Man*, New York.

Wilson, G. K. (1979), *Unions in American National Politics*, London.

Woodward, J. (1958), *Management and Technology*, London.

Woodward, J. (1965), *Industrial Organization: Theory and Pactice*, London.

Woodward, J. (ed.) (1970), *Industrial Organization: Behaviour and Control*, London.

Work in America (1973), Report of a Special Task Force to the Secretary of Health, Education and Welfare, Cambridge, Mass.

Wright, E. O. (1976), 'Class boundaries in advanced capitalist societies', *New Left Review*, No. 98.

Zeitlin, M. (1974), 'Corporate ownership and control: the large corporation and the capitalist class', *American Journal of Sociology*, Vol. 80, No. 1.

Zoll, R. (1978), 'Centralisation and decentralisation as tendencies of union organisational and bargaining policy', in C. Crouch and A. Pizzorno (eds.) (1978) *The Resurgence of Class Conflict in Western Europe since 1968*, London.

Index